BUCK ROGERS
— IN THE 25TH CENTURY: —
A TV
COMPANION

By Patrick Jankiewicz
Foreword by Erin Gray

BUCK ROGERS IN THE 25TH CENTURY: A TV COMPANION

"Buck Rogers in the 25th Century: A TV Companion"
By Patrick Jankiewicz

Published in the USA by:
BearManor Media
P O Box 71426
Albany, Georgia 31708
www.bearmanormedia.com

ISBN: 978-1-59393-171-1
Printed in the United States of America
Book design by Robbie Adkins, www.adkinsconsult.com

Also by Patrick Jankiewicz

You Wouldn't Like Me When I'm Angry! A HULK Companion
(BearManor Media)
Just When You Thought It Was Safe: A JAWS Companion
(BearManor Media)
As Contributor
Stan Lee Conversations
**(University Press of Mississippi, edited by the very Canadian
Jeff McLaughlin)**
Starlog Presents Star Trek's Greatest Guest stars
(HarperPrism)

Dedication Page

This one's for my favorite Ambuquad, Steve Jankiewicz!

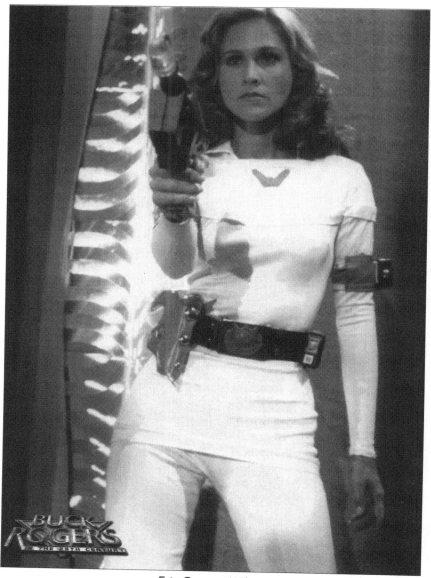

Erin Gray as Wilma

"To the Stars"
Foreword by Erin Gray

At my first comic con decades ago, a promoter was escorting me toward the con hotel when we walked past a line of eager fans snaking round the building. I asked who the fans were waiting to see. "You," the promoter replied, "Colonel Wilma Deering."

Buck Rogers rock-  eted into my universe in 1978. At the time, I was filming a TV mini-series, "Evening in Byzantium." I didn't want to do this strange sci-fi show, and, in fact, had to be cajoled into auditioning for the part. But when filming began, I quickly realized there was something about this character, this leader of the Earth's defenses clad in a body-hugging jumpsuit that demanded attention. Even now,

Erin Gray and daughter Samantha. Photo: Pat Jankiewicz

after 35 years, Colonel Wilma Deering can still command a room.

The show and its characters have become seminal in television's sci-fi canon, but for girls who watched the show growing up, Deering's character was a cultural marker pointing to the future and all its possibilities. Young girls drew inspiration from Colonel Wilma Deering. She helped them see that it was possible to reach for the stars. And for me, playing Wilma Deering was a life-changer. Buck Rogers was a space-age comic book hero far removed from the comic book princesses I'd grown up reading and a world away from the gender dynamics I was used to. As a child of the fifties, a daughter of divorced parents, and an actress in a world that thought my sexuality should be at the service of a man, my strength for the bedroom not the boardroom, to become a role model in the era of the power suit was a kick in the pants.

My generation of women weren't raised to be leaders. No one encouraged us to imagine beyond our culture's gender restrictions. Run my own company? Ha! Back in the day, it would never have entered my mind. In 1969, I was turned down for a credit card because my husband wasn't on the application. It didn't matter that I made over six figures as a fashion model or that I'd been on the cover of the company's catalogue.

As a single working mother, my mom was once told she couldn't buy a house without a husband so her advice to me was simple. Go to college, but not to study math, not to make discoveries, and certainly not to become an advocate or a leader. "Go to college, Erin," she said, "and find a good husband." Then along came Colonel Wilma Deering. Portraying her allowed me to wear a cloak of strength, to learn how a strong woman advocates, to see how a strong woman takes action.

Over the years, I've met women who've shared that Wilma Deering is the reason they joined the Marines, became pilots in the Israeli army, world-class markswomen, police officers and paramedics, and I'm thrilled when I'm reminded that Wilma's sexual presence in her skintight white spandex not only awakened many young men's libidos, but it also showed women that their sexuality was their own to command.

Once at a convention, after a number of young men shared how much they loved Wilma when they were adolescents, my son insisted I have t-shirts printed saying, 'Yes, I know I was your first.' Over the years, I've come to learn that a leader knows how to unite others and delegate, seeks knowledge and reaches deep within to find the courage to face fears rather than be controlled by them. A leader has the determination to turn challenges into opportunities. Colonel Wilma Deering helped me become a leader in my own life.

In this book, "Buck Rogers in the 25th Century: A TV Companion," Patrick Jankiewicz takes a close look at the impact of this culturally iconic television show. It seems fitting that Patrick should write this book as he was one of my first interviewers in Hollywood. Patrick presents wonderful insights into the film business and its history, and he has interviewed many, including *Buck Rogers'* co-creators, Buck Rogers himself, as portrayed by Gil Gerard who with his wit and charm can still make me laugh until I have to beg him to stop, the cast and crew of the movie, and the TV series.

He's also gathered behind the scenes stories and memories that will delight anyone who grew up in the company of Buck Rogers, Colonel Wilma Deering, Dr. Elias Huer, Hawk, and of course, lovable Twiki.

Pasadena, 2015

Introduction

Unlike *Star Wars'* Luke Skywalker, a farmboy who found religion, or *Star Trek's* Captain Kirk, a military man who loves his work for the duty, camaraderie and adventure it brings, the *Buck Rogers in the 25th Century* TV Series was all about sex. This is an impressive achievement, because there is no sex on the show.

Buck Rogers is a 534-year old fighter pilot who has literally been out of circulation for centuries. Although he is revived in the 25th Century, Buck finds to his delight that he is in a future full of impossibly beautiful women in improbably revealing costumes. Wilma Deering, Princess Ardala and other alien enchantresses are frequently enlisting Buck's aid or vying for his undivided attention. Unfortunately, Poor Buck is trapped in this future full of impossibly beautiful women in improbably revealing costumes where sex never comes up directly. It's like he's in Aldous Huxley's *Brave New World* without the orgies!

While the show was purportedly about a hero out of time battling aliens, a hero stolidly played by Gil Gerard (a square-jawed leading man who was seemingly created by combining the DNA of Lee Majors with Robert Urich), the subtext of the *Buck Rogers in the 25th Century* TV series is repressed desire. This is best represented on the show by Erin Gray's Wilma Deering. Her perfect body encased in a latex cat suit, her hair pulled into a tight bun, her feelings toward Buck held back by her position in protecting Terra, the re-named Earth rebuilt as a Utopia and the bastion of the future.

She needs no romantic distractions, because Wilma is entrusted with nothing less than the safety of her planet. Upon first meeting him, she dismisses Buck as "a barbarian," but Wilma's yearning for Buck and dedication to duty are what the show is truly about. She represents both the sexual appeal of the future and it's repressive nature much like the show itself, which was constricted by running on Thursday Nights at 8:00 p.m. on what was then quaintly known as "The Family Hour."

The women on the show are shot as beautiful and shiny as any of the robots or spaceships. They are an essential part of the show, hinting at the allure and yes, danger that awaits Buck in this exotic 25th Century. In honor of this, guest vamps from the show will be referred to respectfully as "Buck Babes," because that's what they were on the show. *Buck Rogers* would push at sexual boundaries by implying rather than stating explicitly. Incredibly, *Buck Rogers* even snuck a hooker into its "Vegas In Space" episode. It seemed more daring than its recently cancelled sister series, *Battlestar Galactica*, which had a prostitute in its pilot episode and quickly lost its nerve and changed her into a nurse when it went to series. *Buck Rogers* would get away with implying naughtiness, by never explicitly showing it.

Buck himself is too good-natured to verbalize his desire for these strange and erotic women of the 25th Century, but these opinions are expressed by a stubby extension of Buck's Manhood, his robot sidekick, Twiki, who states what the gentlemanly Buck cannot. The robot's head even resembles a penis! As Buck's 'member,' he gets to utter things no one else in the show is allowed to mention. Because he clearly represents Buck's junk, it makes the scene where he meets Princess Ardala hilarious. The gorgeous space royal looks down at Twiki and coos to Buck, *"Who's your charming little friend?"* Every woman wore butt-hugging spandex and had so much rouge on their cheeks, they almost glowed in the dark.

Although the episodes are played straight, Twiki manages to comment on an actress' wardrobe, body or sex appeal. He even hails Wilma with a "Hey, Babe!" and has a (carefully implied) love affair with a female robot in one episode. The suggestion of sex was omnipresent throughout the series. It was coy and hinted at, but it was there. For example, in one episode, femme fatale Ardala creates several clones of Buck and takes them to her private chambers, locking the door. Kane, her lackey, naively wonders, "What could she conceivably be doing with three Buck Rogers for almost an hour and a half?"

Buck Rogers in the 25th Century 's unspoken sex subtext is why Julie Newmar's War Witch torments the handsome young scientist Kodus (Donald Petrie) while simultaneously hitting on him. She has him strapped to an apparatus that displays him before her and has him tortured in agonizing pain before he passes out. "Don't kill him," she commands her henchman. She glances where his lower regions would be as he hangs off camera and says "If you kill him, he's of no use to us and I plan to use Kodus...*In a variety of ways!*"

The hint of sex is why The Satyr seeks out his wife, as do other satyrs in a second season episode. The first thing the Satyrs do is grab the beautiful young mother, drag her inside a house, throw her kid out and slam the door. The onscreen moppet is assured (as are the kids at home) that the Satyrs are "just looking for food," but it's pretty clear what they want. The subtext is there if you're looking for it.

That's why the foreword to this book is by Erin Gray, not Gil Gerard. As much as I dig Gil's Devil-may-care hero from the 20th Century, everybody who asked about the book wanted to know and talk about her. There were plenty of questions about Buck, Twiki, Ardala, Huer and various guests, but EVERYONE had questions and comments about Erin and her alter ego, Wilma Deering. Because of this, it seemed appropriate that the lady be the one to discuss the show and its impact.

A busy actress who helps out several charities in her free time, Erin Gray had never really discussed her work on *Buck Rogers* outside of interviews at the time of the series. I had the honor of doing an interview with her, looking back on the show for a magazine and it was a fascinating, incredibly honest story.

Erin tells you everything, she's cool, funny and always interesting. Her stories about the show were amazing. They indicated to me there was a book in this. A lighthearted action adventure series that had all sorts of drama going on behind the scenes.

Erin's always been a household word in my house. Several years ago, my big brother Tom sold a script to Steven Spielberg. I tagged along for this momentous occasion, as younger brothers do, and on the way in, Tom had to make copies of the agreement for the meeting. Stopping to do that, we ran into Erin Gray, who gave me a hug.

Later, after his contracts were signed, Tom was carrying a big check with a lot of zeros, but seemed struck by a strange melancholy. I asked him why. "I know I should be happier," he mused, "But all I can think is *that you got a hug from Erin Gray!*" This led to a Jankiewicz family catchphrase, if someone did something impressive, they would always be asked: *"but is it better than a hug from Erin Gray?"*

-Patrick Jankiewicz
Claremont, California 2015

AUTHOR'S NOTE

On the Universal Studios backlot years after the rise and fall of the *Buck Rogers in the 25th Century* TV series, I was getting a guided tour by my friends Mick & Cynthia Garris. Mick wrote an episodic being filmed, so the day was pretty joyous...Until we walked back to his office.

Going past a dumpster by Soundstage #28, I noticed a large craft laying on its side like a beached whale. Another similar large object laid ignominiously nearby.

"Oh no," I said, touching it delicately, finding it to be sturdy and in perfect condition. "What is it," asked Cynthia, a charming blonde actress/singer who had never seen a *Buck Rogers* episode, otherwise she would realize this poor battered prop was A Very Big Deal, immortalized in toys and on lunch boxes. "It's a Starfighter from *Buck Rogers*," I said sadly, running my hand lovingly along the plywood fins like it was The Ark of Covenant. "—and that brown thing over there was a Draconian Marauder." "Well, that's why they call it show *business*," joked Mick.

Both giant props were spray painted with the word TRASH and unceremoniously tossed by the dumpster, too big to go in, Both waiting to be hauled off and ditched. It was a beloved part of childhood and seeing Buck's ship lying there like a family dog hit by a car bothered me more than I cared to admit.

My eyes kept going back to the hastily scrawled TRASH. That stung, but somehow the word fit. *Buck Rogers in the 25th Century* was trash—glorious pop culture trash made as a disposable commodity to cash in on the post *Star Wars* science fiction trend of the '70s and '80s...But it was the kind of beloved trash that has been respectfully spoofed and honored by such hipster culture-excavating shows as *South Park, Robot Chicken, The Simpsons, Family Guy* and *Futurama*, all of which have referenced Buck. Pulling *Buck Rogers in the 25th Century* out of a pop culture landfill and examining it in the fresh light of the post ironic modern day seemed like an interesting challenge.

The views and standards between men and women from the '70s and '80s are shockingly different than those of today. This contrast is clearly on display in the series, the way the show changed itself between seasons—going cheaper and cruder, rather than embracing it's better episodes, which felt like the third season of the original *Star Trek* (*indeed, classic *Trek* writer D.C. Fontana actually contributed to *Buck Rogers in the 25th Century*, even if she hid behind a pseudonym.) The second season tried for an even more dumbed-down *Star Trek* approach and lost much of the magic of the better episodes of the first season.

The show also had many interesting guest stars, classic actors, cult movie stars and an eclectic mix of personalities—a pre-Oscar Jack Palance, a post *Halloween* Jamie Lee Curtis, original Buck Rogers Buster Crabbe, doomed Playboy Playmate Dorothy Stratten (tragically murdered soon after her episode and later played in a TV movie by Curtis), interesting young actresses like Kimberly Beck, Morgan Brittany, Judith Chapman, Anne Lockhart and Pamela Susan Shoop, character actors like Henry Silva, Michael Ansara, Cesar Romero, Roddy McDowall, Anthony James, Woody Strode, Peter Graves and Frank Gorshin, horror stars like Robert Quarry, William ("Big Bill") Smith, even cult movie icons like Paul Koslo, Mary Woronov, BarBara Luna and Sid Haig, and big stars of the '80s era, (Gary Coleman & Judy Landers). There's even several of the first TV appearances of then-unknown Dennis Haysbert. Clearly, *Buck Rogers in the 25th Century* had something for everybody.

Buck in NASA outfit from Awakening.

Buck Rogers Begins

Created in 1929 by Philip Francis Nowlan, *Buck Rogers in the 25th Century* began as a popular pulp about World War One veteran, Anthony Rogers, who is investigating strange incidents in Pennsylvania coal mines. Inhaling radioactive gas in an abandoned mine, Rogers is thrown into a state of suspended animation, a condition he stays in for 492 years. Finally revived in 2419, he teams up with future female adventurer Wilma Deering against such adversaries as Killer Kane and Black Barney in a future full of spaceships, space pirates, deadly robots and aliens.

The idea for turning Rogers into a comic strip hero began with the president of The National Newspaper Syndicate, John Flint Dille, who shrewdly felt he needed a comic strip set in Outer Space (remember, this is 1929!). Dille asked Nowlan to translate his character to the funny pages. He also had a crucial suggestion for the science fiction hero: change Anthony's name to "Buck Rogers."

Buck proved an immediate hit, inspiring Alex Raymond's better known hero, Flash Gordon, who later eclipsed Buck in popularity. When *Flash Gordon* became a blockbuster serial for Universal Studios, they took note of the older space hero. Wanting to cash in on their success with Flash Gordon, the studio launched a 12-chapter serial adaptation starring their Flash, Buster Crabbe (his hair dyed dark to make his Buck superficially different from his Flash Gordon), with Constance Moore as Wilma Deering.

It also gave Universal a chance to re-use props and sets from *Flash Gordon*, cutting costs in their frugal 25th Century. After that came a short-lived TV series in 1950, remembered only because Hitchcock blond Eva Marie Saint played Wilma. In *The Right Stuff*, his brilliant book on America's space program, writer Tom Wolfe mentions how the character was a mantra when it came to justifying spending in the race for Space and The Moon: "No bucks, No Buck Rogers." From there, the *Buck Rogers* franchise went into suspended animation that it would not emerge from until the character's 50th birthday.

But none of that matters. The real inspiration for a new *Buck Rogers in the 25th Century* TV series came on May 25, 1977, with the release of *Star Wars*. As George Lucas' epic fantasy became a runaway hit, Hollywood took notice at how much "dough re mi" could be made through space dogfights, beautiful princesses and cute robot sidekicks.

Of those who paid close attention to *Star Wars'* opening, Glen Larson was especially impressed. Prolific TV producer Larson has had a long career of creating TV series that resembled recent hit films. After *Butch Cassidy And The Sundance Kid* came out, Larson created *Alias Smith & Jones*. Right after Clint Eastwood played a trucker with an orangutan in *Every Which Way But Loose*, Larson created *BJ And The Bear*, about a truck driver and his chimp, which was inexplicably named 'Bear.' After Burt Reynolds played a stuntman in *Hooper*, Larson created the show *The Fall Guy* about a stuntman who solves crimes, his show *Automan* came after Disney's much anticipated *Tron*. Larson also brought caped hero *Nightman* to TV after Tim Burton's *Batman* came out, among many others.

"Glen was famous for coming up with TV shows that borrowed from popular movies that had just come out or movies that were about to open with a lot of excitement around them," said the late ABC Executive C.Z. Wick. "Everybody knew that and Glen was famous for it. Plus, he could get the projects going very quickly, sometimes even before the movie he was knocking off came out!" Larson's copycat shows led writer Harlan Ellison to playfully dub him 'Gran Larsony.'

Naturally, *Star Wars* quickly overtaking Steven Spielberg's *Jaws* to become the highest grossing film of all time, inspired the derivative producer. Larson decided to do the biggest *Star Wars* takeoff ever attempted for Television, *Battlestar Galactica*, for ABC-TV, about "a ragtag fleet" looking for Earth, as they are being hunted by a merciless group of robots known as The Cylons. The pilot cost seven million dollars and the show ran a then unprecedented one million an episode.

Because of *Battlestar Galactica*'s hype and anticipation among TV viewers and the studio, Glen Larson became the small screen's go to guy for sci-fi. While there had been a proposed *Buck Rogers in the 25th Century* three part miniseries being set up in 1977 (where Buck had a cuddly alien pet/sidekick), NBC and Universal threw it out and asked Glen Larson to start from scratch. Turning it down, Larson later reconsidered, which proved to be a cunning cost cutting move. With two expensive projects, *Battlestar Galactica* at ABC-TV, *Buck Rogers in the 25th Century* at NBC, essentially being the same type of show, it would allow him to cheaply recycle props, FX, costumes and even sound effects between both programs.

For the revamp, Buck was upgraded to an astronaut and shuttle pilot. This was a smart move, as there wasn't much a guy investigating West Virginia coal mines could offer in the 25th Century, other than a sore back, union grievances and Black Lung. With his pilot film coming out in 1979 on the character's 50th anniversary, Larson and *The Outer Limits* creator Leslie Stevens came up with their own take on Buck.

The pilot movie, *Buck Rogers in the 25th Century*, pulls him out of the coal mine and made him a 20th Century pilot. Being a top gun, Buck would have the swagger and humor to hold his own in the far future. There would be concessions to the modern *Star Wars* era—a beautiful princess, a cute robot sidekick ("Twiki" instead of R2D2), action and many space battles. But in the pilot, the script emphasizes that despite being 500 years out of date, Buck is clever, good with his fists and his instincts.

Burt Reynolds In Outer Space

"(Our Buck) has adult appeal, sophistication," Larson boasted. "The easiest way (to explain it) is really to say that if you were going to take Burt Reynolds and put him in a Space movie. This is what you wind up with. It's a guy from now thrown into an environment 500 years in the future. This gives him an opportunity to use hip, flip so-forth dialogue. My assessment of (NBC's original miniseries) is that it was a kind of very square, cartoon-type approach. They took themselves too seriously. (Our approach is) what would happen if somebody was cryogenically suspended for 500 years and he suddenly found himself in this new environment? His personality would relate back to now. That's a great opportunity for a writer."

They envisioned the space hero as a futuristic James Bond, good with the ladies, a wisecracking hero who could improvise solutions no matter the deathtrap and larger than life villains. Indeed, for the pilot, they cast James Bond's very first villain, Joseph Wiseman, who battled Sean Connery in *Dr. No*. Glen Larson unsuccessfully pursued *Spy Who Loved Me* Bond girl Barbara Bach for the role of Princess Ardala. This was 1979, the same year Bond producers tried to pander to the *Star Wars* crowd by sending 007 into Space in *Moonraker*, now regarded as the series' worst entry.

Larson hired *Star Wars'* designer Ralph McQuarrie and the film's Academy Award-winning Special Effects designer, John Dykstra, to provide *Galactica* a bit of *Star Wars'* authenticity, scale and grandeur for TV. "They used craft designs for *Buck Rogers* that I actually did for *Battlestar Galactica*," Ralph McQuarrie remembered. This was a wise move, as McQuarrie designed the iconic X-Wing and Tie Fighters *for Star Wars*. The Terran Starfighters that Buck and Wilma defend the planet in were originally conceived as Vipers for *Battlestar Galactica*.

Legendary artist and production designer William Stout also did some conceptual work for the show. "I did a lot of designs for weapons, armor, spaceships and costumes," the artist shrugs. "I believe the only things of mine they ended up using were my insignia designs."

The movie would pit Buck against his most popular comic strip nemesis, Princess Ardala, whose father Draco commands a race of evil aliens.

The Draconia

One of the smartest moves that Larson and Universal Studios made was to postpone the project and form a effects shop to churn out mattes, models and visuals for each episode, known as Hartland. Once up and running, Hartland cranked out FX for the pilot turned movie and then on a weekly basis for *Buck Rogers in the 25th Century* and later *Galactica 1980*—essentially doing *Star Wars* every week on a TV budget.

Production designer Paul Peters recalls that "During Buck's hiatus, this started out at Doug Trumbull's Future General (FX shop), where Princess Ardala's flagship, The Draconia, was two years in building application and actually took three weeks to shoot. It was David Garber, Wayne Smith, Richard Deersearch, myself and several other people (building it).

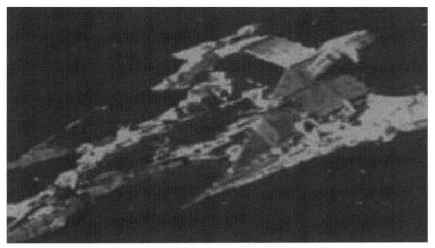

The Draconia.

"During the turnaround, we realized we were going to need our own environment to carry this and by that time, *Battlestar Galactica* was fairly far along and we knew we'd be picking that up and at that point, *Buck Rogers* was going to be a syndicated series of shows. We put together this incredible facility that Universal owned and operated offsite," he explains. " it was not on the backlot, but nearby in North Hollywood, that employed 130 people.

"Some of the best technicians, electricians, designers of the time, came together to work at Hartland. We were allowed to have fun, we were allowed to deliver some images that had some magic to it. Everything was delivered in-house. We had three different sections of model shops, full machine shops optical, processing and matte departments, a full service facility. Every week we delivered two equivalents of the feature on print, 30 or 40 different shots of motion control and animation, we didn't miss an episode, we didn't miss a shot. Sleep was not an option, generally speaking. A great team and great facility."

Princess Ardala's flagship, The Draconia," was the most expensive miniature ever built for television," says *Buck Rogers'* visual FX supervisor, Peter Anderson. "It cost more than The Starship Enterprise or the title craft in *Battlestar Galactica.*"

"It started at Doug Trumbull's shop. Where The Battlestar Galactica was an armature, designed in layers and kit parts, The Draconia was designed from scratch, model molded, the best fiber optics   Unfortunately, the delivery date for the movie was close at hand and they were still working on it. It was several hundred thousand dollars at that point and they said 'We gotta roll it out onstage and start shooting it!'

"Every single shot that ever played of The Draconia in the feature film and the TV series after that was from a round-the-clock three weeks of shooting," Anderson sighs. "When they blew it up, we designed it to have 27 different explosions, there was interactive lighting gags and so on. By the time we got it to the optical department, they said 'We can afford to do three (explosions).' It is probably the most incredible, prettiest piece of sculpture I ever had the opportunity to lay my eyes on. The filming of it was just marvelous. It was incredibly beautiful. I wished I had (the Draconia model) for a couple more weeks just to do it justice."

"The Draconia was also a huge set," Peter Anderson says: "When we walked in, there were parts of the original wall of Dr. Huer's office and then you would open the door and suddenly, you were in a Draconia hallway. I pitied the poor art director!"

"I Hated Star Wars!"

Universal Studios hired actor Gil Gerard to be their Buck, as the actor was recently in the studio's star-studded hit sequel, *Airport '77*. The character of Buck was meant to be an adventurous Han Solo type. When the producers cast Gil Gerard, the actor seemed to fill the bill. Unfortunately, when promoting the film to the genre press, he was asked his opinion of *Star Wars*, a movie that was the basis for his show far more than the *Buck Rogers* newspaper strip.

"I hated *Star Wars*," Gerard told *Fantastic Film* Magazine, "it bored me to death." He disliked "All of it. I really just didn't care for it. I had no interest in the characters whatsoever. I didn't care whether they lived or died. I didn't find them funny, sympathetic or interesting. Perhaps I was over prepared for it, because when I went in, I was distracted by the special effects. I was like 'THIS is what everybody's raving about?'" To his credit, he did praise Steven Spielberg's *Close Encounters Of The Third Kind*.

With their hero in place, the studio saw hundreds of actresses before model-turned-actress Erin Gray was cast to play Buck's love interest, Wilma Deering. Gerard and Gray were both popular commercial actors at the time, not yet known to the general public. *Buck Rogers* marked Gray's second acting gig ever.

While *Battlestar Galactica* was serious and straightforward, Larson's *Buck Rogers* was intended to be lighthearted and sexy. This proved to be a smart move, as the leaden, painfully earnest *Galactica* lacked the fun of the more humorous *Buck*, earning bad reviews and less than stellar ratings.

Larson had a daring idea for *Buck Rogers*—make the pilot a movie that the public had to pay to see! He had experimented with this before after the *Battlestar Galactica* pilot aired on TV in 1978. It was quickly released into theaters with deleted scenes re-inserted and '70s Universal gimmick "Sensurround" added. Sensurround was basically a giant speaker that would rumble at headache-inducing levels the back rows of the theater during explosion scenes.

"When we first wrote *Buck Rogers*, we immediately wanted to go to the movies with it. It felt like a movie. It had the potential of a movie. There's a certain uniqueness to great visual effects that allow a broader access to an audience," Larson said triumphantly. "We're pioneers in a way, trying to make a new idea work."

"A TV movie had never become a feature film before, instead of running on TV first," he continued. " It happened because the cast and crew did such good work, a buzz started at the studio as the dailies came in. An Office on the 12th floor of The Black Tower looked at the footage—Lew Wasserman and Sid Sheinberg's office and they said, 'We want this as a feature. We don't want this as a pilot, we want to release this as a feature' and the studio told NBC, 'After (it plays in theaters), you will have first shot at it.' We did go back and do a little more work on it."

The movie had a theatrical run before it slipped onto the TV screen that fall in slightly different form, leaving many viewers feeling ripped off.

Governor Bill Clinton

When *Buck Rogers in the 25th Century* briefly played in theaters in '79, It had its world premiere in Little Rock, Arkansas, with, then Governor/future President of the United States, Bill Clinton in attendance. There, Clinton and Gerard formed a lifelong friendship.

"*Buck* premiered in Little Rock, where Gil is from, and we all flew back for it. That's where I met Bill Clinton, who was governor and came to the premiere. I really thought it was odd that the Governor of Arkansas was making eyes at me in front of his wife and my husband," Erin Gray laughs. "I was an attractive girl used to guys hitting on me, but this seemed inappropriate. Bill couldn't help himself, he was pretty clearly coming on to me...He kind of slimed on me, a real good ol' boy come on. "

Season 1
"Awakening"

Season 1, Episode 1 & 2
Directed by Daniel Haller
Written by Glen Larson & Leslie Stevens

Cast
Buck Rogers...Gil Gerard
Princess Ardala...Pamela Hensley
Wilma Deering...Erin Gray
Kane...Henry Silva
Dr. Elias Huer...Tim O'Connor
Draco...Joseph Wiseman
Tigerman...Duke Butler
Twiki...Felix Silla
Delta Section...Caroline Smith
Supervisor ...John Dewey Carter
Pilot...Kevin Coates
Comtel Officer...David Cadiente
Technician...Gil Serna
Draconian Guard...Larry Duran
Draconian Guard...Kenny Endoso
Officer...Eric Lawrence
Tigerman #2...H.B. Haggerty
Wrather...Colleen Kelly
Pilot...Steve Jones
Pilot...David Buchanan
Wingman...Burt Marshall
Dr. Theopolis...Howard F. Flynn
Computer Council...John Rayner
Computer Council...Guernin Barry
Voice Of Twiki...Mel Blanc
Opened in theaters March 30, 1979
First aired on television October 12, 1979

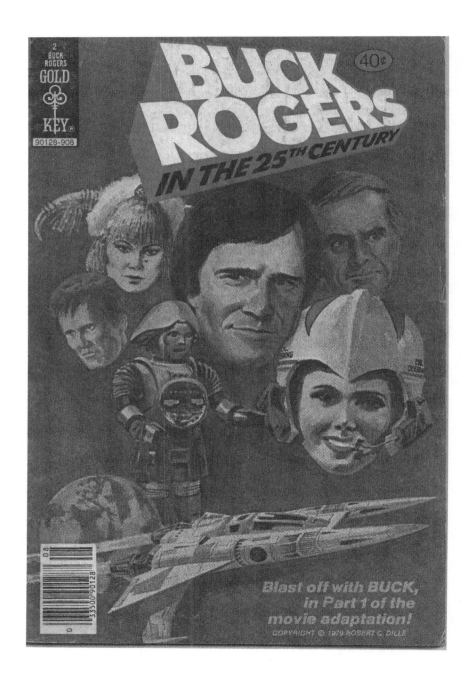

Narrator William Conrad grimly announces "In the year 1987, at The John F. Kennedy Space Center, NASA launched the last of America's Deep Space Probes. The payload perched on the nose cone of the massive rocket was a one-man exploration vessel, Ranger III. Aboard this compact starship, a lone astronaut, Captain William Buck Rogers, was to experience cosmic forces beyond all comprehension.

"An awesome brush with death in the blink of an eye, his life support systems were frozen by temperatures beyond imagination. Ranger III was blown out of its planned trajectory into an orbit a thousand times more vast. An orbit which was to return the ship full circle to its point of origin, it's Mother Earth not in five months but 500 years . For 500 years, Buck Rogers drifted through a world in which reality and fantasy merged into a timeless dream."

In 1987 (The future, at the time the pilot was made in 1979), after Ranger III is damaged, the ship begins icing up, the controls aren't responding and quickly freeze over. Buck himself is also frozen. His ship drifts aimlessly through the galaxy for 504 years, before being discovered by the Draconia, of the Draconian Empire.

A Draconian Pilot reports to "Killer" Kane, "There is something about the ship, I've not seen anything like it." Kane is the right-hand man of the gorgeous Princess Ardala, daughter of Draconian leader, Draco. He's an Earthman who defected to help Draco, Ardala and The Draconians conquer Earth. Upon hearing Kane's report, the tempestuous Ardala is excited that they are bringing in Buck. A mystified Kane says, "He's alive. The man lives, I'm not sure why. The ship is antiquated."

Intrigued, Ardala immediately wants to know if the pilot shows "any defects from the ordeal?" Finding out he's perfectly preserved, she giddily tells Kane, "I've never met a 500 year old man before—Prepare him for an audience!" Drugged as he comes out of his 500 year slumber, Buck sees Ardala, and believes he's dreaming.

Groggy, he looks up at her in wonder. *"Are you a real, live Princess?"* An amused Ardala says, "I think we've given our Captain too much medication." As the two examine him and notice the American flag on his uniform, Ardala remembers that "The United States of America was an empire on the planet Earth some centuries ago."

Realizing he's useless to them in his present condition, they opt to render him unconscious again and send him back to Earth, where their ships cannot penetrate the planet's defense shield. Kane plants a microtransmitter on Buck's ship to map a safe channel through Earth's Defense Shield. Kane tells Ardala that her father can use it to attack.

Hurtling towards Earth, Buck awakens again and still believes his encounter with Ardala was a dream. Excited about being home, he sings "Chicago Chicago/ you're my kind of town." He tells NASA to "Pull out your cards and backgammon boards, Lucky Buck is back!"

Receiving no response, he adds, "C'mon, you turkeys, get off your duffs and give me some info!" Delta Quadrant, future Earth's communication system, thinks he is speaking a "foreign language" and the craft seems to be moving too "slow and erratic for any conventional spacecraft." Flying alongside in her starfighter, Colonel Wilma Deering hails Buck, "Attention, Alien Spacecraft." "Watch who you're callin' an alien," Buck wisecracks, "you're not so familiar yourself!"

Deering tells Buck to follow her down, "the slightest deviation off course and your ship will be incinerated!" Because of her cold and commanding tone and references to him as an alien, Buck thinks Wilma is Russian and mockingly taunts her with "Das Vadanya." Wilma guides Buck's shuttle to a landing strip. "Wait'll the guys at The Cape hear this—Buck Rogers sets down in the middle of Red Square," he chortles.

Seeing the docking bay as Wilma walks up to him, Buck says "Hey, babe, this is quite a setup." "It's COLONEL Deering, Commander of Earth's Defenses," she says icily, before calling Buck a "barbarian." Wilma takes him to meet Dr. Elias Huer, a kindly scientist who helps protect the planet. Huer has studied the 20th Century and considers himself something of an expert on the era, so to meet a man from that time is a thrill for him.

"My name is Dr. Huer and I'm very pleased to meet you," the scientist says. Instead of a greeting, Buck says "If I'm dead, I obviously didn't make it to Heaven." Although they are in New Chicago, Dr. Huer cautions him that it's unlike the place he grew up in.

"There is nothing like Chicago left on Earth, Captain," he says sadly. Earth has gone through World War III and a nuclear winter since Buck's disappearance. All that's left of Earth is this futuristic city, built on the remains of Chicago, now known as The Inner City. It's a domed city, to protect the inhabitants from the radiation that has claimed the rest of the planet. Buck is crestfallen, as Huer tells him "We are trying to ease you into your situation slowly...My administrator Dr. Theopolis will take over."

New Friends

Buck is surprised when Dr. Huer brings in a small mechanical man. He smirks and asks "what is that?" "This is Twiki," Huer says by way of explanation. "He's your Drone." Twiki's function is to bring Buck up to speed on the ways of life in the 25th Century, but Buck has an opposite effect on the impressionable ambuquad. Twiki begins spouting late '70s slang, ceaselessly busting out one-liners and catchphrases because he is so enamored with Buck. This makes him one of a kind amongst his fellow robots and becomes a running gag throughout the series

Essentially, Twiki is the audience surrogate for kids watching the show. He's the one who shows them how fun it would be to hang out with Buck. By the end of the two-parter, he tells Rogers, "Buck, you're my kind of guy."

Around Twiki's neck is an electronic face, which says to Buck, "What an attractive man you are, Captain Buck Rogers." Huer tells Buck that this is Dr. Theopolis, "a member of our computer council. He also controls The Inner City's environment." Care of the environment and intergalactic diplomacy have been turned over to these computers. Long after Earth was destroyed, the computers built the city to protect what was left of planet Earth so it wouldn't be dependent on other worlds for food and water.

"I hope you will enjoy sunset tonight, Captain," Theopolis adds. "I'm programming a hint of mauve, suitably peaceful."

"It seems a little too programmed," Buck says of the 25th Century. He notes that being around Wilma makes it seem "more of a dream than a nightmare."

Buck is given an automated apartment, the lights dim and his bed rolls out when he says the words 'I want to go to bed.' He jokes it should be something else, something more subtle when they get to know him better. Buck sneaks out of The Inner City to see the old neighborhood, now a post nuclear hellhole full of mutants called Anarchia. He, Twiki and Theo are saved from certain death by Wilma, who rescues them with troops and a futuristic tank. In the movie, he thanks her for being so "ballsy."

Huer explains that Earth shipping lanes are being attacked by Marauders, voracious space pirates whose raids jeopardize an about-to-be-signed treaty with the Draconians. This will allow the aliens docking rights on Earth. Wilma doesn't believe Buck's story and feels he's an agent of the pirates. She frets, "those pirates would do anything to prevent our signing this trade treaty with Draconia."

Buck finds that to be too much of a coincidence and suspects it's being orchestrated by The Draconians. He insists that he's been on The Draconia, but Huer and Wilma react with disbelief. Only Buck realizes that the beautiful Princess Ardala and her father are planning to conquer Earth. Wilma discovers the microtransmitter on Buck's shuttle and believes her worst fears confirmed. Led by the overzealous Dr. Apol, one of Theopolis' fellow computers, the computer council feels Buck is a traitor who should be put to death. Theo offers a spirited defense that wins Buck a temporary reprieve. Wilma wants to test Buck's knowledge of The Draconia. Dr. Apol goes on record as being against the reprieve, a subplot dropped by the film.

Wilma tells him they have a good faith agreement with The Draconians. "Good faith is for bureaucrats," Buck scoffs, warning that if they don't listen to him, they're "sitting ducks." Deering calls Draco, Ardala's father, "the greatest leader the world has ever known." Buck tells her "A word of caution, Colonel—beware of Greeks bearing gifts." When she misses the reference, he says "Forget it. Guess I come from a time that was hopelessly paranoid."

Col. Deering—who teaches Buck how to fly their Starfighters—worries to Huer that Buck "could attempt to discredit the treaty with the Draconians," She requests she get to "spend some time with our Captain—saving Earth cannot be a waste of time, despite having to endure the Captain's company." Wilma says "The Captain belongs to me until I expose him."

Huer and Theopolis privately note that Wilma has never been this emotional about anything—or anyone—before. Despite Wilma's misgivings, Dr. Theopolis says "He's a good man, I feel it."

Ardala has the pirates attack The Draconia, to avert suspicion of her true motives. Buck goes into battle against them and destroys several Marauders, he even manages to save Wilma. Ironically, she directly causes the death of another female pilot, Lieutenant Wrather, who is blown up when Wilma orders her to ignore Buck's sage combat advice.

Rogers helps Earth's Defense Force battle the remaining pirates. As a 20th Century combat pilot, he is used to instinct and skill, while in the 25th Century, pilots rely primarily on their computer guided weaponry.

"Let's see how you like a little old-fashioned red dogging," Buck taunts before destroying a pirate in combat. When he wipes out the last of the Marauder ships, he uses another football term to her, "that's called blitzing the linebackers!"

Buck stops their attack and saves Wilma, so Ardala announces a party to thank him. She brings greetings from her father, Draco, who praises Buck for 'saving' The Draconia.

With the reception thrown by Ardala and The Draconians, Buck is in attendance, hoping to get Ardala to reveal that she met him previously. At the ball, Buck tastes futuristic alcohol. As he drains his glass, Twiki toasts him with "L'Chaim!" Princess Ardala arrives wearing a stunning midriff and horned headpiece. Ardala denies meeting Buck before. Kissing her hand, Buck explains "I never forget a knuckle." Everyone dances stiffly and joylessly in the ballroom.

"I see dancing has come a long way in 500 years," Buck mutters to Twiki. He has the Drone get him a rose for Princess Ardala. When she sees Twiki, she asks "Who's your charming little friend?" Twiki, looks Ardala up and down, and comments "Wotta body!" Ardala has a bald, muscular, tattooed bodyguard named 'Tigerman' who takes an immediate dislike to Buck, even snarling at him.

As The Draconians carry on their assault on Terra, Buck knocks out a Draconian guard and steals his uniform. Undercover, he sabotages their hidden Pirate fleet. Their Marauders explode on deck before Ardala can mount the invasion. Engaging in a brutal final battle in the film with Tigerman, he blows him up after kicking him in the crotch, he leaves him unconscious.

Buck is pinned beneath heavy debris as a magazine of unused laser torpedoes tear The Draconia apart internally. Twiki lifts it off him as Wilma once again comes to their rescue, landing her Starfighter on the crumbling deck to retrieve Buck, Twiki and Theo. Ardala and Kane jump into an escape pod, as Draco's hologram rages about punishing his daughter and Kane. The Draconia erupts.

Wilma says "Let's go home," to which Buck teases "Mine or yours?" In the TV version, a grateful, Wilma, Huer and Theopolis invite Buck to join them on Earth's Defense force. He declines but they know he will be there if they need him on a case by case basis.

One of the loose ends of the pilot was in the original ending, which showed up on TV, where Theopolis reveals that Buck was not the traitor—even though they almost had him put to death. Addressing his fellow computers, Theo exonerates Buck and puts the blame on the real spy.

The original script had Kane fix one of the Computer Council to betray Earth. "Members of the council, I am sad to say it is one of our own kind, a computer programmed by the turncoat Kane before he defected to serve Princess Ardala...Programmed to appear normal but betray our secrets." The guilty computer, Dr. Apol, is short -circuited and pleads just before he runs down like H.A.L. the computer in *2001: A Space Odyssey*. This will be used again with a female computer in "The Plot To Kill A City."

The pilot script by Glen Larson and Leslie Stevens (dated Feb 2, 1978), follows the final product pretty faithfully with a few major exceptions. The biggest one being that Twiki didn't talk! Introducing Dr. Theopolis and Twiki, the show's answer to C-3PO and R2-D2, Theo (as he's commonly called) speaks in an officious, prissy voice like C-3PO while Twiki, doesn't talk at all, he beeps and squeaks, just like R2-D2.

Before *Buck Rogers in the 25th Century* opened in theaters, Glen Larson told the press, "Twiki's voice is still being worked on... It's a computer voice, not in a language you'd understand. It talks in some kind of binary code that only Theo understands." This was a direct steal from *Star Wars*, where the squat little robot R2-D2 would beep his complaints or displeasure, only to have it translated by C-3PO. Happily, a famous voice actor had other ideas.

Enter Mel Blanc

Mel Blanc, the voice of Bugs Bunny, Daffy Duck, Yosemite Sam, Sylvester The Cat, Tweety Bird, Barney Rubble and Fred Flintstone's prehistoric dog, Dino as well as hundreds of other cartoon characters, was brought in to provide Twiki's computer sounds Apparently, "Beety Beety Beety" is Mel's take on Binary code. When Blanc playfully threw in a wild line as a joke, where he said "Buck, you're my kind of guy," the producers realized letting Twiki talk would allow them more comedy relief in the movie and show.

The voice makes Twiki interesting, To have this blank child-like face emit Blanc's deep baritone is intriguing. You don't expect Twiki to sound like that and this makes most of his surprising comments unexpected and funny.

Story Editor Alan Brennert realized one could throw in a wise-crack or quip from Twiki—who had an inanimate mouth so you could easily dub in lines for him anywhere—and lighten up a dour "episode that was about as cheery as *A Long Day's Journey Into Night!*

"That sound effect Twiki would make? We would spell it B-e-e-t-y, for when he would say, 'Beety beety beety' in scripts — we tried to get out of doing this, but we were actually told that Mel needed to know when to put in the beetys," Brennert sighs comically. "But no one ever told us why he chose that sound. Glen Larson might've worked it out with him, but my only contact with Glen was when we all rode up in an elevator with him once by chance."

The pilot script has Twiki walk in, as Buck asks, "What the Hell is that?" The script notes that "Twiki enters from the sliding room and half hobbles towards the door Buck had been staring at earlier. He is no more than three feet tall, obviously made out of metal in semi-human form. His manner of walking and carrying his head is more reminiscent (sic) of a chimpanzee."

Based on this description and the way he's depicted in pre-production drawings by William Stout, Twiki was apparently going to be played by a chimpanzee like The Daggit—the robot dog on Glen Larson's other space show, *Battlestar Galactica*. This approach proved difficult on that show when the female chimp got tired, she would tear off the robot dog head and hurl it across the set. Obviously, by the time *Buck Rogers* was ready to shoot, they needed a more efficient method for their robot sidekick. Just as *Star Wars* had little actor Kenny Baker play R2-D2, *Buck* used little stuntman/actor Felix Silla for Buck's rough and tumble robot sidekick, Twiki.

Once Twiki had a voice, he was given the best line in the film. Going outside the domed city with Buck, he complains *"I'm freezing my ball bearings off!"* That line was dumped before the pilot ran on TV.

Phallic Headed Robot

Ironically, some kids watching the show thought Twiki's head had a certain phallic shape that resembled a penis. "Not at all, not at all," said the late Glen Larson, who insisted "He did not look like that, he was just a robot."

Oscar-winner FX artist Mike Lantieri, who worked on Twiki during the show, says "I don't think Universal Studios, a big corporation, would have wanted or allowed a robot on the air if they thought he looked like a penis!" Story Editor Alan Brennert insists, "I never, ever looked at Twiki and thought of a penis. I never, ever heard anyone say that he was designed to be phallic."

Story Editor Anne Collins Ludwick confesses that "Frankly, I never really 'got' the Twiki character – I found his 'beety-beety-beeties' silly and annoying and his truck driver interjections too jarring to be comical. Plus, he always looked to me like exactly what he was – a little person dressed up like a robot. Or maybe it was just *the disturbing shape of his head...*"

Some of the actors noticed that shape to Twiki's head: "Oh, Gil noticed that immediately," laughs Erin Gray. "Personally, I never noticed or thought Twiki looked like that, but Gil Gerard sure did," Felix Silla grins. "Right from the beginning—When I was in the full costume, Gil used to say, *'Here comes Twiki, the world's largest dildo!'* I would say, 'Fuck you, Gil' and we'd both laugh."

Dumping Draco

Another element that fell out before the series was Princess Ardala's father, Draco, played by Joseph Wiseman. His holographic image appears, courtesy of Ardala, promising a new age of cooperation with their "interplanetary pact." Draco the Warlord assures Earth, "By my command, the unarmed Draconia will descend to your lower atmosphere and remain there to serve as a museum of our technology." As he tells Earth he is addressing them from his home planet, Kane laughs to Ardala, "If they only knew that is a recording and that your father is actually halfway here with his attack force!"

Buck knows it's a trick and says to Ardala, "Did that light show come all the way from Daddy's kingdom or do peaceful conquests bore him?" An incredulous Wilma hears Buck's theory and laughs in disbelief, "Conquests? This is a mutual trade pact!"

Draco shows up again in holographic form in the climax, when Buck sabotages The Draconia. As his pirate ships are being blasted while Draco is still thousands of miles away, he accuses Kane of being a traitor working for The Earth Directorate, snarling "If either of you (Kane or Princess Ardala) survives this greatest debacle our realm has ever known, you'll answer to me!"

Producer Larson found Joseph Wiseman to be "a guy who's perfect for the role. You see him and you know why. He's a Fu Manchu, a Dr. No, a Ming (The Merciless). We've tried to make the whole texture of this picture differ drastically from *Battlestar Galactica* because *Galactica* is very pragmatic. *Buck* has that contemporary feel on it's side, against *Galactica's* sort of futuristic robots and things."

Draco's scenes were deleted from the TV series—Ardala seems more of a femme fatale when she speaks for the entire Draconian empire, rather than working as a pawn for her father. Draco was dumped after the pilot movie and Wiseman appeared as a different character in the episode "Vegas In Space." "I assumed (Draco was dropped) because Joseph Wiseman was too expensive for our budget." jokes Alan Brennert.

Wiseman, a white actor, looks a bit silly dressed like a mandarin in Asian style makeup (a term Asian actors decry as "yellowface"), which may be another reason Draco was dropped. He wouldn't be missed, as Pamela Hensley is so much more effective when Ardala is in charge.

Futuristic City

The most impressive set in the pilot film wasn't a set at all, but an actual location in downtown Los Angeles. The then new, futuristic looking glass Westin Bonaventure Hotel (whose designer, John Portman, also gave Detroit it's similar looking signature

Draco.

structure, The Renaissance Center) added production value to the pilot in a pivotal scene between Buck and Wilma.

With its great size and funky design, it's almost a character in itself. Because of its futuristic setting, *Buck Rogers in the 25th Century* could go to very few outdoor locations other than this or Vasquez Rocks. It's wide glass elevators are a very recognizable movie location now, from Clint Eastwood battling a killer during *In The Line Of Fire* to Arnold Schwarzenegger and his horse using the elevator to chase a terrorist in *True Lies*, a movie he did with *Buck Rogers* guest Jamie Lee Curtis.

"The Westin Bonaventure was huge and new and looked like something from the future," says Erin Gray. "It looks great in the film, just a beautiful backdrop as Gil and I walk and talk. You can tell it's not a model. I was also impressed when we shot there because Gil noticed all of the pilots in the background were male except for me. He shut down production until they could put some women in the background in uniform so I was not the only one. He said, 'C'mon, guys, it's the 25th Century, Wilma should not be the only female pilot!' I agreed with him on that."

The Bonaventure looms over Buck and Wilma.

The romantic banter between Buck, Wilma and Ardala is a highlight of the pilot film.

"I always believed gallows humor was important to a drama and it's the most fun," Glen Larson said. "I had the most fun with these quasi-love scenes. I hate to think I'm a hopeless romantic, but I think there's room even in a space opera for that kind of thing. *Buck Rogers'* (comic strips) like Flash Gordon in the books and artwork, had some of the sexiest stuff you've ever seen in your life! I don't mean tawdry, just gorgeously done, sexy scenes. And I felt Jean-Pierre Dorléac was the perfect guy to capture that look."

Dressed to thrill

To capture the sensual tone of the *Buck Rogers* comic strip, Glen Larson hired beautiful women and the perfect guy to dress them in a science fiction setting. He brought in Jean-Pierre Dorléac, who designed the title character's super suit in *The Greatest American Hero*, Brooke Shields' striking raggedy bikini in *The Blue Lagoon*, Christopher Reeve and Jane Seymour's period accurate outfits of *Somewhere In Time*, and Larson's own *Battlestar Galactica*. What made him especially perfect for the show was his erotic costumes for the women of the sexy Jane Fonda sci fi film, *Barbarella*. Dorléac's work on *Buck* was equally memorable, particularly in what Princess Ardala was wearing or not wearing, as the case may be.

"The costumes Jean-Pierre designed for Princess Ardala—even the costumes he didn't design for her, were amazing," Larson joked. "She (Princess Ardala) was naked for the entire series! I think one of the problems you can have in Outer Space is that it's inaccessible to a lot of the audience, so one of our goals was to do a human drama with *Buck Rogers*...Whether it was on a sci fi stage or any other stage, so it would translate for the mass audience. Beyond a certain core audience, will they like it? So that was our goal: have some fun with it and if it could be romantic, too? That's great. Jean-Pierre's outfits helped set the tone."

Jean Pierre Dorléac also designed Buck and Wilma's iconic white flight suits. "These were specific ideas that were in the script, that this world Buck was revived in was a very sterile society that was extremely well-organized," the designer explains.

"Unfortunately, I only did the feature. I did that and immediately went onto *Somewhere In Time* and *The Blue Lagoon*. Science fiction wise, I have done a lot. I did *Max Headroom*, all of *Quantum Leap*, *Battlestar Galactica*, *Heart & Souls*, *The Greatest American Hero*."

Ardala in horned headdress.

The Emmy-winning Dorléac' feels, with Earth's Defense Force's costumes, "It's the old adage—if it ain't on the page, it ain't on the stage.' Glen (Larson) gave me all the ideas (for the wardrobe). The white outfits were supposed to be very antiseptic, clean and very military-looking. His NASA uniform—the one he's wearing when he gets frozen in the shuttle? That was just the actual NASA space uniform of the time, not my design.

"When it said in the script 'Buck changes into an Earth costume of the (25th Century) time,' that's what I had him do,. He wore it for uniformity and Glen specifically told me he wanted that white sterile look, with that rainbow insignia. That rainbow insignia that Buck, Wilma and Earth's Defense Force wear is very interesting, since the gays made a similar logo for the Rainbow Coalition years after we did *Buck*.

"I am very pleased that, after all these years, the costumes are as contemporary today as they are—the big clunky boots, lycra and cotton clothes that people are wearing now are exactly what was done in the film, as well as shirts being worn out as tunics. I never thought I was prognosticating the future, but I am very pleased that it really does fit well with where we are now."

Ardala

Princess Ardala, played by Pamela Hensley, an actress whose previous claims to fame had been playing the love interest in *Doc*

Savage, Man Of Bronze and James Caan's government appointed girlfriend in *Rollerball,* she stood out as the exotic Ardala in her form fitting, eye-popping costumes. One of the designer's main challenges was dressing Ardala and the alien race she represented.

"With Ardala and the Draconians' look, I remember Leslie (Stevens, *Buck Rogers* co-producer/co-writer) coming to me and saying 'We want this very Mongolian opulent.' I went 'That's an oxymoron, there's no such thing as Mongolian opulent!' But we did end up taking a lot of ideas from Mongolian design. The rest of it was my crazy ideas from designing it at 2 o'clock in the morning! Personally, I love the movie, I always have. I did *Somewhere In Time* the same year that I was nominated for the Oscar for that, but I'm just as proud of my *Buck Rogers* work.

"Mongolian opulence' was my buzzword, but as I pointed out to Leslie, there was no such thing because The Mongolians were very poor and wore a lot of handmade things that were very tapestry looking, but that was the look I wanted for Princess Ardala and The Draconians," says Dorléac.'

"We had to invent the concept of the Draconians, which made it so much fun.. Pamela Hensley was one of the most delightful actresses I ever got to work with. Pamela was a sensation and Erin (Gray) was sensational too, but Pamela had to wear the most skimpy, exotic clothes—because Erin's character was the 'good girl' in Buck's life, she didn't get to dress like that. Remember Ardala's costume with all the beads? We had one girl on that shoot whose only job was to run around and collect all the beads off the floor!"

"Coming up with the look of these aliens and Princess Ardala in particular, was a lot of fun. The whole movie was a great delight, one of the best times I had in the world to do a feature," the designer says with a smile.

"Pamela was a riot to work with, as everybody (on *Buck*) will tell you. When they gave out the big silver balls at the disco scene, Pamela was saying (in a little girls' voice voice)'Look what my daddy got me for Christmas!' She was wonderful to work with—Pamela was the craziest one of them all...She was like dealing with Mae West.

"This story may be a little off color, but I'm gonna tell it anyway. When we made her beaded outfit, we measured her completely beforehand and made the outfit out of muslin. We finished the costume, she came in and did a final fitting. She put it on and stood in front of the mirror and she said 'Jean Pierre, darling, you're going to have to loosen my groin or I'm going to be cross-eyed with delirium in two hours!' I said, 'It can't be that tight, we measured everything!' She said 'If you don't believe me, just look' So I was on my knees in the fitting room, I lifted the pearls and sure enough, everything was hanging

Jean Pierre Dorleac, photo by Pat Jankiewicz.

out. I dropped it quickly and Pamela said, '*What's the matter, darling, did it wink at you?*'"

As for Ardala's rams horn headdress, "That is part of a Mongolian costume concept—they actually wore hats that were very similar to that with shapes like that, they were not beaded or had beads hanging down, they had fringe. The concepts were from Mongolian design, as were the Mongolian helmets, all of which came from Asian culture.

"On *Battlestar Galactica*, I had a great deal to do with the look of The Cylons, but Twiki and the other robots in the *Buck Rogers* film were something I had nothing to do with," Dorléac adds. "They wanted Cylons to be a reptilian race originally, that were designed for stuntmen over 6"7 who originally had to ride horses that were cut from the film because they couldn't see with the masks and kept falling off the horses!"

Gil Gerard remembers, "When Pamela Hensley first walked out in the scene in her horns, beads and midriff, the crew and I were stunned! I thought that was great, her in that costume on that big sound stage...I thought she carried it off like nobody else could have—Pamela was incredible as Princess Ardala."

Felix Silla, the actor who appeared onscreen as Twiki, was equally amazed by Hensley. "That scene where Gil and I go to the reception on her ship, I remember Pamela Hensley coming out in that costume and looking so regal—what a body and those horns, she looked like a real princess!"

Erin Gray was equally impressed with Ardala. "Pamela Hensley was just delightful. I liked Pamela because she was a great broad! I mean that in an affectionate term, women who are broads say it like it is, no bullshit, they are honest and funny, strong, confident in who they are and in their sexuality and Pam had all that in spades. I thought she looked fabulous, handling herself beautifully on set."

"There was never any drama with Pam," Gray says with admiration, "I really wish we had become better friends, but when she was working on the show, I wasn't and when I was working on the same episodes, she wasn't. We were both Buck's love interests, so we were rarely in the same scenes. We do finally get to interact in the first season finale, 'Flight Of The War Witch,' so that was fun."

Hensley later married E. Duke Vincent who ran Aaron Spelling's TV empire and, except for reading some books on tape and writing two cookbooks, she stepped completely out of the public eye.

Opening Credits

The movie tries for an ersatz James Bond credit sequence, where Gil Gerard lays on giant glowing letters of BUCK ROGERS' name, as Erin Gray and Pamela Hensley try to kiss him awake, along with several nameless actresses in a '70s Disco sequence. Instead of John Barry's iconic 007 theme, we have Kipp Lennon warbling 'Suspension,' whose silly lyrics include "what am I/Who am I/What will I be/Where am I going and what will I see?" This works far better as an instrumental, which is how it will be used, played with lyrics in only one other episode, 'Flight Of The War Witch.'

"That song, 'Suspension' was Glen Larson's creation. My contribution was the opening music and the floating space ship music," says composer Stu Phillips. "That came from just a moment of inspiration—in those days, only minutes were spent writing cues. Not days. Except for that song, all of the music in the movie was by me."

Erin Gray in silly Buck movie opening credits.

Composer Stu Phillips

Stu Phillips, the man who composed the themes to some of Glen Larson's most memorable shows (Including *Knight Rider* and *Battlestar Galactica*) wound up doing the honors on *Buck Rogers* Because "I had been working with Glen since 1974 and I was generally his first 'go to guy."

Was it difficult for him to compose for *Buck*, as he'd just done another Larson space show, *Battlestar Galactica*? "Unless my memory fails me, I believe that I had already completed the main season of *Galactica*. Also, I only did the the original pilot and the first two episodes of *Buck Rogers*, so I don't recall any conflict. What I did to (differentiate the two shows is) change the flavor of the music by two things.

"Number one, I added bass guitar and drums to the *Buck Rogers'* action cues. I also tried to be less classical in as much of the music as I could, Number Two, I made it a little more pop flavored, as *Buck Rogers* was a bit more Tongue-in-cheek, whereas *Battlestar Galactica* attempted to be more serious."

Art Director

To direct the pilot, Larson hired Daniel Haller, explaining "Daniel Haller made Roger Corman's films successful, because he was the art director on many of his films. "

Daniel Haller himself praises "Paul Peters, the production designer. Paul gave a lot to the pilot film. We were lucky that this was postponed a year. I went on to do other things and while I did that, Paul kept on contributing to the film and designs. Being an art director myself, I thought it was wonderful. I had pay or play on *Buck*, so I got paid when it started, got shut down and re started, so I was paid three times for this one job."

Although Paul Peters turned down *Battlestar Galactica*, he agreed to do *Buck* and brought a modular design to the series, as well as tweaking and recycling some *Galactica* sets

"I had been an art director and had done one show, so I knew the process of being a Production Designer and doing multiple interviews, speaking to the director, the producer," says Paul Peters. "In those days, the art department said 'You're it. Go see Glen Larson and here's the director.' After one season of working on *The Six Million Dollar Man*, I got the reigns of this thing. That's amazing. The fact that it was delayed enabled me to have more time and what better teacher/mentor could you have than a former art director?' It's to Dan Haller's credit that this turned out so well."

Dorléac' remains grateful to his director to this day. "I have to say this about Dan—he saved a costume in this for me. Princess Ardala's purple costume when she meets Buck after he comes back. I designed the thing when they cut the scene. I said, 'Dan, I've got this $10,000 costume and it's never gonna be seen,' so Dan put the scene back in the film for me!"

Future Disco

In the most jaw-dropping scene of the pilot, Buck attends Princess Ardala's ball aboard The Draconia. There, our hero instructs the musicians to "just let yourself go" which, in a movie from 1979, meant playing generic synth disco music! He has them re-create '70s Earth disco while he does The Bump with Princess Ardala. The scene draws unintentional laughter at revival screenings.

"What are you doing," Ardala asks, watching Buck gyrate. "It's called gettin' down," he tells her. "It's a little before your time, if it frightens you..." To which Ardala responds, "Nothing frightens me."

"What happens if we bump together," The Princess asks. "We automatically become Man and Wife," quips Buck. Twiki dances, exhorting the crowd to be "Groovy, get down!" Wilma watches and says, "It's disgusting!"

It's ironic that Chicago resident Buck Rogers brings back Disco, as Chicago is also the city where Disco died. "Disco Demolition Night" on July 12, 1979 (exactly three months before the *Buck Rogers* pilot film showed up on TV on October 12, 1979) at Chicago's Comiskey Park, was meant to be a fun diversion during a slow White Sox season.

After the Sox played The Detroit Tigers, Chicago W-LUP DJ Steve Dahl was supposed to blow up a crate of disco records. Instead, thousands of rowdy, disco hating rock & roll fans stormed the field, burning disco records and hurling them onto the grass. The field a smoldering shambles, The White Sox were forced to forfeit the second game to Detroit for the first time in history.

Two Tigermen

One can't help but notice that Princess Ardala's bodyguard Tigerman is noticeably shorter in several scenes. "There's a good reason for that," Dorléac' chuckles. "Duke Butler, the first Tigerman, was discovered at the Universal Studios Tour. He was hired immediately, sent into wardrobe and I don't think he had ever been on film before. He didn't have any lines in the film, I think he just growls twice. Anyway, we finished shooting the film and they called us back for re-shoots.

"Erin had to re-shoot a quick scene talking to Buck, so for that one shot, her hair is sprayed blonde instead of making her blonde, because Erin was a brunette. And they called Duke back for Buck's fight with Tigerman at the end of the film. When they tried to bring him back, the studio found Duke was gone! He had left town and moved to Minnesota or someplace. So they hired another guy (H.B. Haggerty) and tried to make him look as much like Duke as they could; but he was much shorter and much hairier, as you can clearly see in the film."

Tigerman Duke Butler with Ardala and Kane in Awakening.

The second Tigerman played the role in every subsequent Ardala episode until "Flight Of The War Witch," where he's replaced by a large black bodyguard The Princess dubs 'Pantherman.'

Anarchia

In the coolest concept of the pilot, Buck learns that outside the perfect world of the 25th Century are the scorched remains of post nuclear Earth. Buck's 20th Century hometown is now in ruins. Sweet home Chicago is now known simply as "Anarchia."

Buck begs Wilma, "Tell me about the holocaust (that ended the 20th Century)." "I can't," she says sadly, as it occurred long before she was born. Buck says "Until I hear it and feel it, it isn't real. Look, I lost everything that was important to me—a mother, father, brothers, sisters, a woman I cared for. Until I hear something that will convince me different, they're waiting for me in some other time and space." Anarchia is the twisted, smoldering ruins of what was once Chicago. Hearing that Buck wants to go there makes Twiki observe "He's crazy!"

Theopolis tells Buck, "Even armed forces are afraid to go into Anarchia at night." Buck sneaks into Anarchia with Twiki

Buck and Twiki in Anarchia.

and Theopolis reluctantly accompanying. Finding himself in the wreckage of what was State Street, Buck realizes they are being stalked by radiation-scarred mutants, The mutants use pipes to bang on fire hydrants and other hunks of metal to alert other mutants there are strangers among them.

Chased by the mob of deformed survivors, Buck cuts through a cemetery, where he finds his family grave. "This is where my parents were buried," he cries. "What happened? There's only one (tomb)stone, no date."

Theopolis explains, "only a few fortunate ones were buried at all, it happened so fast. Families were buried together. Dates became unimportant as all systems broke down. Finally, there were no more armies or fighting. Only starvation, contamination and lingering death."

Mutants trap Buck, Theo and Twiki. Buck uses over the top judo kicks in a hokey martial arts style that can only be described as "Buck Fu." Twiki manages to take out a mutant, too,

As Buck is overwhelmed by dozens of mutants, Wilma Deering arrives with troops in a futuristic tank and saves them. "I kinda like it out here," Buck tells her. "It's a bit primitive, but IT IS the South Side of Chicago!" That Wilma comes to their rescue shows she cares about Buck.

The mutants have an interesting look, with rags over their faces and head coverings over open sores. Costume designer Dorléac' says, "Because they are suffering from radiation burns, I feel they are not going to go out in public with their faces exposed; they would cover their faces to prevent more damage."

As interesting as Anarchia is, it's surprising that the ongoing TV series never returns to it. Buck makes a passing remark about it in one later episode, but there are no more references to it or further adventures to be had in the intriguing post-nuclear environment. This was deliberate.

Alan Brennert, the show's Story Editor, reveals that "(*Buck Rogers* producer)Bruce Lansbury banned all mention of Anarchia on the belief—and I agreed—that it would only make viewers think, 'Why are these guys running around the galaxy when they've got this shameful mess in their backyard that they haven't fixed?'"

Gil Gerard feels, "It would have been nice to re-visit Anarchia on the series, but we couldn't have...By that time, the backlot of (20th Century) Fox where we shot that had been plowed under and they built all these condominiums and it was all gone~

"Anarchia was the backlot of Fox, they were preparing to tear it down, so it was perfect, this rotting city with piles of rubble all over the ground. That's why we used it. They had false fronts of buildings so you could have these mutant guys chasing Twiki and me flitting from window to window. I thought it would be cool for Buck to go back there not because Dr. Huer sent him on a mission, but simply because he was curious. This is the last remainder of his century, after all."

Buck Memories

ERIN GRAY: "When we shot the movie, I found an original *Buck Rogers* Pal/Solar Scout Pin at an antique store, from the Buster Crabbe serial and was in cereal boxes. I took this *Buck Rogers* cereal box pin, copied it in wax and duplicated it in brass. I had duplicates made for the entire cast and crew as Christmas presents, so everybody got one. I gave Gil a gold one, the crew got the brass ones. For the 25th anniversary screening at the Egyptian Theater in Hollywood, all the guys wore their pins. I was touched—that really meant a lot to me."

GLEN LARSON: "It all started long before television with the serials for *Buck Rogers* and *Flash Gordon*. I will say, I hate to learn a lesson after many years, but there's something in the process. Seeing the pilot movie again years later was a lesson... There's a lot of scenes I especially love in the pilot movie, but normally, when you make a movie, you have previews.

"You go see it with a crowd in a theater and I wish we had done some previews (to fine-tune it before the movie originally came out). I used to have a reputation for having earmarks all the way to the lab because I wouldn't let go of the print. I wouldn't let go of the film (because) you can always do something a little bit differently. Seeing the pilot again 25 years later, there was probably a thousand places I would recut. Don't let the 'BEETY BEETY BEETY' of Twiki talking get on top of something else."

SAMANTHA HISSONG (Daughter of Erin Gray): "At 12, I came to The Egyptian Theater for a 25th anniversary screening of the movie, *Buck Rogers in the 25th Century*. That was the first time I had ever seen the movie. It was so strange to see my Mom on a DVD cover with a gun in her hand! I never actually saw the movie until my Mom brought me to that screening of it. You really don't think of your Mom running around with a big laser gun!"

Buck Facts

- At the time the show was on the air, The Universal Studio Tour had a Special FX display, where one lucky audience member would be selected to wear Buck's helmet and pilot a Starfighter before a green screen.
- Pamela Hensley was billed before Erin Gray in the movie.
- Princess Ardala has 29 sisters to replace her if she fails her father.
- Romantic rivals Wilma Deering and Princess Ardala both refer to Buck as "Our Captain."
- In the first season episode "Vegas In Space," Rogers once again brings up his nickname "Lucky Buck."

- Vic Perrin (Uncredited Draconia Voice) was the narrator of *The Outer Limits* TV series. In *Buck's* theatrical version, the Draconian voice was provided by TV star William Conrad who was also narrator on the *Buck Rogers* TV series. Conrad was also the uncredited narrator of *The Fugitive* TV series.
- Wilma's tank fires blasts that sound just like the sound from the guns on *Battlestar Galactica*, another Glen Larson/Universal production. To save costs as Universal did with the serials, many *Galactica* props and sound FX showed up on *Buck Rogers*. Both shows even used some of the same guest actors.
- President of The United States Bill Clinton is a close friend of Gil Gerard. As Governor of Arkansas, Clinton attended the film's charity benefit premiere in Little Rock and has been friends with Gerard ever since. During Clinton's Presidency, The White House requested the SyFy Channel, which was showing *Buck Rogers* reruns at the time. Coincidence?

Since the pilot had been altered to make it more of a 'movie,' it needed to be altered again to fit the needs of a weekly TV series. For example, Henry Silva's Kane clearly desires Princess Ardala. When he's replaced by Michael Ansara on the weekly series, the character seems to be a sycophantic eunuch.

- Conceptual designer William Stout is thanked by Michael Crichton in *Jurassic Park* because the author was inspired by Stout's dinosaur art while writing the book.
- Anarchia reportedly used the soon to be bulldozed backlot on MGM as well as Fox.
- Like the 1979 movie *Buck Rogers*, 1999's *Star Wars Episode One: The Phantom Menace* also concerns itself with broken trade pacts leading to an intergalactic war.

The Weekly Series

To handle *Buck Rogers in the 25th Century*'s complicated visual effects, Hartland proved up to the task, handling enormous FX at a breakneck pace They would take an assembly line approach to speeding up spaceship models and optical plates (CG was still years away), and deliver them on a weekly basis, some shots of which took the original *Star Wars* months to accomplish, because they were so time consuming.

Starlog announces that Buck Rogers *is coming to TV.*

Bruce Lansbury, producer of *Mission Impossible*, *Wonder Woman*, *Wild, Wild West*, *Fantastic Journey* and brother to *Murder She Wrote's* Angela Lansbury (he produced that show, too), found Hartland made the show easier to produce.

"Getting involved in the high degree of technology available at Universal's Hartland complex, (they) can provide to the highest level, truly state-of-the-art special effects," he told the genre press. "They ought to be better than *Galactica* (from) last year, because now the complex is better put together. We have an army of people working solely for *Buck Rogers*."

The weekly series was being touted by Lansbury as "a light action-adventure in the 25th Century. Buck is a character out of his own time, our time, lonely and a loner, a maverick. We're shifting Dr. Huer's character a bit from the movie version, so that he becomes the senior operator in the World Defense Agency—don't hold me to the agency's name, we might change it and Wilma Deering is the equivalent of a Colonel under Huer in that agency. In the series, she's not merely a Squadron Leader, so we can go into stories of greater variety."

Lansbury compared Gerard's Buck to James Garner on *The Rockford Files* and Cary Grant in *Gunga Din*, feeling the hero is "very useful because as a 20th Century Man, he has faculties and talents that 25th Century Man has allowed to atrophy. Buck uses his head more than they do, their society has so much of their thinking done for them by the council of Computers, people have forgotten how to use their hands and their heads.."

Stargate BR: 1

As noted, the weekly series would downplay Anarchia and add other pockets of civilization, including New Phoenix and New Detroit. New Chicago would no longer be referred to as "The Inner City." One of the innovations *Buck* brought to sci fi shows was the use of the Stargate. While stargates are an accepted concept now, *Buck Rogers in the 25th Century* was the first to use it regularly on a weekly basis, long before the likes of *Star Trek: Deep Space Nine* or *Stargate SG1*.

"Alan Brennert invented a device for us whereby we don't have the time problem in star travel. He's calling it a 'Star Gate,'" Lansbury said back in 1979. "Essentially, (it's) a black hole phenomenon. You punch out your destination on a ship's computer, arrive at a Star Gate, there's an explosion of light, and you disappear, to re-appear as many light-years away as you programmed yourself to be."

Story Editor Brennert recalls, "All I was doing was borrowing an old concept from Andre Norton, among other pulp writers, but it was something we'd never seen on TV before, so I take some pride in that. Plus, I was finding a way to justify the interstellar distances traveled by these dinky little fighter jet-like ships. I was determined that the science—or pseudo-science—in *Buck* didn't seem arbitrary and absurd, as it did on *Battlestar Galactica*."

Action Figure

Buck Rogers in the 25th Century movie and TV series produced many spinoff products, comic books, lunch boxes, tee shirts, posters, Colorforms and of course, action figures. Buck, Twiki, Draco, Dr. Huer, Tigerman, Draconian Guard and Kane were all made into toys, as well as plastic replicas of Buck's Starfighter and The Draconian Marauders. There was briefly a Wilma Deering doll, too.

"Those were all reminders that I got screwed royally on the merchandising by Universal," Gil Gerard chuckles ruefully. "I nev-

Buck Rogers *action figures. Photo by Gina Sheridan.*

er got a dime for it. It was nice that they made it, but what it became was another sticking point at how badly handled everything having to do with *Buck Rogers* was.

"The toy people were saying 'We can't get enough of this stuff, it flies right out the door, we need more...' and I find I'm being totally ripped off by the studio! My agent made a bad deal and actually bragged about the percentage of the merchandising he got me, but he made a mistake. In order for me to get paid for anything, they needed to put my name *and* my likeness on the box. They had my name on one box and my likeness on another— as long as they didn't put them together, they didn't have to pay me anything, so I was really pissed! I thought it was a pretty good likeness of me, though. With the DVDs, they said 'It's not really a likeness of Gil, it's just a generic male figure.'"

Erin Gray notes wryly, "Poor Wilma Deering only got a tiny action figure—she was totally cheated out of having her own larger doll. They made a large and small doll of Twiki, but not Wilma! That would have been nice..."

Gil Gerard: Buck Rogers lives!

Although he's done a lot of TV series, films and movies of the week, Gil Gerard knows how the public will always see him—in white spandex, with a beautiful girl and trusty robot sidekick in tow, off to save the day...and his planet.

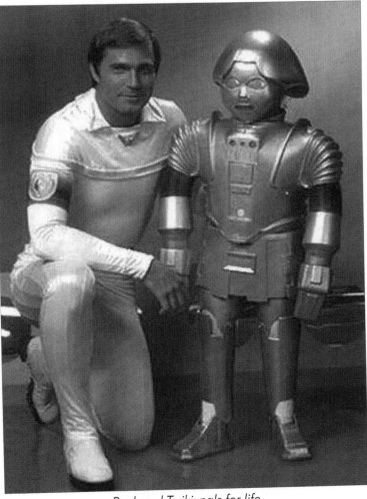

Buck and Twiki, pals for life.

"It's funny," the actor says with a shy grin, "because the people watching the show will never know how much I hated that white suit! It was a job that I did. I was an adult, I didn't think of him as an iconic figure, I was playing this character Buck Rogers and doing the best job I could with it and just having a good time. To me, that was it. "

As the star of *the Buck Rogers in the 25th Century* TV series, Gil Gerard had a lot riding on the show. "I wasn't a hardcore science fiction fan growing up," he offers. "I never really wanted a trusty robot sidekick when I was a kid and I didn't have imaginary friends."

How did it feel in 1979 to be Gil Gerard, an actor with a hit movie, a hit TV show, his own action figure, his face on a lunchbox and 10 year old boys idolizing him? "I was more interested in the 17 and 18 year old girls," Gerard jokes. "It felt good, *it was good*. I just enjoyed it and had a great time!"

Gil Gerard is funny and full of Southern Charm. The Man who would be Buck was born Gilbert 'Gil' Gerard on January 23, 1943 in Little Rock, Arkansas.

"I was named after my Uncle Gilbert, as was my cousin Gilbert, so we were the three Gilberts," he laughs. Gerard attended the University of Arkansas, but dropped out. "I worked as an industrial chemist at a chemical company run by Arkansas Governor Wynn Rockefeller, but acting was something I always wanted to do. I thought about it while I was working as an industrial chemist, because I really wasn't happy doing that.

"After going through the card file of my life experience, I decided I wanted to be an actor. I lied and became an industrial chemist without a college degree. I don't recommend it because you spend all your time waiting for the other shoe to drop and that's not a good way to live your life, " he confides. "but at the time... The guy who hired me said he knew I could do the job because I had enough knowledge of chemicals and chemistry. He then said to me, 'Do you have your degree?' and I said, 'Yeah.' He never checked.

"After that, I resigned from my various jobs, went to New York, started going to acting school and worked driving a cab 12 hours a night. I went to school during the day. I began to work as an actor (in-

Gil Gerard, photo by Pat Jankiewicz.

cluding a bit part in *Love Story* that wound up on the cutting room floor). I studied under Philip Burton, who was Richard Burton's adopted father.

"I heard that Richard was like a street waif and Philip took him in, took care of him and became his father, while training him in acting. Richard actually came to my class' Christmas party and read *A Child's Christmas In Wales* to all of us. It was amazing, he was a magnetic personality. I just sat there listening, so impressed—all I could say was 'Wow!' That's where I started and then I studied with David Learnt in New York, at The American Place Theater.

Buster Crabbe, Gil Gerard, Erin Gray on Buck Rogers.

I started working as an actor and always asked questions. After everything I have done, I am still learning."

Gerard became popular in commercials— promoting cars for Ford Motor Company and print ads for Camel Cigarettes. He was also a frequent guest star on shows like *Baretta* and *Hawaii Five-O*. He starred in daytime soap *The Doctors* and played lead Moonshiner Eddie Joe in the hillbilly romp *Hooch*, which he also produced. From there, he co-starred with Yvette Mimieux in the TV movie *Ransom For Alice* and then wound up in the star stud- ded cast of *Airport '77*.

"When I did *Airport '77*, I had the great pleasure of working every day with Christopher Lee," Gil Gerard says happily. "The stories that guy has got, just a ton of 'em, all great, funny tales from his own life. I truly enjoyed hearing them. Chris and I used to sit on this set of a VIP Lounge for the scenes on the airplane, because on the *Airport* movies, you had to be on the set every single day whether you were in the scene or not. Because it was set on a 747—shot on Universal Studios' Stage 747, which you have seen in a million movies and TV shows.

"It was a very constricted set, so if the director moved the camera a foot, you might actually be in the background, so Christopher Lee, Joseph Cotton, Olivia DeHavilland, Jack Lemmon, everybody sitting on that plane had to be there on that set every single day, whether you were in the scene or not. It got old after awhile, I lived across the street from Universal Studios, so I would say to the Assistant Director, 'Can I go home and do my laundry?' the A.D. would reply 'I can't let you, man, if the director needs you and you're not here...'

"I'm the last passenger to get off the plane in that. I joked around with Jack Lemmon on that, too. Every morning, Jack Lemmon would come in, I would say 'Hey, Jack' and he would go, 'Fuck you, Gerard!' It was great! He would get a huuuuge cup of coffee to start the day. I had a great time, being around those guys."

After a guest shot on *Little House On The Prairie* ("I came in to re-decorate the Ingalls kitchen!"), that show's producer/star Michael Landon was so impressed with Gerard, he asked him to star in a pilot that Landon wrote and directed for him, *Killing Stone*. Gerard played Gil Stone, a man who spent a decade behind bars for a crime he did not commit. Released, he tries to pick up the pieces of what's left of his life. While waiting to see whether or not the pilot movie would become a TV series, the actor was then invited to take a trip to the 25th Century.

"I became Buck Rogers when I came out to California and had just done that series pilot for Michael Landon," he states. "*Killing Stone* was something that I really wanted to do. Universal called and said they wanted me to do *Buck Rogers in the 25th Century*, but I turned them down. They called three times and I turned them down all three times.

"I didn't want to play a cartoon character. I was not a big fan of *Batman* (with Adam West), so all I could think when they offered *Buck* to me was 'Boff/biff/bam,' those silly sound balloons and other crap they did on *Batman*. I decided I wasn't going to play a cartoon character. I didn't want to do that shit. I was excited about this project that I was gonna do with Michael Landon and I was pleased that he was talking about bringing in really good writers to do really good stories—that was really how I wanted my career to go.

"Finally, Universal called my agent called and said 'Will you read the script for *Buck Rogers*?' He read it and called me up. My agent said 'Listen, it's not what you think it is. You should give it a read' so I did and I liked it. Buck wasn't some one-dimensional cartoon character, he was a guy who had both humanity and a sense of humor. I also realized the Landon project was dead, it just wasn't gonna go. Since I liked the *Buck Rogers* project, I decided to just go ahead and do it."

The show's take on Buck as a man appealed to him.

"I liked the sense of humor and the kind of tongue-in-cheek attitude that Buck had in the original script. I also liked the fact that there was a thing going on between him and Wilma Deering, where she was very by the book and straight-laced while Buck was more flying by the seat of his pants, being a fighter pilot and all.

"That relationship with Wilma was interesting and kind of fun, contrasting the uptight personality of Wilma with improvising-as-he-goes-along Buck was fun. Buck was always saying 'C'mon, let's respond to what's going on, everything isn't A, B, C, D, E.' That's why I wound up taking it. Halfway through shooting, we learned it was gonna be a feature film, which was cool."

"One of my favorite scenes in the pilot movie is the moment where I visit my family's grave in old Chicago. I really liked that scene, where Buck realizes "Oh My God, there they are!" You felt bad for him."

Of his co-stars, "I really enjoyed working with them, Erin, Tim and Felix. That's why it was easy to like Twiki in the show, because I know and enjoy Felix, the man inside him. We are still friends today," he says warmly.

His show had a lot of colorful guest stars. "Oh, I loved all the great character actors we had on the show," Gerard says pleasantly. "Frank Gorshin, Cesar Romero, Sam Jaffe who was in *Gunga Din*! Sam played a judge on an episode, Roddy McDowall was amazing—we even had Peter Graves on the show. They were truly great! I liked Julie Newmar, she was a sweet gal.

"I got to work with Buster Crabbe, the original Buck Rogers," he marvels. "Buster was great, we became really good friends after that. We didn't really work together on the show(they communicate via radio between Starfighters), so I came in especially to meet him on a day he was working—he was the original Buck Rogers, and I just thought out of respect, I should be there to say hello to him.

"We hit it off, had a great time talking and became friends. He invited me to New Mexico for a dinner with an astronaut who landed on the Moon. We stayed in touch and he was a truly great guy, I used to pay a dime to see a John Wayne movie and watch the serials, Johnny Mack Brown, Jungle Jim , Lash Larue, Roy Rogers, Gene Autry and of course, Buster's *Buck Rogers*! Little did I know....Saturday at the movies was the equivalent of TV today. My Mother would give me a quarter and that was bus fare, movie, popcorn and a coke! I was at the movies all day."

"I remember something Buster said to me about his *Buck Rogers*. Everybody laughs at the fx of his serials, but he said to me, 'You realize the FX were cutting edge for our time—those ships with a sparkler stuck on the end, smoking away were amazing FX for their time'—and he said, in 50 years, people will be laughing at the special fx of this show.' Occasionally, I will look at one of my *Buck* episodes with that thought in mind and the special fx still hold up, in my mind. They're getting a little creaky, they aren't cutting edge like CGI, because they were long before CGI," Gerard admits. "They're okay so far, they aren't sparklers coming outta the back end yet, Thank God!"

His favorite guest star "has to be Pamela Hensley," he proffers. "Pamela was great, I loved her. She was terrific, a wonderful person and a very good actress. Her character, Princess Ardala, was the closest to camp that we actually got on the show but she was direct, she played her with a great deal of humanity and feeling.

"There was one particular scene in an episode where she demands that I marry her or she'll destroy Earth or some shit (in 'Es-

Buck and Ardala.

cape From Wedded Bliss'), but there's a scene, a private moment where she's in her chambers, looking in the mirror and she's feeling very sad that I don't want to marry her. It's a very touching scene. I was standing off to the side because we had other scenes in that area and I said to her, 'Goddamn, you are so touching in this scene, all the people watching are gonna hate me for not marrying you!'

   "She was so incredible, you watch that scene and think 'Poor Ardala.' It was such a vulnerable, touching scene she did, I knew everybody would hate my guts because Buck was being such a jerk. I really loved her to death, a great, classy woman as well as a good actress. Fun to work with, I really liked her. Haven't seen her in 35 years, but I liked her a lot. I have fond memories and thoughts of her."

Does he cringe watching the scene in the pilot, where he takes Ardala and re-invents disco dancing? "No, because I got screwed on that," he smiles. "We worked for two weeks with a choreographer and then it came to shoot that scene of Ardala and I dancing. The director (Daniel Haller) said, 'Oh no, we can't do that, 'I'm not gonna do that—I would be here (on this one scene) for three weeks! I just need the two of you doing this,' Gerard mimes bouncing in place, "and then I'm just gonna cover it. So all of the stuff Pamela and I worked on, became her and I doing this," Gerard explains, doing the bouncing again.

"He had us do that, so we could do all the repartee—I would dance off, come back and then do my repartee with Ardala. Because the director said we can't do it, all that was thrown out, so I go over to the guy playing the music to get a beat. Of course, in the finished scene, there was no beat—I didn't know what kind of music they were gonna use. I was hoping to God I would be dancing to whatever beat they came up with and I had to work my way back to Ardala on my own. All we ended up doing is bouncing in place. Watching it the first time, I thought '*Fuck—talk about taking it on the chin in that scene!*"

"I was impressed with the people who became stars after doing our show," the actor adds. "With Jamie Lee Curtis, I was very gratified to see her career take off after she did the show and went on to bigger and better things. Jamie Lee was great, terrific, just a wonderful girl. She did a great job on the show (in the episode 'Unchained Woman'), but also as a human being, she was really great. She actually baked a couple pies and brought them to the set—she was just so sweet and nice.

"I'm proud of the people on the show who went onto great things. Dennis Haysbert, who was in a couple first season episodes before doing our second season as the original helmsman on The Searcher, did great. I didn't realize he did that on our show until I had a very nice meeting with him at a Myrtle Beach Celebrity Golf Tournament," Gerard says with a tinge of pride.

"Dennis came up to me and said, 'I know who you are—I was on your show! You probably don't remember, but I was the helmsman on your spaceship!' I was surprised—and happy—that he had a good experience on the show. He then told me, 'You were so nice to me, it kept me in the business.' He told me that I talked to him about hanging in there. I was very touched that he remembers it as a positive experience."

Working in the sci-fi world took a lot of getting used to. Flying a spacecraft was a unique experience for the actor.

"Those spaceships were not as fun as they looked," Gil Gerard says dryly. "The Starfighters we flew were large models on a giant gimbal that we could sit in, they were just huge! You would go three stories up off the ground, shooting against a blue screen. It was long and tedious—there were times where it took them so long to set up, I fell asleep up there. When we were shooting, they never knew what angle the bad guys would be coming in, so we had to do all these variations on 'Watch out!' I would be sitting there, saying 'Watch out!' in every direction, because they had not made up their mind yet in which direction it was all gonna go!"

"I keep the model of my starship from the show in a Lucite case. I had it designed and put a mirrored thing on it. All the guys at Hartland signed it on the base. It's the ship that I did all the dog-fights in and it actually says 'Captain Buck Rogers' on it. I love that thing."

"I remember, in the movie, for the scene where I get frozen in the space shuttle, I actually fell asleep. After they covered me in all the fake ice, I forgot what the makeup girl sprayed on me, but it looked like shampoo. I was really asleep," he says with amusement. "We were usually shooting a lot at 4:00 in the morning, all these long hours sitting in that Starfighter mock up on a gimbal high up on a soundstage. Sometimes, I would be so tired, I just fell asleep. We worked really long hours on the show.

"There was a period where we were doing two episodes at once, working about 20 hours a day. Since I was in practically every shot, I remember walking into the scene and saying 'Wait a minute—who are the bad guys in this?' I literally didn't know which episode we were doing, because I was doing another episode of *Buck* on another soundstage. I was so busy, because I was in al-

Buck changing into satyr.

most every scene. If I wasn't with someone in a scene, I was off in another scene."

He appeared on the cover of *TV Guide*, but had little time to savor it. "Y'know what? Sometimes when I look back on that whole period, I wish that I wasn't so damn busy, because maybe I could have appreciated it more," the actor reflects. "It seemed like I was on an endless run of working, getting on a plane Friday night, flying all night somewhere and doing personal appearances all weekend, getting on a plane Sunday night, and getting up at 4:00 in the morning to go back to work, till I was on that Friday night plane again! .

"Go Go Go, that's how it was. I remember sitting down and doing 300 promos for radio stations, 'Hi, This is Gil Gerard, tune into *Buck Rogers in the 25th Century* tonight on KNBC in Wichita!' That was on the time when I was supposed to be relaxing between shoots. It was a continual thing, I was going all the time."

"Connie (Sellecca) and I were newly married when I did *Buck*. She wasn't doing anything at the time, it was before the birth of our son, Gib and she started *Greatest American Hero* after that. She did a show called *Flying High* before I met her—and then she got *Beyond Westworld*. I met her on a plane coming back from New York to L.A. and we got together. She got *Greatest American Hero* a year into *Buck*, and then she got *Hotel*.."

He also had to wear spandex. As a TV action hero trying to keep his waistline under control, his formfitting white costume did not help at all.

"I hated the white suit! HATED IT! It was two layers—I had to wear a body stocking under it just to get that thing on," Gerard groans. "It was hard, it showed everything, so I had to make sure I was in great shape for the entire season. If I had a bad day (eating), it really showed! It was tight, so it wasn't stretchy and you can see it stretching in pictures from the show. Poor Erin's outfit was so tight, she needed a slantboard between shots.

"I never, ever liked wearing the white suit," he says distastefully, remembering the agony it caused him. "Wearing it, I kept trying to put my hands in my pockets and I couldn't! There wasn't even an opening in the pants... It's all because of Gene Roddenberry."

Gene Roddenberry? "Yeah! When he did *Star Trek*, he sewed their pockets shut, so after that it was inevitable—in the future, Man can't put his Goddamn hands in his pockets," jokes Gerard. "It was so tight, the pants had ribs. At the end of the day, I would take it off and I literally had ridges in my skin from wearing it! It was also hard to have casual sex in that thing!" (Erin Gray teases, "The lack of pockets never bothered me, I never had a problem knowing what to do with my hands!")

Doing fight scenes on the show was always a highlight of every episode, as Buck broke out his unique form of martial arts and laid out Mutants, Draconian Guards or anyone else unlucky enough to mess with him.

"Those fight sequences were fun because they weren't hard at all. I just did the close-ups and my stunt double would do the rest of it! (Legendary wrestler 'Judo') Gene LeBell stunt doubled for different people on the show, including Tigerman. He was a former wrestler, and a lot of fun. I enjoyed working with him—it was always fun to have a fight scene with Gene.

"Speaking of the action scenes—I remember Erin would make the gun sound when she fired her ray gun," Gerard says fondly. "I did something similar on the pilot I did for Michael Landon. I did a fight scene in it and I'm going (makes punching sounds) when I suddenly realize what I'm doing and just said, 'I've been a kid too long!' I'm doing sound fx for fisticuffs. Michael busted up and we had to re-shoot it."

Buck's Duel To The Death...With The Writers!

Doing the show, the actor frequently complained to the press about the quality of scripts for the show. This led to a heated meeting with the writers over the script for the episode 'Escape From Wedded Bliss.'

"There wasn't much ad-libbing on *Buck Rogers*, we pretty much just stuck to the script. I did a lot of rewrites on the thing, whether they (the writers) liked it or not," he says frankly. "I remember being not particularly pleased with the first five scripts. I read them and hated them all...Buck was a loudmouth, a rube, he didn't have a sense of humor and I found him obnoxious. It was everything I didn't want him to do. I wanted Huer to tell Buck to 'Shut up!'

"I called a meeting with everybody, including producer Bruce Lansbury and the writers, and I said, 'I know you asked me to hold off (judgment until the series got going), but I can't. If you keep going in this direction, you're gonna write a show that I don't want to do.' It was my face up there and I didn't want to be embarrassed.

"There was one particular writer who really treated me like I didn't know what the fuck I was talking about and who physically turned away every time I said something. I pointed this out to Bruce Lansbury, who was also in the room, and said 'They're not listening to me' and he said 'yes, they are.' I said 'Bruce, I'm not stupid— I wasn't born last night, I can tell when someone is not listening and when someone really doesn't care what I have to say and she (writer Anne Collins) really doesn't want to hear what I have to say.'

"I said, 'I don't like this character, I don't like what's going on with Buck, Wilma and Twiki going out and solving intergalactic crimes! Jesus Christ, man, you have a 360 degree periphery and you've narrowed it down to a detective show!'

"'Look, This is *Buck Rogers*, this is the universe...It's not a crime show, it's not *Wonder Woman* or *Quincy!*' It was a tense meeting only because I was being treated as if I were an idiot. Had they come up with legitimate answers to my questions about the show, I was willing to listen, but I got my back up because I was being treated as if I didn't know what the fuck I was doing. I wasn't about to stand for that. That's why, obviously, those writers and I were going to be unable to work together.

"They weren't listening to me," he insists, "so that was it. A bit of a blowup. Most things like that, I prefer to let them stay where they are, that was a private meeting and things like that happen all the time in Hollywood. Then it became a big pissing contest, when it was just business. I don't like dirty laundry being aired."

While the show got huge ratings by today's standards, it was only a midlevel success at the time. Things were dire at the time, because NBC was a dismal third place network in the ratings back when there were only three networks, with flops like *Supertrain, Hello, Larry* and *Pink Lady And Jeff,* so every show was pressured to do better.

"*Buck Rogers In The 25th Century* should have been seen as one of the bright spots on their schedule but, lucky me, I had a show on when Fred Silverman ran NBC, so he never really cared for it. I used to call him 'Freddy Silverlips'—not to his face, of course! He *was* the head of the network, after all..."

For the second season, the network and studio tried to appease the actor by replacing producer Bruce Lansbury with John Mantley. The show dumped every element and supporting character of the first season except Wilma and Twiki, who joined Buck on an exploratory mission in deep space. Ratings dropped like a rock.

"I really didn't like the second season, but oddly enough, I really liked some of the scripts," he admits. "What I didn't like was the scenario. I didn't like us being stuck on this ship and going off to search for stuff. It seemed stupid to me, so contrary to Buck Rogers. What happened with the second season is I just gave up, because there was nothing I could do. NBC obviously thought John Mantley was their golden boy, Silverman brought him in supposedly—this was Mantley's story, so who knows if it was true, so I was like 'Fine, you want this stuff? Go right ahead.'

"I was sad that they lost Tim O'Connor and I felt badly that the whole franchise was decimated. They not only got rid of Tim, but Princess Ardala, Kane, New Chicago, all of the stuff that was there and established who Buck was and his home, all of the sudden, we dump all of that to go off on this damn spaceship going into Outer Space. They were interesting characters and they should have been kept on the show.

"When did we become *Battlestar Galactica* and *Star Trek*, wandering around the damn universe? It's about a man out of his own time, it's NOT about *Star Trek* or searching for the 'lost tribes of Earth,' it's about this guy coming to grips with the fact that he's back on Earth 500 years later, everyone he knew and loved is dead and everything he knows is gone. That's the story, not this other crap.

"Mantley was like (mimes a disinterested shrug). John Mantley talked shit about me in a very bad way and I didn't know about it until I read a clipping. Mantley's gone now—I didn't kill him, but I'm not sad he's gone."

Some of the second season stories "I liked only because, had they been on Earth, it would have been perfect. Buck needed to be on Earth, having experiences with people on Earth including survivors of the (nuclear) holocaust, which I think would have been an interesting show for the audience," he asserts. "I really enjoyed The Satyr."

"Everybody loves watching movies or shows set in the future only because they are interested in seeing what the idea of the future is—people love *Blade Runner*, which sees a future where it's always raining and everything is very dirty," he smiles. "That's a filthy future—at least New Chicago was clean!"

The actor looks great now, having undergone a gastric bypass for a Discovery Channel documentary. He also retained his friendship with former President of the United States, Bill Clinton.

"I met him during his first term as Governor," Gerard remembers. "I did the world premiere of *Buck Rogers* in Little Rock to benefit retarded citizens. It was Bill's first term as Governor, we met and became friends. He's a good guy; we've been friends for about 30 or 35 years. Bill liked the show, and I like him a lot.

"He and I as friends mostly talk about family and shit. One time, in California, Bill and Hillary came up and stayed at my house by the beach. Bill and I went for a long walk and Hillary babysat my son Gib while we were gone. We got together after he was elected president and even went to church together that first Christmas, right before he was inaugurated.

"My son, myself, Bill, Hillary and Chelsea all sat on the same bench in church. Bill was nice enough and gracious enough to be part of my Discovery documentary, *Gil Gerard: Action Hero Makeover*, where I had my gastric bypass."

The actor says that since the surgery, "My life has been great — I lost 154 pounds and that saved my life. My waist was 66 inches, now its 33 inches. I feel great, much better than I ever did! Erin and Felix also did the documentary with me. Discovery didn't want anybody knowing. They didn't even tell me Felix knew. He lives in Las Vegas, but Felix came in when I had the surgery. I was touched by that."

He still does the occasional SyFy Channel movie or show. "I do stuff like *Bone Eater* for them. It sounds like a bad porno, but it's actually a Native American legend composed of six war chiefs that will become an incredibly powerful beast," he laughs. "Me and Bruce Boxleitner survive—the cast was all sci-fi heroes. Me, Bruce, Bill Katt, all guys who played science fiction TV heroes."

Next up for Gil Gerard "Oh, getting up in the morning," he jokes. "I figure that's the first thing. Staying on this side of the grass is important. I did some documentaries that I produced and I will be directing one of them. Life is good!"

Erin Gray:
25th Century Fox!

Let's face it, the appeal of the *Buck Rogers In The 25th Century* movie and TV series was not the flashy special FX, the cute robots or wisecracking leading man, it was Erin Gray.

Wilma in white flight suit.

As Colonel Wilma Deering, Commander of Earth's defenses, Gray made the future look promising. Clad in a skintight Cat-suit that audiences were asked to believe was a military uniform, Gray's sexy heroine teamed up with recently defrosted 20th Century survivor Buck to defend the planet and occasionally the galaxy. Decisive, clever and in command, Gray's Deering was one of sci-fi TV's strong, independent females.

Armed with a gun and a grin, she helped Buck foil plots from enemies both domestic and intergalactic, thwarting angry androids, alien invasions, vixens and many other menaces.

"I loved Wilma Deering. She was how I wanted her to be, strong and asserting, the first female colonel. Wilma was Commander of Earth's defenses. She was cute and had a nice butt, but you *didn't* mess with her; she was in charge," Erin Gray giggles. "I think many guys would like to be dominated by me!"

She performed in assorted movies, SyFy originals and TV shows like the sitcom *Silver Spoons*. Gray even squeezed in a *Friday the 13th* flick, *Jason Goes To Hell*. "That one revealed that Jason Voorhees is my brother and I love him dearly," she grins. The easygoing actress is still proud of her spaceborne alter ego.

"Wilma was only my second acting part ever and it was hard to begin my career in science fiction," she declares. "Because in science fiction, nothing is normal. A door is not a door, a light switch is not a light switch—science fiction changes everything! As an actress, I never realized I would have to learn so much about guns. When you train to be an actress, you imagine that you will be playing Queen Elizabeth, but in reality, the first fifteen things I was in, I was always carrying a gun.

"On *Buck Rogers*, they handed me the gun and I thought, 'How cool—I'm in a space suit on a space set and they have actually given me a ray gun!' I remember that I was in one of my first scenes, I had to run around a corner, dive and fire on the bad guy. I go through the whole thing, aim at the bad guy and I go, 'BANG! BANG! BANG,'" she blushes. "The whole crew cracked up. The director said to me in front of the crew, 'No, Erin, we put in the sound FX later. We don't need you to make them!'"

One of her favorite perks on the television series "was having my own Starfighter. I have to say, having your own Starfighter is a real thrill! What amazed me about sitting in the cockpit of it is how I was surrounded by pieces of technology that were re-purposed for my spacecraft. There were parts of a radio here, pieces of a typewriter there and the whole thing looked like a toaster at my house.

"It would always kill me when the crew would say, 'We're gonna do a pickup shot of you in your Starfighter...' I would say, 'Okay, where's my Starfighter?' They would tell me, 'It's too expensive to bring it in, so we're just gonna sit you here on a stool.' 'Wait a minute,' I would say, 'I know you're only doing a head shot, but I am in a battle scene in my Starfighter. Could I have something to help me have a sense of where I am?' They gave me a broomstick to use as the Starfighter's joystick, so I could pretend I was flying."

"Remember my helmet when I flew the Starfighter? My helmet was 'one size fits all' while Gil's was tailored to his head. My helmet slid like a bobblehead, so if I had to look around on the show while wearing it, you would notice my whole body turn. Otherwise the helmet would be in a different direction."

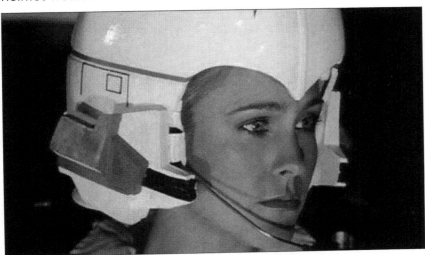

Erin Gray, in helmet flying ship.

FILM FOX

No one was more shocked than Gray when Universal Studios decided to turn the *Buck Rogers* TV pilot into a feature film. "We did the first two hours of *Buck Rogers in the 25th Century* as part of a ten hour miniseries. I was originally told it was gonna be a miniseries. We were called back to production in March to finish shooting what was supposed to be a miniseries and suddenly it was a film, but no one had bothered to tell me. All I knew is that when we came back, the cameras were different and the pacing was different. Months later, I got a call saying that it was now a feature film that would play in theaters and I needed to do some pick-up shots for it. Gil told me, 'Yeah, we're doing a film!' And I said, 'Nice of someone to finally tell me!'"

Although she was excited to be part of a major motion picture, she had some concerns.

"As an actor who cares about her role, I look at something and make choices on where the arc of my character is going and how she relates to something. When I did the film, I asked 'Is there a script for the movie?' 'No, but here are sides (dialogue) for today.' I read them and I said, 'I'm a little confused...I know I did a scene very similar to this six months ago, so tell me where we are in the story. Is this before or after the trial sequence?' I got answers like, *Just do the lines.'* I didn't like that about the movie."

In the film, Wilma is tough, humorless, not as winsome as she is in the series. On the show, she's far more curious about Buck and his 20th Century customs.

"I don't think Wilma in the movie differs that much from the TV version in the first year." the actress opines. "In the movie, Wilma was equal to a man—I liked that a lot. They kept that for the whole first season of *Buck Rogers in the 25th Century.* She was completely softened for the show's second season and I was really saddened by that. I didn't want to play a typical female role, a damsel in distress," she says, lapsing into a Minnie Mouse falsetto. "'Ohhhh, Buck, are you alright? Can I help you, Buck?' I was wringing my hands all through the second season. "

FUTURISTIC FRIENDS

She was pleased with her supporting cast, particularly Tim O'Connor as her boss, Dr. Elias Huer, and robot friends Twiki and Theopolis.

"Oh, I loved playing with Tim O'Connor—Tim was so good as Huer," she praises. "We were terrific together and I always felt

Twiki and Wilma.

secure working with him. I also liked Wilfrid Hyde-White (who replaced O'Connor as new scientist Dr. Goodfellow in the show's
second season), but I really missed that camaraderie with Tim in
Season Two."

"Twiki was played by Felix Silla," Erin Gray adds. "Normally, Felix would be sitting in a corner with the Twiki helmet off, smoking
a cigar. Felix was a forty-five year old man with three kids, who
would visit him on the set. They were all twice his size. It was
interesting to see him be a parent on one hand and on the other,
watch him say, 'Let me put my cigar out, pull on my Twiki hat and
go back to work.'"

Unfortunately, Twiki's fussy computer companion, Dr. Theopolis, "was one of the most difficult co-stars I have ever had. That
little face on Theo was battery-operated, and the connection was
always loose! We would be doing a scene and Theo would just
fade out halfway through it. We always had to wait for someone
to run in and change his batteries!"

She found it easy to work with robots. "The whole point of
acting is to bring truth to something that's not there,' she proffers. "Be it a robot, an alien or a person, you just have to make it

believable and bring truth to it. Whatever works for you. I would be looking at Theo and thinking about my little boy's darling face!"

LEADING LADY

While Gray had a great chemistry onscreen with Gil Gerard, she found him somewhat enigmatic off-screen. "There were problems with my leading man that I just didn't understand," she says quietly.

"The first indication that we had problems was literally the first day *Buck Rogers in the 25th Century* aired on television. After we did the feature, I thought everything was fine. It was gonna be a big TV series. That first episode aired and I came onto the set at Universal Studios saying, 'Wow, wasn't that a great episode last night? That was—' when I suddenly noticed that everyone was just sitting around. 'Ummm, why isn't anybody working? What's wrong?'

"The crew all looked at me in surprise. 'You mean you don't know?' 'Know what? What's going on?' 'Erin, we've been shut down.' 'Why?' Nobody would tell me. I finally got it out of the script supervisor. 'Erin, Gil refuses to come to work. He wants your credit changed.' On the first night it aired, the credits read 'Starring Gil Gerard and Erin Gray'

"He wanted 'Starring Gil Gerard' first and on a separate card, 'Co-starring Erin Gray.' I was a Universal Studios contract player at the time and I was only making $600.00 a week as the female lead on a major TV series. The studio had me under contract, so they could do whatever they wanted with me, but Gil had them by the...well, you know!"

Despite being the star of one of the few midlevel hits NBC had at the time, she was still a contract actress working for a pittance. "When the studio asked me to do the Golden Globes, I told them 'I don't have a gown or the money to buy one.' They finally provided me one so I could go. A certain amount of anger and resentment starts to build up...You're making me work these long hours for no money and having me bleach my hair every couple of weeks?!'"

BUCK vs. WILMA

Doing the series, "I was sad to see many episodes where Gil would cut the humor. It always amazed me that he would cut the jokes, because there is no one funnier than Gil Gerard, no one can make you laugh harder than Gil. He has a great wit! There were times on the set, you would say "Gil, shut up for five seconds'; because he was making you laugh so hard, I had a stitch in my side from laughing.

"Gil has such wonderful charm and that's what made Buck so special as a character. Why would you want to get rid of what made you so different and more special than any other leading man out there," Erin Gray queries. "He had a triple A sense of humor, he's fabulous, we are still friends, but it stunned me that Gil would cut the show's comedy. The script girl and I had an ongoing bet over how many jokes Gill would cut. We made it a game for the crew when the new scripts came out.

"There were bets over how many jokes he would take out of this or that episode. I would say 18 jokes would be cut, someone else would say 25 and we would go through the jokes we all thought he would cut. He would come in and then we'd get the rewrites and he cut almost all of them. I heard he wanted to do more 'action hero' stuff and took it seriously, but he was the king of wit and charm, it was one of his strengths! That was phenomenal, that he would cut something he was so perfect at."

"Early on, he was quite funny. I'm a straight man, not one to play jokes, but Gil talked me into playing one on a friend of his. We were just getting to know each other, when he talked me into going down to LAX (airport) to meet his business manager, Joel. He said 'Here's what you're going to do' and pointed Joel out.

"I come out and 'accidentally' bump into Joel. I say, 'OH MY GOD, JOEL! How great to see you! Don't you remember me? After that fabulous weekend together? It was the best sex I ever had, but I know we had a lot to drink...' I really played it up, the best performance of my life. All I remember is Joel's eyes getting bigger looking at me as he wracked his brain trying to remember me. Meanwhile, his wife is behind him coming closer and closer. I keep playing it up, about that night. His wife finally walks up and says, *'Honey, who is this?'* That's when Gil popped out from behind a pillar and says, 'Joel, meet my new leading lady!' I had never seen someone squirm so much in my life."

"There was a lot of laughter working on the show, most of which was in a famous *Buck Rogers* outtake reel. Gil and I started playing jokes on each other. After working such long hours, your energy would be down in the dumps at 3 a.m. and you would try to boost morale by being funny. it became a running competition to see who could have the raunchiest, most risqué joke that day. We would joke to keep things going, so there would be all this good stuff for the Christmas reel. One week before the Christmas party, somebody stole the reel from the editing room!

"This contest started when I would sneak into dailies every day. Because I was fairly new to the business and wanted to learn more, I would sit down in front and listen in to what the editor and director were saying—what shots they took and why. Day after day, Gil would crack the crew up after every scene.

"I saw in dailies, just before the slate guy would say what scene it was, Gil was always cutting up, telling jokes, being 'Mr. Charming' while I was always 'Miss Serious'...I was only asking technical questions, like "I'm supposed to walk over here? Okay, got it!' Everyday, I looked at it and even though I was a newbie, I realized that this was not giving the best impression of me to all the producers and executives from the black tower who came in to look at dailies, so I decided to change my image.

"I began on 'Planet Of The Slave Girls,' in a scene of me and Brianne Leary. I told the cameraman, 'When the director says cut, just keep the camera rolling.' I didn't realize he was risking his job because film is really expensive, but he did as I asked and I said to Brianne, 'No matter what happens, when the director says cut, keep looking at me!' We were dressed in skimpy slave girl costumes and we were about to be thrown into Kaleel's volcano to our inescapable death.

"Brianne says to me, 'Oh Wilma, I'm sorry—there's no way Buck is gonna save us, we're going to die!' CUT I then said, 'Y'know, it's really tough being an egg. You only get laid once, eaten once and It takes 10 minutes to get hard!' The crew guys were falling off the ladders and the next day in dailies, the editor and the director threw up all their notes when I said that! They were like, '*What did she just say?*' That started the competition from that point on."

The sci fi press had stories from several crewmembers on *Buck Rogers* recalling Gerard's behavior, including behind-the-scenes attempts to diminish Gray's role. "I never knew about any of that, until it ran in *Starlog* Magazine," she confides. "You must understand, I was so happy to be a working actress, it truly was all of my dreams come true. I was a leading lady with a great role. If they gave me a script, I did it. I didn't get into fights with the producers. When I read those articles in *Starlog* about what was going on behind the scenes of my show, I was like, 'Whoa!' I had no idea how much he was doing."

After the initial credits holdup, Gray found things occasionally tense with her leading man. "He did remind me a few times that the show was called *Buck Rogers*—I got the drift. I thought, 'Okay, fine. I don't need to do anything, I will just let my white spandex speak for itself!'"

SPANDEX!

Her least favorite part of the 25th Century was the male audiences' favorite: her formfitting spandex uniform. 'I couldn't stand those spandex stretch suits," she says with a good natured moan. "They looked good, but I wanted to burn 'em all! Everyone liked Wilma's demeanor, but being in those stretch suits meant I couldn't sit or bend my knees, so I came off as tough and rigid. I would get a headache from being in those suits, it was like a full body girdle. In those days, they didn't have spandex that expanded, so Wilma didn't bend a lot.

"When I first saw the spandex costume I would have to wear, I said 'Do I have to wear it to lunch,'" she laughs. "I came from the modeling world, so I was a little more comfortable than the average girl on the street would be with that outfit. I was one of the original *Sports Illustrated* models. It was just another wardrobe fit. What I didn't realize was that I couldn't sit down for long, because it was like wearing a girdle from head to toe!

"Guys telling me how much they loved me in spandex growing up is happily balanced by an equal amount of girls telling me I empowered them or inspired them to set their goals on a higher level...as well as, um, inspiring a lot of young men," she says sheepishly.

"My husband (Richard Hissong) was the director of Photography on *Friends* and in one of my favorite moments ever, (*Friends* star) Matt LeBlanc saw me, screamed, 'OH MY GOD, IT'S COLONEL WILMA!' He came running across the stage, hugged me and

Wilma leaning and smiling in purple catsuit.

said, 'You don't understand, every Thursday night at eight o'clock, my Mom and I would sit there and we would watch you!' I hear that over and over again, 'My Dad and I,' 'my brother and I,' we don't have that so much anymore. Now everybody is in their own room watching separate shows, not really experiencing those family TV moments.

"*Buck* had something for everybody; there was humor, there was drama, there was," she playfully strokes her own hair, "sex appeal— a leading man with a twinkle in his eye and of course, Twiki... but for me, I'm always pleased so many girls loved my character. I was delighted to play a strong woman. It was a changing time for women and to be part of that was really terrific."

WORKING MOM

The shooting schedule didn't make it any easier. "Those long hours were hard on me—I was a young mother making one quarter of what a teamster on the show was making. Because I was a contract actress, I came in before Gil and worked long after Gil went home, but I was the one with a baby at home and I really resented that," Gray sighs.

"My young son Kevan was at home missing Mommy and I was missing him. That took a real toll on my family and me. Kevan was too little to remember that, but I missed my baby. Part of me never realized when you commit to a series, you are committing your life. Being the star of a series is no 9 to 5 job. Your child is only young once and you need to be there. It wasn't until the cast of *Designing Women* fought the studio to bring their babies to work did the situation change. I didn't even argue or bring it up. I never asked, this was only my second real part and I didn't want to get in trouble."

"Kevan was three. The first time he was ever on set was when we were at the studio on *Buck Rogers*, I get to the stage...It's the entire Draconian flagship, covering the entire set. I make myself small against the wall so nobody will see me and Kevan hiding against the wall, so we can see the scene, but I didn't read the call sheet...The director says into his megaphone, 'Okay, we've only got one take here, guys. Is everybody ready? Rolling! ACTION!" Suddenly, the whole Draconian flagship is exploding, bodies flying everywhere as stunt teams leap through collapsing debris.

"Buck is running through the ship with Twiki in his arms and they are coming right at me and Kevan. Kevan doesn't say a word until Buck falls at my feet, covered in debris. Kevan wails, '*MOMMY— BUCK ROGERS IS DEAD!*' Gil comes out from beneath the rubble, grins and throws a large piece of debris at Kevan. He catches it and with big eyes, looks at the large boulder in his little hands and then at Gil and I, as if to say, 'this does not compute according to my limited knowledge of size and weight!' Unfortunately, the second time he came to set, he got to watch a Space Vampire draining me. Poor Kevan, when his frat found out who his mother was, they gave him the nickname 'Twiki.'"

SULTRY SIDEKICK

Erin Gray spent the early years of her life in Honolulu, Hawaii. "My spirit will always be in Honolulu," she says happily. Moving to Southern California, she began modeling as a teenage girl.

"I started at fifteen. There aren't a lot of professions where a woman can make a lot of money, go around the world and set their own hours, so I'm not gonna complain. I mean, how often do women make $150.00 an hour? The problem was, there wasn't much stimuli in being a model. I could not put on one more nurse's uniform, or stand in front of a mirror and look at my own face for the umpteenth hour." With that thought, she went into acting."

Glen Larson, producer of *Buck Rogers*, played a big part at the start of her career. "Glen exec produced the first thing I ever acted in, *Evening In Byzantium*, which Glen Ford starred in with me and Michael Sloan wrote. I got the part because Glen's real life wife didn't think Karen Valentine was pretty enough to be his wife!

"The last day of shooting *Byzantium*, an all night shoot after six weeks of filming, I got a call from the studio saying that I was supposed to come in and test for *Buck Rogers in the 25th Century*. I said, 'Gee, d'ya think I can go home and take a nap and shower first?' They said 'No, we just want you to come in and test.' It was probably for the best, because I wasn't thinking or even worrying about what I was doing—I just said my lines and tried not to bump into furniture, which is the best thing for an actor! It worked and I got it."

Her favorite episodes of *Buck Rogers* were "whenever Wilma went undercover. I loved that; put a wig on me and I had fun. Whether I was posing as a spy, a millionaire or a slave girl, it was always cool. Episodes like 'Olympiad' were great, too, but the one I really loved was with the vampire."

SPACE VAMPIRE

The show, 'Space Vampire,' pitted brave Wilma Deering against a Vorvon, a literal Space Vampire who feeds off life essence, not blood. To spare Buck's life, she gives herself over to the undead creature, who drains her to the thrill of teenage boys everywhere.

"I have to say, shooting that story with The Vorvon was my favorite experience on *Buck Rogers*. I had so much fun working with the director Larry Stewart on that. He was very caring and had a great sense of humor. That's my favorite episode and the one fans always ask me about. The gentleman who played The Vorvon, Nicholas Hormann, had this swollen purple head and fangs... To this day, I have no idea what he really looked like, but he was very nice to work with..."

Space Vampire seduces Wilma.

Battle Of The Network Stars

Besides *Buck*, Gray was one of the most athletic contestants on *The Battle Of The Network Stars* competitions. "You will notice every *Battle Of The Network Stars* event I participated on, my team won! What really ticked me off is The Networks never allowed a woman to be captain of a team. I was furious about that! They wouldn't let me be captain. Our captain was a former NFL player (Bubba Smith) who didn't know which way the front end of a boat was...And our first challenge was to get that boat out of the ocean!

"One Team Captain(actor) Robert Conrad loved me because I was very competitive and had a real 'bring it on' attitude. I loved every *Battle* I did. You got $50,000 if you won, so damn right I was angry if our captain didn't know the front end of a boat from the back! One female on a team had it in her contract that her hair could not get wet, even though she was very athletic. The late Mary Fran couldn't really swim but dog paddled so her team wouldn't lose. I worked hard for that and won every time."

One particular competition showed more of her than she intended. "*Battle Of The Network Stars* once gave me a swimsuit that when I dove into the water was completely see thru. Even I was embarrassed—*Everybody in the world saw Wilma Deering's nipples!* On *Silver Spoons*, they always told me, 'Erin, put a bra on! But truthfully, I never wore them. They just made sure my wardrobe had an extra layer on it."

Dairy Queen In Space

Season Two of *Buck* changed everything from the show. "There were episodes in the second season that I liked, like the one with the little people who think off my wardrobe("Shgoratchx!")—that was fun! I also have a very special place in my heart for Thom Christopher, who played Hawk. He was a wonderful addition to our show and an incredible gentleman. To this day, he's one of my favorite people. He added class and style, a terrific actor."

"But during that second season, I really wasn't happy, The joy was gone for me," she admits. "I will always appreciate the fabulous opportunity of starring on a network show, but there was a drop in quality. It was harder for me to justify being away from my child and I had a lot of stalkers and death threats during the second season. One note was delivered to me through my dressing room door on the Universal lot. It was a nude drawing of my body covered in knife wounds that said, 'I'm watching you and I'm going to get you.'

"At a moment like that, you question doing a job. Is it worth being an actress when your life is being threatened? They found that person. I didn't have a driver and would sleep in my trailer if we wrapped late and had an early call the next day. So to find that in the middle of the night on a dark and empty lot is scary."

Season Two also dropped Dr. Huer, Wilma's mentor. "When we lost Tim O'Connor, I lost part of my my heart and soul on the show," she confesses. "Tim O'Connor was a pillar of strength for me; I didn't have a lot of experience before I did the show, so I really leaned on Tim for advice, for help on how to understand a scene, he was always there for me. When they dropped him from the show, it broke my heart. I was shocked. I was even more shocked and saddened at the way Tim found out he wasn't coming back—they told him at the first season wrap party.

"Dr. Huer was a very important part of the series. He was a father figure to Wilma. They replaced him with Wilfred Hyde-White, who could never remember his lines, which took a lot of takes," she says, still fuming at O'Connor's firing. "They dropped Tim and brought in a bunch of other guys. Frankly, I didn't think any of the new characters were worth losing Tim for."

She got a funny shout out on the hip cartoon *South Park* in the episode 'TheSubstitute,' when Cartman and the boys reveal their standard of beauty is 'Erin Gray as Wilma Deering in Season Two of *Buck Rogers in the 25th Century.*' "I owe the creators of *South Park* a very big 'thank you' for that," Gray chuckles.

"Not only was I was quite shocked to hear my name repeatedly mentioned on *South Park* and what they thought of me, the great thing was, I was up for a job and the producer wasn't sure about hiring me—he wasn't even sure I was known enough I to warrant hiring me. But when he heard me mentioned on *South Park*, he gave me the job...So I have to thank the creators for that honor! My husband just played that *South Park* for me today! Thank you, (*South Park* creators) Matt and Trey. I was surprised they thought Wilma was even hotter in the second season, so they must be 'leg' guys! Second season was my Dairy Queen In Space outfit."

Tai Chi

She's become a devout practitioner of Tai Chi. "I love it. Tai Chi is the art and discipline of energy. The entire field of Chinese medicine is based on Tai Chi. I was the Aerobics Queen of the valley until I discovered it. I did a TED Talk, on how acting is dangerous to your health and Tai Chi heals you."

Today, Gray runs *Heroes For Hire*, which provides guests for comic cons and sci-fi conventions. Her client roster of 150 includes stars from hit genre shows like *Arrow, Supernatural, Smallville, Star Trek, Game Of Thrones, Torchwood* and the fan favorite King of cons, Bruce Campbell.

"I am blessed to work with such great people," she professes. "In the office, we always say 'please God, bring us another Bruce!' Bruce Campbell is just a wonderful human being. Working with people like him, John Barrowman, Katie Cassidy, Giancarlo Esposito, John Carpenter and Alana Huffman is a dream."

Doing conventions as a guest led to a life-changing conversation with another genre TV star. "I was at a convention sitting with (*Babylon 5* 's) Julie Caitlin Brown, an actress who became an agent. The two of us talked about how the promoters needed to improve their connection to Hollywood and up their presentation in terms of what they provide for actors.

"Julie was talking about wanting to get pregnant and work from home and I was thinking the same thing. We were sharing our thoughts on becoming agents. She went out the next week and became an agent. I thought, 'Wait a minute, that was my idea!' When I started doing it, Gil (Gerard) asked me to bring him to a con. Gil said, "I will give you 10%.' I said 'No, I'm your friend.' He said 'I'm gonna make you earn it' and he was right, he did," she laughs fondly. "Gil plays golf with Marc Singer(star of *V* and *Beastmaster*). He asked me to represent him at cons, so I said 'Okay, 10 %' and that's how it began."

"I was going through a divorce and bankruptcy, and had a child in private school. I went to a seminar at the Chicago Museum of Broadcast Communication; [*Batman* actress] Julie Newmar and [*Star Trek* actress] BarBara Luna were there, and they started talking about conventions. I had never heard of anything like that, and when they told me about them, my reaction was, 'Oh nobody

Erin Gray practicing Tai Chi by Pat Jankiewicz.

would remember me and the show. It was over 10 years ago.' This was about '91 or '92. A year later, BarBara called me and said, 'Erin, you're going to this place at this time,' sending me to my first convention..'

"BarBara got me to do conventions. She said, 'You're gonna go to this, you're gonna have a great time and you're gonna thank me later.' She was right and I did," Gray concedes. " Now I go to far more conventions as an agent than I do as a guest."

Gray plays a self important genre actress on Felicia Day's hilarious *The Guild*. "How fun it is to play a character playfully making fun of me and my character, especially written by Felicia Day," she asks. "What an honor, I loved it! I got this sweet phone call from Felicia, saying 'Erin, I have written this part for you, but if you don't want to play it...?' I said, 'What are you saying? You wrote a part for me? Of course I want to play it. Felicia, I adore you, I'm there!' I love my character, Madelyn Twain. I read it and laughed so hard, I howled. I just love going out and playing with those guys.

"Felicia is a perfect example of what you can aspire to be, she writes, creates and acts...Legendary Pictures bought her company, which gives her more room to write and create. There's so many opportunities in science fiction today. I wanna play the president of the United States...I was envious when Mary McDonnell played the president of the Universe on *Battlestar Galactica*, I just want a great part like that!"

"My daughter Samantha, after trying it, ultimately decided not to go the acting route. She's 22, a brilliant writer. I always encouraged her, 'be an actress, be a writer, don't limit yourself! 'I tell her, 'Look at Felicia Day, she does everything.'"

And whatever happened to her famous outfit? "After two years of the show, we were cancelled and they asked me if I wanted to keep my spandex suits. I said "burn them!" I had just spent two years in those head to toe girdles and after two years in them, I wanted to burn 'em myself!

"Fortunately, a friend of mine bought them, sold them at an auction and made a fortune. Duh, wish I had thought of that! They were sooo tight. I'm not a collector, I didn't want anything from *Buck Rogers*. Had I known I could have put my daughter through private school and college with the money my friend made off of selling them, I would have taken them all!

"I do have my Starfighter. The guys at Hartland gave me the model of my Starfighter. Gil has his and he was smart—he put his in a nice little box with a mirror. I put mine on a shelf and left it there for 30 years! The show *Hollywood Treasures* came to me to buy it when they learned I actually had it.

"I took it down from the shelf for them after 30 years and realized I should not have had it by a heater," she says, doing a face palm. "It was warped! *Hollywood Treasures* was kind enough to build a box for me to put it in. I personally think mine has character. The model maker from *Star Wars* and *Star Trek* said mine was a 'unique design' that took 30 years of a long, slow heating process to warp and create. Personally, it looks like it's been in a lot of space battles!

"Still, *Buck Rogers* has never really left my life because I run into fans of it on a daily basis! The fact that it has lasted over the decades is an incredible milestone. For me, there's many emotions mixed together from the show, ups and downs, good and bad times, funny times. Great relationships and not so good ones. I treasure them all. There was a *Buck Rogers in the 25th Century* marathon on SyFy Channel one Christmas, so we put it on in every room of the house as a joke with the sound turned down. Nobody sat down to watch it, but it was fun that it was on."

"Today I am a proud grandmother to the world's cutest five year old girl," Erin Gray says with a broad grin. "Her name is 'Logan,' but I call her 'Lolo' and whatever Lolo wants, Lolo gets! She's adorable, brilliant and, since I teach Tai Chi and martial arts now, Lolo is taking classes with her daddy, my son Kevan. I watched her win a match with a girl taller than her, which made this proud Grandma even prouder..."

Tim O'Connor: Dr. Huer

Tall, silver haired Tim O'Connor, with his bright blue eyes, looks like someone you can trust, which is probably why he has spent much of his acting career playing various authority figures like generals, priests, cops and doctors.

Dr. Huer.

On *Buck Rogers in the 25th Century*, he was Buck's trusted mentor, Dr. Elias Huer, Wilma Deering's superior, whose task was to protect Earth (or "Terra," in *Buck* speak) from enemies across the galaxy. Dr. Huer usually sent Buck and Wilma to handle problems he could not resolve through diplomatic channels. He's a father figure to Buck, even though Buck is hundreds of years older than Huer.

"I was born in 1927 and I remembered Buck Rogers in the comic strips from 1933," Tim O'Connor enthuses. "When the producer, Glen Larson, asked if I wanted to be part of his *Buck Rogers* movie and television series, I said, 'Yes, I would!' I was happy to be offered a job as a regular on a series, but even more so because I remembered Buck Rogers so fondly from childhood. I loved the comic strip so much and the serial with Buster Crabbe in 1939.

"I remembered it in the funny papers so well, I was so excited to read it every day and of course, to play Dr. Huer, who I loved in the strip—except Dr. Huer was bald in the comic strip—a total skinhead! Glen Larson told me the idea of what the series was gonna be. Because I loved Buck and knew the characters, it was a thrill to do the show."

"I saw Dr. Elias Huer initially as brilliant, but also a little strange. He would make ordinary, common mistakes, despite being so smart. For example, he has a plant, which is rare and unusual in the Buck Rogers' 25th Century world, and he was given this by Buck. The plant was beginning to grow in his office. The way I saw it, he was very leery of this plant. When the plant brushed against him, he jumped back. He spoke to the plant and began to take on a personality. That's how I felt about that and wanted to kick around that take. The producer didn't see it that way at all and simply wanted me to keep Dr. Huer more serious and he was quite right.

"As Dr. Huer, it was my job to gather all the information and identify what the new challenge was going to be that week, to both Buck and the Earth, and then I would send Buck and Wilma off to solve it. They were the action characters and it was my job to send them to prevent us all from being sent to certain oblivion," he notes wryly.

"I liked working with Gil and Erin very much—they were a charming, good-looking young couple. Dr. Huer was a kind of

Tim O'Connor gets serious with Wilma and Pantherman.

father figure—he got involved with Buck and Wilma, but he was always a bit closer to Wilma than he was to Buck.

"My character was unsure of what kind of relationship Wilma and Buck had and Wilma was occasionally troubled by her relationship with Buck and would talk to Dr. Huer about it. The reason being that Wilma and Huer knew each other longer, before they found Buck frozen, so their relationship was closer. Huer knew that Wilma was hurting a little in her relationship with Buck and that would distract her from whatever their mission of the week was, so he would talk to her about it and support her That's how I saw him."

In the original pilot/movie, Dr. Huer is a little more distant from Buck. "I agree with that, but only because he had more responsibilities in the film, his job running the defense of the Earth essentially made him like the head of the CIA. I tried to keep him more personable and down to Earth after that. I tried to make him as intimate as I could, with the dialogue I had to work with. I have forgotten how the devil I got involved with *Buck Rogers*, but I do remember the first shot that I was in. It's the first time I met Buck, which was also the first time I met Gil and Felix (Silla, Twiki the robot) at the time and I remember how impressed I was about

Dr. Huer closeup.

the series. I really liked it and I was glad to be part of it."

Huer has two assistants on the show, computerized Dr. Theop-olis and Twiki, who becomes Buck's robot sidekick. With impres-sive skill throughout the series, O'Connor adroitly delivers tons of expository dialogue to the talking clock and robot.

"I have always worked with robots," O'Connor jokes. "Serious-ly though, I began to enjoy it more as the series went on, work-ing with those two robots," he says triumphantly. "The voice that

Eric (Server) did as Theopolis was wonderful when I first heard it. Theopolis was a very interesting idea and concept, these computers helping Huer run the planet. I like when Buck is put on trial by the jury of Theopolis and the other computers in the movie—I wish they had taken some time on the show to explore it more.

"I actually ended up talking to Theopolis as though he were an old friend of mine. I remember, there was an episode where we are under attack, literally being bombed ("Escape From Wedded Bliss") and I got intimate with Theopolis under a desk once!

"Things are falling down all around us and we are under my desk as I have my arm around him to protect him. I remember turning to him, Theopolis, and saying in a concerned voice 'Are you alright?' That was pretty funny. I kind of liked that. It was interesting and we brought it all to life. Theopolis and I defend Buck against any accusation, but I was always left at home when they would go off into adventure. I think Princess Ardala actually brought me through a black hole once (in "Flight Of The War Witch'), but usually I was left at home while Buck and Wilma went on the mission."

"I quite enjoyed Twiki, too. I remember meeting Felix Silla and seeing what he had to go through in that costume he wore as Twiki, how he handled it, wearing a sweatband around his head to keep all the sweat from pouring into his eyes was just incredible, Everyone took care of themselves on the show, but we were all kind of careful with Felix to make sure he would get a breather, because that Twiki costume got very hot very fast. Felix and I had worked together on the movie *SSSS* before *Buck Rogers in the 25th Century* —he was a seal boy in a freak show and I was the carnival barker. We did that for the producers of *Jaws*."

O'Connor "was born and raised in Chicago, just like Buck Rogers," he jokes. "I loved movies and when I came out of the service—I was in boot camp and would have been sent to Japan, but the war ended. I thought I would like to be an actor but didn't think it was possible until I ran into a guy that I went to grammar school with. He was going to a radio school in downtown Chicago. They taught engineering, writing, analysis and acting. Since I was on the G.I. Bill, I went to the school and that was the start of my career."

Tim O'Connor was an alien on Wonder Woman.

Besides *Buck Rogers in the 25th Century*, O'Connor guested on many sci-fi shows, including Rod Serling's *The Twilight Zone*, *The Outer Limits* (with future Kane Michael Ansara), *Wonder Woman* and even *Star Trek: The Next Generation*. "When you do science fiction, I find you don't try to do anything, just respond to what's said to you from your soul. It's from your soul. You are the character and the character is you."

Seeing his likeness immortalized in *Buck Rogers* toys and comics was a shock for the actor. "I was very surprised by that," he admits. "Like Erin once said, 'We never knew anything about that, we just saw them years later and we were impressed.' There was a Dr. Huer of me as an action figure with a removable tunic, which pleased me."

One of O'Connor's highlights on the series was when original Buck Buster Crabbe came in ("Planet Of The Slave Girls"). "Oh, I was so delighted when Buster Crabbe guest starred," the actor says , still excited about meeting a childhood hero. "I didn't know him, had never met him before then, but I certainly knew of him! I watched his *Buck Rogers* when I was a much younger person and there he was, on the set! He really didn't look that much different. He looked good and when he played that character, I was really rooting for him. The serial came out when I was about seven, so I was smitten with the idea of Buck Rogers, and here he was, my Buck Rogers!"

Another guest he liked was Pamela Hensley's Princess Ardala. "Pamela had to go around in these flowing costumes that were also very revealing. She had to work in them and spend the day dressed like that in these chilly soundstages. Despite this, she was always animated, funny, nice, always there in the scene, a good actor and total pro. I also liked Michael Ansara, as her assistant, Kane. I had worked with Michael Ansara before, on *The Outer Limits* and a couple other things. I really enjoyed him as Kane, but I hadn't seen him since the show."

The second season of *Buck Rogers in the 25th Century* dropped Dr. Huer. "I knew the show was changing in the next season, but I didn't realize what had happened—I was dropped and didn't know why until I saw the season premiere. They couldn't use me if they were going to change the show as radically as they wanted to. They would have had to change the character of Dr. Huer so radically, they had to get a new one and they did. They brought in Wilfrid. who was a wonderful actor "

O'Connor still looks back fondly on his life in the 25th Century."When you are a regular on a TV series, people start to greet you like an old friend—that was a nice surprise to me when it first started happening. I am greeted by all kinds of people who walk up to me, saying 'Hello, Dr. Huer!' or 'You look just like the guy from that show!'"

Felix Silla: Talking With Twiki

Buck Rogers' best friend is his plucky robot pal, Twiki. Little Twiki frequently joins Buck on dangerous missions and occasionally saves the day. Actor/stuntman Felix Silla, a tough 3"11 Italian, enjoyed playing the astronaut's durable sidekick.

Twiki closeup.

Silla was no stranger to costumed creatures. "I was born in Italy in 1937 and came to America in 1955. I traveled with the circus for awhile, riding bareback and doing other tricks, about six or seven years, and then I started doing stunts, doubling for kids in movies.

"I was an alien (Talosian) in the first episode of *Star Trek*, I played Cousin Itt on *The Addams Family* with John Astin and Carolyn Jones, and I was a gorilla in the original *Planet Of The Apes*," he shrugs. "I was the baby gorilla in that scene with Charlton Heston running loose, my line is 'Mother, it's a human!' after Heston runs across us in the museum.

"I was an Ewok in *Return Of The Jedi*, I'm the one on the hang glider, and one of The Dinks—the alien race in the desert, in Mel Brooks' *Spaceballs*." He was even one of Danny DeVito's Emperor Penguins in *Batman Returns*. "Our penguin costumes were so good, I fooled a penguin! A real penguin walked over to me and studied me for a minute, before he could tell 'That guy's not real.'"

"I doubled Drew Barrymore in *E.T. The Extraterrestrial* , when she's trick or treating in the ghost costume, and the little boy in *Poltergeist*, which was a fun movie to do . I doubled Short Round in *Indiana Jones And The Temple Of Doom*. Every action thing you see Short Round do was actually me. Steven Spielberg was one of the best directors I ever worked with, nice guy, very smart man. He does all his homework the night before he comes to the set. When he's on set, he never hollers at anybody, he's easygoing because he did all his prep work the night before."

He landed Twiki on *Buck Rogers in the 25th Century* "when a gentleman I used to go to church with in Panorama City told me something was coming up that I might be good for. When *Buck Rogers* started up, my friend made sure I was asked to come interview for it with a bunch of other little people. I was chosen to play Buck's robot friend, Twiki. That's how I got it, through my friend—he was one of the producers on the show, Glen Larson.

"*Buck Rogers* was originally going to be a TV miniseries, but there was such a great reaction to the dailies, Universal Studios made us into a movie released in theaters instead. When it came out, the movie made a lot of money and then we came back as a TV series. I enjoyed every day on *Buck Rogers*, just going to work on the Universal backlot with Gil Gerard and Erin Gray was a lot of fun.

Felix Silla unmasked.

"We laughed a lot on that show, many funny things happened on the set, our outtakes were hilarious—missed cues, blown lines, Gil and Erin telling jokes, we laughed a lot. Well, at the Christmas wrap party for Season One, we were going to show them all on a blooper reel, but someone stole the reel! They never found it.

"Because it was a fantasy show, everything had to be built for it, so we hardly ever went on location off the lot because almost every set for it was on the backlot. I loved the show because we made it at Universal Studios, just 10 minutes from my house!

"I used to have a Twiki license plate on my car when the show was popular. Fans of the show liked it but other drivers would pull alongside and ask me, 'What the hell's a Twiki?' That plate hangs on my wall now. I truly enjoyed being Twiki, everybody liked him."

The biggest challenge for the actor was wearing Twiki's mechanical costume. "Being in Twiki was hot, very hot, and sometimes hard to breathe in. It was all fiberglass, the Twiki body, chest, back and head was all fiberglass, so it wasn't that flexible." Silla says. "The skirt and sleeves on Twiki were hard rubber.

"His arms and legs were also hard rubber, so most of the time, I couldn't sit down...It was like walking around in a suit of armor. Dr. Theopolis, who I wore on my chest, was no problem. Happily, I could take Twiki's face off between shots and smoke a cigarette. The skirt on the lower part of Twiki's body made it hard to sit. If I was allowed to sit, or Twiki was sitting in the scene, they had to take the bottom half of the costume off, that skirt, so I could actually sit down. "

"Twiki had no fingers, his hands were like clamps, so I could pick stuff up with no problem. I don't know if he was meant as a takeoff on R2-D2, but I saw him as a different thing. They looked differently and acted differently from each other. You could understand what Twiki was saying, but R2-D2 just beeped. Twiki was Buck's best friend.

"It was very difficult to talk inside the Twiki mask and, as I said, also hard to breathe in it. When it got hot in that suit, boy, it was terrible. I could see through the eyes, they were actually mesh screens. For the Starfighters, they had giant mockups and it was always hard to ride in them with the Twiki costume on. The one good part about that was, because you only saw my upper half in the fighter, I didn't have to wear the whole costume!"

Being Twiki in a metal shell meant "it was hard for me to walk up and down steps. When I went on a mission with Buck Rogers in his Starfighter, Gil would have to pick me up physically and put me in his spaceship. Every time we had to do those scenes, Gil would joke, 'Hey Felix, when did you get so fat? You are heavy!' I would say, 'Shaddup, Gil' or 'Fuck you, Gil' and we would laugh. Gil was a good guy, very happy go lucky. Gil was always on time and went right to work. I found him easygoing.

"Erin Gray was a wonderful lady. They were both great to work with. Gil and I had a lot of fun working together, even today when we meet up to do conventions, we laugh and joke like we did on the show. A lot of great things happened that first season of *Buck*; one of my two daughters was even born that year in 1980.

"Twiki's voice was done by Mel Blanc, who was also the voice of Bugs Bunny. There was one great day where Mel Blanc came onto the set and I got to meet him. We had a picture taken together, but I never got a copy. He just sat and talked and told us all great stories."

Twiki has a jaunty walk as he enters a scene on the show. "When we did the very first episode, I put on the costume for the first time and asked how they wanted to see me walk. Daniel Haller, directing the pilot, told me 'Just walk normal, Felix, that's what I want. Just walk your normal walk and it will be fine. ' He was right—I did and it was, they would play the Twiki music when I came in. I liked Daniel, and I thought he did a great job with the pilot movie."

There was one major change to Twiki from script to screen. "In our pilot script, Twiki didn't say anything. He just stood there as a sidekick for Buck and Dr. Theopolis was the brain who talked for him. Twiki would say something computerized to Theopolis , who would translate for Buck and Wilma. When they got Mel Blanc, it made sense to have Twiki talk, which made him a more interesting character."

Twiki sees a lot of action in the pilot, even joining Buck on a dangerous trip to the ruins of Chicago. "I remember when we did the scene of Gil and I at the cemetery after we enter Anarchia. It's the scene where he's looking for his father's grave when we're attacked by mutants. It was shot at night on the Universal backlot. Before we started filming, I told Gil, 'I need to look out for rocks, vines and stuff that would trip me or make it hard for me to run on before we do the scene.' Gil said to me, 'I will give you about ten feet—you can run ten feet ahead of me and I will follow you.'

"It was fine, the cemetery was on a little hill. The camera was on a track on the left side with Gil and I running full speed on the right. Suddenly, I fell—I fell flat on my face! I thought, 'Oh My God!' I worried about what happened to the costume, whether I had scraped or broken Twiki's face. It turned out nothing happened to the costume, it was fine, so the director yelled 'cut.'

Anarchia at dusk.

"One of the camera guys saw me fall, jumped over a small cemetery wall, picked me up under the armpits and lifted me up, then asked Daniel Haller, 'What do you want me to do with this guy?' That started strangling me, as I kept saying, 'Put me down, put me down.'

"What he was doing by lifting me up that way, was making the hard fiberglass Twiki body pull up around my neck and actually choke me! I finally got really mad and yelled, 'God damn it, put me down—you're killin' me!' He goes, 'Oh, Okay.' The costume was fine, so we just did the scene again and got it."

Silla had a lot of adventures as the amiable ambuquad. "Sometimes I had to do stunts as Twiki...The one where the three girls kidnap me ('Twiki Is Missing') had a scene where Twiki is floating away in Outer Space. I did that stunt myself, I was up on cables to simulate myself floating in Space in my Twiki suit. That was hard, spinning in a harness on that show. Anything that seemed too dangerous, I just refused to do it. Why do something if you're gonna end up getting hurt? Money isn't everything. Happily, I never got hurt playing Twiki."

Twiki about to get snatched in Twiki is Missing.

Of the show's two season run, "My favorite episode was the Olympics one, where Buck and I attend the ceremony in the 25th Century ('Olympiad') and I really liked the one we did with the girl who got killed (Dorothy Stratten), where we went on the space cruise ('Cruise Ship To The Stars'). That one was fun, because Twiki actually got a girlfriend...I loved that Twiki had a robot girlfriend. Patty Maloney played Tina, my silver and gold robot girlfriend. Patty and I are friends and the exact same size, 3"11.

"'Cruise Ship To The Stars' meant we spent a week with Dorothy Stratten; The Playboy Playmate. I got to talk to her all the time during the shoot. A really wonderful girl, it was too bad that happened to her. She was murdered by her husband, but I never saw him on the set, she was always alone."

"One of the most enjoyable things about the first season is that we had a special guest star every week, like Dorothy Stratten or Jack Palance. We had a lot of big names—Cesar Romero, Roddy McDowall, making each episode was wonderful because of that."

Of all the guest stars, Silla was truly impressed by Pamela Hensley's Princess Ardala. "Oh man, to see Pamela in her Princess Ardala costumes," he says wistfully. "Boy, she looked amazing! Pamela was hot, and I mean HOT! She was friendly too, a sweet lady and every episode she was on was a lot of fun, just a blast."

Actress Patty Maloney is credited with playing Twiki in the episodes 'A Blast For Buck' and 'Space Vampire.' "I did not know that, I thought I did 'em all," Silla states. "Actually, I wasn't replaced—she played Tina, but I might have had to go off and double some kid. I thought I played Twiki in every episode. Patty and I are the goblins in the original *Don't Be Afraid Of The Dark*."

Silla knew *Buck* was in trouble during Season Two. "The first season was great, but we went down the tubes in that second season because they changed producers. We lost Bruce Lansbury and brought in a new guy, a different producer, John Mantley, who did *Gunsmoke*.

"He came in, took over the show and screwed everything up. He brought in Hawk the Hawkman, who was an alright guy, but they should have left it alone. As Twiki, I was on the show all the time during the first season. On the second, I was hardly on the show at all. Here and there, that's it. Twiki's time got cut down, because they brought that other stupid robot in, Crichton. They brought that big robot in and the stupid thing broke down all the time! It was just terrible.

"Mantley changed everything and the ratings nosedived. Nobody liked it. Mantley only knew westerns, having done *Gunsmoke* for 18 or 20 years, but he knew nothing about space shows. Westerns were all he knew, so he changed everything including Twiki's voice!"

In the second season, Twiki's voice was changed from Mel Blanc, whose 'Beety! Beety! Beety!' was an iconic part of the show to a squeaky voice provided by Bob Elyea. "It was funny because everybody got upset when they changed Twiki's voice, a lot of viewers were mad and sent angry letters.

"The first season we had Mel doing it and he was great. Mantley got rid of Mel and just had one of his friends do Twiki's voice. They were probably paying Mel pretty good money. Nobody liked the change. The second season was just so stupid, starting with that terrible voice for Twiki. They never explained why Twiki had a new voice in the second season opener.

Tim O'Connor, Felix Silla, Erin Gray and Gil Gerard today. Photo by Pat Jankiewicz.

"I preferred the first season. I loved working with Tim O'Connor, who was so great as Dr. Huer. Tim was much better than the other guy (Wilfrid Hyde-White). The first season, the cast was smaller and it was better. Tim didn't come back and they claimed he wanted more money and used the other guy, the old man, Hyde-White. He played Dr. Goodfellow and they brought in the guy playing the captain, Jay Garner. I didn't like him or the old man. The old man was fine, but we had to drag him along and he couldn't read the dialogue. He needed large cue cards so they had to spend more money the second season, rather than just keeping Tim.

"The real reason is that Mantley was trying to save money by bringing his friends in. Mantley got cheap, that's why he got rid of Tim O'Connor. Even today, poor Tim has no idea why they didn't bring him back," Silla says sadly. "No one asked him or said anything to him. They just changed the whole show, Mantley told us the first season was too expensive. He dumped Tim and brought in a whole bunch of other people! If it's supposed to be less expensive, why dump one guy and replace him with five more show regulars? How does that make sense? The show was great the first year, they should have left it alone.

"We didn't like it, nobody liked the second season. Gil Gerard was upset, because dumping Mel gave it a lesser quality. Nobody liked the new guy's voice for Twiki and viewers kept demanding to know why they did that. They had to spend more money, as they dumped the new voice and eventually brought Mel back that season.

"Nobody gave Gil or I an explanation because they didn't consider it our business. Mel Blanc was brought back as Twiki's voice because Gil told Mantley, 'If you don't bring back Mel, we're not gonna come back to work.' They brought Mel back, Twiki regained his voice, and then Mel had a really bad car accident (on California's notorious 'Dead Man's Curve'). He was in bad shape and he passed on a few years later. I only met Mel that one time on the set."

"During the second season, John Mantley had no idea what to do with *Buck Rogers in the 25th Century.* Was the show for kids or adults? Gil tried telling him and the studio that they were killing the show, but no one would listen to him. They never even told us if we were coming back or not for a third season," he says, still irritated by that. "Same thing they did to Tim O'Connor. They never told him he wasn't coming back for the second season and never told Gil, Erin or I that it was cancelled. They never said anything to us, just cancelled the show. *Buck Rogers* was replaced by *Hill Street Blues,* which started with low ratings but became a big hit."

Although Buck, Wilma and The Searcher are overrun by telekinetic alien dwarves in 'Shgoratchx!,' "I couldn't play one of the little guys in that because I was too busy playing Twiki in the same episode. It was fun to have all those other little guys around, because they were all friends of mine who I had worked with many times, including Billy Curtis, Harry Monty and Tommy Madden, with a couple other friends. If Twiki hadn't been in that episode too much, I could have been one of them. "

Several guest stars remember Silla complaining during every break about how hot the costume was. "That's true," Felix laughs. "That costume got pretty damn hot!

Buck Facts

- In 2008, Twiki was nominated at the Nick At Night TV Land Awards for "Awesomest Robot." He lost.
- Twiki had both a large and small action figure by Mego.

Story Editors
ANNE COLLINS &
ALAN BRENNERT

Writer/producer Anne Collins Ludwick served as Story Editor/ producer on many shows, including *Wonder Woman*, *Matlock*, *Fantasy Island* and *Vega$*, but nothing prepared her for *Buck Rogers in the 25th Century* , where she bonded with both producer Bruce Lansbury and co-Story Editor Alan Brennert and found herself in battle with the show's leading man, Gil Gerard.

Emmy-winning writer/producer/novelist Alan Brennert was brought onto *Buck Rogers* as Story Editor, after writing four episodes of the live action Lynda Carter *Wonder Woman* for producer Lansbury. It was one of his first professional gigs in Hollywood. Collins Ludwick and Brennart became friends and came up with some of the best episodes of the show's run.

"Once he hired on as Supervising Producer of *Buck* in the spring of 1979, Bruce Lansbury asked me to come aboard as story editor," explains Anne Collins Ludwick. "Working with him on *Wonder Woman* for the previous two years had been an absolute blast, so I immediately said yes. Right after that, we coaxed Alan

Maintenance Androids were a recurring Alan Brennert motif.

Brennert, who had written a couple of wonderful scripts for us on *Wonder Woman*, to join the staff as well.

"And may I insert right here that I 'discovered' Alan – while looking through writing samples of would-be freelancers for *Wonder Woman*, I read his spec screenplay and, as clichéd as I know this sounds, my heart started pounding, because I knew I had just read something by an exceptionally talented writer.

"I could not get to the phone fast enough to get him in for a meeting, and the rest is history," She says proudly. "Soon we were all commuting to Universal Studios, where Bruce was ensconced in the Producers' Building near the fabled Black Tower, while Alan and I toiled away in a writers' building beyond the sound stages at the edge of a large concrete ditch – L.A.'s version of a river. I seem to recall that among the other writers headquartered in our building was Don Bellasario, who, of course, went on to create a string of extraordinarily successful TV series. (including *Magnum P.I., Quantum Leap* and *JAG*.)

"Early on we met with Glen A. Larson, who created (this version of) *Buck Rogers* and many, many other TV series in the late '70s / early 80s. I remember him as being a very decent, approachable, down-to-earth guy with a good sense of humor and a tireless ability to pitch and, in many instances, write plot lines and characters that audiences found instantly appealing. I distinctly remember admiring the gold records on his wall commemorating his former days as one of the Four Preps, having spent my early childhood singing along whenever the radio played 'Down by the Station,'" she laughs.

"Glen envisioned *Buck Rogers* to be a light-hearted, action-adventure, science fiction/fantasy series, with humor and pathos naturally arising from its fish-out-of-water main character. The studio saw *Buck* as a way to get more mileage out of its existing *Battlestar Galactica* props and effects, while the network no doubt saw the series as a way to parade gorgeous, exotically (i.e. scantily) dressed women in front of a weekly audience hungering for *Charlie's Angels*-type T & A.," Collins Ludwick continues.

"While Bruce Lansbury had to worry about appeasing three masters (creator, studio and network), Alan and I, taking Glen's vision of the show to heart, had to concern ourselves only with the characters – who they were, how they related to each other, and

Wilma, Twiki and Buck flying together.

how they would deal with whatever fantastic situations we put them in each week. We were excited and enthusiastic — this was going to be highly fun," she says.

"Writing for *Buck* differed from writing for *Wonder Woman*, mainly in all the technical, futuristic concepts and jargon we had to employ and which sometimes drove the story. We had to be careful to keep things at least scientifically plausible, whereas in *Wonder Woman* we played with elements of pure fantasy. My favorite character on the series, contrary to what Gil may have thought, was Buck all the way. I loved his humor and his physicality and the sense of loss/homesickness which he was forever forced to suppress, and I loved the interplay between him and Wilma," relates Collins Ludwick. "It was great fun to write."

When he joined the show, Alan Brennert remembers, "I looked at Twiki and thought, 'I have to write dialogue for this stupid thing?' At one point, Anne and I tried to get him killed off, but Twiki apparently had the highest Q rating on the show. He was way more popular than Buck."

"I can't say the experience of writing for Twiki grew on me," he shares conspiratorially, "though I was grateful that, despite the fact that research said he was the most popular character on the show, he never refused to say a line I wrote or tried to rewrite it. Some robots would let that go their heads."

"I also had fun throwing in spaceport voiceovers that about twelve people in the audience probably got. My best one was 'Will Captain Christopher Pike please report to the Veterans Administration.'" Captain Pike, who can only make beeping sounds in his futuristic wheelchair, was Captain of The Starship Enterprise before James T. Kirk takes the helm on *Star Trek*.

Brennert felt "NBC was always harping about giving the show more futuristic elements, but then they objected when I started using the (science fiction) term "Terran" instead of that old clunker 'Earthling.'"

"Bruce decided they couldn't have it both ways, so we ignored them, continuing to use 'Terran,'" he says triumphantly. "The best compliment I can pay Bruce Lansbury is that he's the man who showed me how to cut my work on the page, so it wouldn't have to be cut later in the editing room. I took that lesson to heart and it's served me as both a screenwriter and a novelist. Bruce was great."

"Bruce was great," Collins Ludwick concurs. "Bruce, with his great imagination and sense of whimsy, was the perfect person to shepherd the show that first season. I believe we had a 24 episode order at that point... 22 episodes really, since that order included Glen's two hour modified theatrical release which would serve as the pilot.

"So the three of us began brainstorming story ideas and digesting those that the network and studio threw at us. In the meantime, Alan and I started considering pitches from outside writers. Many of the people we brought in were science fiction/fantasy types whom Alan knew personally or by reputation, since that was kinda his favorite genre back then. For the most part, developing scripts alongside our freelancers and Alan and Bruce was a joy, as was watching the scripts come to life.

"The script for the two-part episode scheduled to air the week after the pilot had already been assigned and was in the process of being written, as was the hour-long one that (classic *Star Trek* writer and one of the first women to write for TV adventure series) D C Fontana had agreed to write. I say this because I have no recollection of ever meeting her, and I have to think that's something I would remember."

"Once completed scripts started coming out of the pipeline, notes started coming back from the powers-that-were, and after the (episode's first) writer had absorbed them and done his or her final pass, we started re-writing," she says. "Sometimes, that meant tossing pretty much everything the original writer had submitted and doing a major overhaul starting with Fade In

"Sometimes this was due to the writer's inability to deliver what we were asking of him/her, sometimes it was due to radical changes requested at the last minute by the studio and/or the network. Sometimes the overhaul was so massive that, after arbitration by the Writers' Guild, I wound up sharing the Written By credit with the original writer. Sometimes, if I had been credited with writing a script I was not happy with (i.e. I'd been required to make changes I strongly disagreed with), I would use my pen name, Cory Applebaum, in a small, passive-aggressive show of protest."

The Story Editor was pleased to meet her leading man. "Can't recall when and where I first met Gil Gerard, but in those early days he came across as friendly, easygoing, good humored, and certainly good looking, with a slight but pleasant Southern drawl," she remembers.

"It was a while before I met Erin Gray who had played Wilma Deering in the movie/pilot. Erin initially did not want to do the series, since that would require her to constantly bleach and, she feared, permanently damage, her naturally dark hair, which was essential to her stock in trade – who could blame her? Tim O'Connor was likewise a true pro – dependable, easy to work with, as was Felix Silla, the guy who had to play the robot, Twiki."

Her trip to the 25th Century left her underwhelmed. "I vividly recall my first trip to the set – the hangar where the starfighter fleet was housed – and being appalled at how cheesy the props looked up close, especially the 'refueling' tubes crisscrossing the floor, which were just clear plastic hoses lined with rhythmically blinking Christmas tree lights. But they looked pretty on TV, and visually sold the idea that energy was being transferred through them, so kudos to the set designer."

Did she have any favorites of her work on the show? "I'm afraid my memories of specific *Buck* episodes are few and far between. I guess my favorite episode would be "Vegas in Space," just because it was my first script for the show. It was very fun and exciting to write it and glimpse it being produced, plus (that episode's guest star) Pamela Shoop's delightful performance will forever make it stand out in my mind. I also remember the way Erin gleefully sank her teeth into—sorry, couldn't resist——the 'Space Vampire' episode."

Brennert feels "'The Plot to Kill a City' came out most faithfully of all my scripts and I think it still holds up pretty well as a cheeky sf adventure story. It had great super-powered villains—something we should have done more of. 'Vegas in Space' was the series prototype and I thought Anne's script captured everything the show should have been, especially that melancholy moment when Buck is recalling his old friend from NASA. And I did enjoy writing for Gary Coleman in 'Cosmic Whiz Kid'—since it was intended to be comedic, most of my funny lines got through."

Collins Ludwick recalls that "Shooting continued at a steady pace through the summer, so that by the time the show premiered in September, we probably had at least 10 shows in the can, maybe 12, maybe even more, I can't remember.

"All seemed to be going well until September; the closer we got to the show's premiere, the more rumblings we heard that Gil wasn't happy with the scripts. As I recall, Gil felt that Buck was taking a back seat to Wilma, that Buck was too flip, too quick with a wise-crack, too slow to let Wilma know who was truly in charge when the shit started flying each week. Alan and I felt we had been pretty damn faithful to the concept Glen had laid out for us that spring (in the pilot film), but suddenly the ground was shifting beneath us. The fun was coming to an end."

Alan Brennert feels "The only significant moment that I don't believe has ever been chronicled is this: Some sort of turning point occurred between filming of 'Vegas in Space' and 'Planet of the Slave Girls' (Although 'Slave Girls' ran first, 'Vegas In Space' was shot before it). If you look at 'Vegas,' you see that Gil displays an impressive range: he's funny, he tosses off one-liners with ease, and then he shifts gears effortlessly for his quiet reverie about his old friend in Houston, dead now with everyone else Buck knew, wondering whatever became of him.

"This was what Anne, Bruce, and I always thought the show should be: witty science fiction adventure with a charming, funny hero whose humor hides the melancholy loss of the world he once knew. After shooting this, the 'shakedown episode,' we called it, Gil went to New York for a week or so, and when he came back he seemed *different.*

"Much more serious, much more all about Buck being serious, and quick to throw jokes out of the scripts," Brennert observes. "Anne and I often wondered whether some of his theater friends in New York might have looked down on what he was doing and convinced him he was a serious actor who should be acting seriously. That's just speculation, of course, but Gil's performances became much more sober when he came back from New York, and I can't think of another explanation for it."

Anne Collins Ludwick remembers "Things finally came to a head on either the day the movie/pilot was to air, or a week after that when the first episode of the show, the two-hour 'Planet of the Slave Girls,' was to air. In any case, Gil demanded to meet with Alan, Bruce and me that day in his bungalow.

"I remember Bruce Lansbury briefing us before we went over there, telling us that 'Gil is undoubtedly extremely nervous because the show is about to air and he's the star. If the show flops, everyone will blame him. He needs to vent, and we need to let him.' Bruce said, 'We need to just sit quietly and listen, no matter how outrageous his complaints may seem. Let's just hear what he has to say.'

"So off we went to Gil's bungalow, where things began cordially enough," Collins Ludwick says trepidatiously. "But soon, Gil began accusing me and Alan of making Buck seem weak, shallow and subservient to Wilma. He started getting very, very negative when it came to the scripts we'd developed. Now, I like to think that, had I been more mature, or at least more experienced when it came to dealing with stars, I would've let his recriminations roll off me and let him get everything off his chest. But being young and inexperienced, I didn't know how to do that, and therefore didn't.

"To Bruce's great chagrin, I started talking back like a sassy fourth grader, which of course only inflamed the situation. Soon accusations and counter-accusations were flying in all directions, until finally I got up and did exactly what Gil told me to do, which was *to get the fuck out of his dressing room.* I never had a meeting like the one we had in that bungalow before or after *Buck.* Never came close."

"How Bruce resisted the urge to throttle me when we left the bungalow, I have no idea," she confides. "I can't recall what he said to me then, but we all went home, the show aired, the sun rose the next morning. Everyone cooled off, and after a few days, Gil and I even exchanged apologies, but nothing was the same after that.

"Reviewers were unkind to Gil and to the show, which (justifiably) angered and frustrated him, and exacerbated his dissatisfaction with the scripts. It was clear that, despite our truce, Gil no longer trusted me to do right by him, and that things were only going to get more and more uncomfortable. So I resigned and left the writing that remained to be done in Alan's more than capable hands. He was soon joined by Rob Gilmer, a great guy and a very versatile writer whom Universal had the good sense to keep in its stable."

She has an amusing response to Gil Gerard's claim that she 'treated me like I didn't know what the fuck I was talking about and who physically turned away every time I said something ,'

"I don't recall (looking away) in Gil's bungalow that much during that fateful meeting, but if I did, it was:

a.) Yet another immature act of passive aggression on my part or

b.) I had spotted James Garner, who was doing The Rockford Files on The Universal Studios' Lot at the time, and his bungalow was very close to Gil's."

Alan Brennert felt the meeting "was a learning experience. Both Anne and I have said elsewhere that we were young and could have handled our interactions with Gil better, but then, the same probably could be said of Gil."

Erin Gray says "We had Anne Collins as a Story Editor at a time when female Story Editors were not that common. She should not have been forced off the show—that should not have happened. Anne and Alan Brennert's scripts were always funny, entertaining and clever, with fun banter and double entendres and I'm sorry that this happened to them. It was only my second job, the producers kept me in the dark, but Anne deserved much better than that kind of treatment, as did Alan."

After the battle in the bungalow, Collins Ludwick says "I soon moved on to other projects, as did Alan and Bruce when the last episode of that first season was completed. Apparently John Mantley took the show in a more serious direction, I never watched, but the series was cancelled after that second season, and Gil and Erin went on to other things as well.

"My biggest regret is that I never got to work with Bruce Lansbury again, except very briefly a decade and a half later on a *Murder She Wrote* episode. He was surely one of the most imaginative, congenial, and decent TV producers ever to oversee a network series. His creative sensibilities colored the shows that epitomized 70s television, *Wild, Wild West, Mission Impossible, Wonder Woman*, and the happiest times of my TV writing career were those I spent under his wonderfully protective and nurturing wing at *Wonder Woman* and *Buck*."

Alan Brennert wasn't quite finished with his tortured time on the show just yet. Writing for the sci fi film magazine *Starlog*, he did a hilariously scathing column called "Confessions Of A Story Editor," where he correctly predicted the demise of the series (before its second season ever aired), exonerated Anne Collins and Bruce Lansbury and laid the blame for the show's failure at the feet of Gil Gerard.

He revealed the star cutting jokes, rewriting scripts like 'A Dream Of Jennifer'(Gerard reportedly rewrote a scene so Buck far outraces Wilma Deering), and giving Erin Gray and other co-stars short shrift, also explaining how Twiki, because his dialogue was recorded after the episode was shot, became the last, best hope to keep humor in the show when most episodes were as grim "as *Night Of The Living Dead!*"

"It was quite cathartic to write at the time," the writer confides. "One thing about that article I did for *Starlog*, somewhere in the last few paragraphs, I talk about why I left the show, citing how — and this is approximately how it was published – 'the stars rewrote the scripts.' In the manuscript I submitted, it was 'star' — singular, meaning Gil — and the good folks at *Starlog* decided for their own reason to make that plural, probably to avoid pointing fingers at one person. This has always bothered me because it implied Erin and Tim were among the reasons I left, when actually they were the nicest people and most hard-working, collaborative actors around. "

Jack Palance using his cape.

"PLANET OF THE SLAVE GIRLS"

Season 1, episodes 3 & 4

Directed by
Michael Caffey
Writing credits
Steve Greenberg (story) &
Aubrey Solomon (story)
Steve Greenberg (teleplay) &
Aubrey Solomon (teleplay) and
"Cory Applebaum" (Anne Collins pseudonym)
Original airdate: September 27, 1979

Cast
Buck Rogers...Gil Gerard
Wilma Deering...Erin Gray

Dr. Elias Huer...Tim O'Connor
Major Duke Danton...David Groh
Kaleel...Jack Palance
Governor Saroyan ...Roddy McDowall
Ryma...Brianne Leary
Dr. Mallory...Macdonald Carey
Stella Warden...Karen Carlson
Regis Saroyan...Michael Mullins
Brigadier Gordon...Buster Crabbe
Twiki...Felix Silla
Voice of Twiki...Mel Blanc
Galen...Robert Dowdell
Major Fields...Sheila DeWindt
Julio...Don Marshall
Female Pilot...Diane Markoff
Woman...June Whitley Taylor
Husband...Borah Silver
Worker...Michael Masters
Guard...Don Maxwell

Buck accepts membership in the directorate and joins Wilma on the planet Vistula. Led by Governor Saroyan in a turban (Roddy McDowall), Vistula is a virtual paradise except for the fact they still have slavery. The slaves are used by the ruling class as servants.

Meanwhile, in a mountain stronghold, Kaleel addresses his ridiculously dressed people (they wear metal headbands and togas), as a wife in the crowd betrays her husband to him. "He says you sell us and keep the money!" Incensed at a follower doubting him, Kaleel's hands begin to glow as he angrily approaches the man and kills him, telling the faithful, "My touch is the touch of truth, the kiss of God!"

When Mutant leader Kaleel poisons the food disc supply of Earth's fighter pilots, Buck and Wilma must stop him. Kaleel is a sorcerer and slave trader, profiting off selling his own people into slavery. They believe he is a god. With their elite pilots down, to defend Earth, a ragtag group of retired pilots and Twiki are recruited, including a legendary pilot, Brigadier Gordon (Played by the first *Buck Rogers* & *Flash Gordon*, Buster Crabbe).

Wilma goes undercover as a slave girl. Befriending another slave, Ryma, she slips off on her own to do some sleuthing. Ryma is sent to Buck by her owner and explains, "I was supposed to be yours tonight." She appreciates Buck's anti slavery stance. He sneaks off to meet with Wilma and finds Kaleel's men sabotaging more food discs at Food Processing Plant 347, a flimsy exterior sign for what is an undisguised soundstage on the Universal backlot.

Stella Warden is Kaleel's right-hand woman. A sexy leather-clad moll, she oversees the attacks on Earth's food discs. With Buck and Wilma on Vistula, Dr. Huer has Brigadier Gordon lead the mission.

A big, pulpy two-parter, there's a lot to like in "Planet Of The Slave Girls"! From Jack Palance full-blooded performance as Kaleel, Roddy McDowall as the clueless caliphate, slave girls and the one/two punch of Brianne Leary and Karen Carlson, it's a fun, energetic two-parter, but nothing tops having two generations of Buck Rogers meeting. Wilma gets to judo flip a guard, Twiki gets to tell somebody "Get off my back!"and fix Carl, an insulting computer.

In the first season, Twiki operates as Buck's Q, building whatever he and Wilma need that week on their missions, including the tracers that Buck and Wilma use on Vistula.

There's a striking scene of Wilma shackled in her slave girl toga, being mocked by Stella. She also gets an impressive 'butt shot.'

Jack Palance is the star of the show, though, screaming *"DON'T be afraiiid—ONLY THE WEAK are AFRAIIIID!"* He's great, and sets the high water mark for Buck baddies. The two-parter was originally titled "Flight To Sorcerer's Mountain" before NBC opted for the more commercial 'Planet Of The Slave Girls."

In the episode, Wilma wants Buck to teach 20th Century combat techniques to cadets. The class instructor, Major Duke Danton, resists until Wilma orders him to let Buck do it. Duke says "So you're Buck Rogers, huh?" "Since the day I was born," Buck quips. Danton and Buck have an immediate mutual antipathy—as both men know the other was involved with Wilma. Buck is laughed at by the class when he mentions something called 'Football.' He urges the class to learn "red dogging," which he describes as "punching a hole through the defensive line."

Danton mocks Buck when one pilot asks Buck to explain 'sacking the quarterback.' Buck obliges by slamming into Danton and proceeds to have a brawl with him before the class. (The show, like the rest of the series, has the most obvious stunt doubles you've ever seen.) Danton wins the fight, but he and Buck start a grudging admiration for each other. David Groh, who plays Danton, comes off credible as both a romantic threat to Buck, being an old boyfriend of Wilma's and as a 25th Century pilot. Groh, who usually played harried modern guys and gangsters, seems to relish playing a macho space pilot.

Buck and Danton put aside their differences to rescue Wilma, fighting nomads in the desert of Vistula to reach Kaleel's stronghold. When Buck pulls out his desert survival gear to protect them from exposure, it's amusing to note their protection is gold lame' suits that leave their faces completely exposed! Kaleel and Stella prepare to kill Wilma and Ryma in a volcano, as Buck takes on Kaleel. Wilma then frees Ryma, who urges her people to rebel and end slavery.

There's some nicely dated late '70s catchphrases in this two-parter, from Twiki yelling "Right On!" to Buck calling somebody "a turkey" and "with all due respect Galen, stick it!" Twiki's line "Curse You, Red Baron" is a reference to Snoopy from the *Peanuts* comic strip.

Buck and Danton talk about O.J. Simpson, "I told you all about him back in the desert, a running back out of USC," says Buck. As this is the future, it seems weird that Buck didn't mention what O.J. Simpson is best known for today, the suspicious death of his ex wife and her friend. This may seem like a mistake, that Buck never mentions O.J. murdering his ex wife and another person in 1994, but it's not a goof. Buck's ship froze in 1987, eight years before it happened

PALANCE

When the episode aired, actor Jack Palance was on a downward slide. Although he once starred in George Stevens' *Shane*, *Requiem For A Heavyweight* and other classics, he was now appearing in low budget junk like *Without Warning*, *Hawk The Slayer*, *Gor*, *Gor II*, and *Cyborg 2: Glass Shadow* (with a very young Angelina Jolie as the title robot).

In the late '80s, he experienced a career renaissance when Tim

Burton cast him as Jack Nicholson's mob boss in the blockbuster *Batman*. This led to appearing in *City Slickers*, playing grizzled trail boss Curly (Who is described as looking like "a saddlebag with eyes"), for which he won the Oscar for Best Supporting Actor. He proved he was hirable in his seventies, by dropping down on live TV and doing a flurry of one armed push-ups.

BUCK MEETS BUCK

Despite Jack Palance' wonderfully over the top performance, hands down, the Most Important Thing about the episode? Buck Rogers meets the original Buck Rogers!

The scene where Gil Gerard and Buster Crabbe fly side by side talking is one of the best in the series.

BUCK ROGERS: "Have we met?"

BRIGADIER GORDON: "I don't think so, Captain. We're from different times. I've been doing this sort of thing since before you were born, Captain."

BUCK ROGERS: "Think so, huh?

BRIGADIER GORDON: "Young man, I know so!"

PETER ANDERSON (Mattes/models): "I had an opportunity to work in the cave sequence on 'Slave Girls' with Jack Palance. We were going to extend the top of the cave wall with a matte painting, because we did original in-camera matte paintings for the show. We spent two hours setting up this matte painting, got everything lined up, when Jack comes back from wardrobe. He's got a super high theater hat that sticks up and goes a foot into the matte line. We said 'Sir, we're not gonna ask you to stoop down, but we need to work out a routine here...' Without even bothering production, Jack walks up onstage and as he gets higher, he carries his hat like a general's armament. He was so tall, he was only a fraction of an inch below the matte line! A true pro..."

GIL GERARD: "I liked Jack Palance and since we didn't really have any scenes together, I came in to meet him one day. Jack was huge—Jack filled the set. He had incredible energy, watching him I just said 'Whoa!' I was surprised he was as big as he was, he was bigger than me, he must have been 6"5, because I'm 6"1/6"2, depending on how good I feel that day, and he was a big man. His presence was incredible—he was really that guy, that character."

TIM O'CONNOR (Huer): "I remember Jack Palance and how wonderful he looked—and what a nice fella he was, such a good actor..."

ERIN GRAY: "With Jack Palance, what I remember more than anything, was that man sure loved to swing that cape! He did more things with that cape on the set...He was constantly twirling it around, trying different things. He gave me the impression that he was still 8 years old! Seriously, watch what he does with the cape in the episode.

"I was really impressed with Buster Crabbe—he came in, seventy-something years old at the time and he had this incredible washboard stomach! The man was really fit, upbeat, had a twinkle in his eye and was really fun to work with.

"One of my favorite scenes in that is when I'm chained up and sweating over a volcano and I committed fully to being a sweaty, chained up slave girl, Good for me! That sort of thing was there for the adults and teenage boys, while the kids had no idea...They were there for the spaceships and robots!

"I surprised myself with the things we got away with on the show, especially some of the things Buck and Twiki say! I did a couple stunt shots in 'Planet Of The Slave Girls' because my stuntwoman's ass was bigger than mine and I worked really hard to keep my ass in shape! So I did a couple minor stunts to make sure Wilma's butt was in shape on camera. My stunt gal was a lovely girl, but my ass was better. Later on, I got Donna Evans to be my stunt double—she had a great body and a smaller ass than mine, so she looked better than me in some of the walking away close ups!"

ALAN BRENNERT (Story Editor): "I liked many of the guest actors on the show—Anthony James, Markie Post and Jimmy Sloyan in 'Plot to Kill a City,' Gary Coleman in 'Cosmic Whiz Kid,' Jamie Lee Curtis in 'Unchained Woman,' but what was most thrilling for me was to write a line of dialogue for Buster Crabbe!"

BUSTER CRABBE (From BEST OF STARLOG VI BUSTER CRABBE: HIS LAST INTERVIEW By Jeff Rovin), on doing BUCK in '79 "The techniques have changed dramatically. When I did a scene in (the 1930s) Flash Gordon, we could merely have been flying a plane or piloting a boat (when he flew his spacecraft). We didn't approach it any special way because, for all we knew, it was 1936. It wasn't anything really special. This time, on the *Buck Rogers* TV show, when I got up in the spacecraft and got comfortable, the director (Michael Caffey) said 'When I say Go, Buster, all you have to do is throw your head back.'

"That's what I did and the fellow with the shoulder camera moved his camera around as if I were taking off. When they added the special effects and sound effects, it was fantastic. The technological aspect is obviously much better now than in the old days and they certainly have much better looking spacecraft today than we had."

ANNE COLLINS LUDWICK (Story Editor/Co writer): "'Planet Of The Slave Girls'—that title still makes me cringe! The powers-that-were had a big hand in coming up with titles. I guess I used my 'Corey Applebaum' pseudonym whenever I was not thrilled with the way an episode turned out, or when I was sharing credit with another writer and was, again, not proud of the final script and/or its production, but I don't recall loathing any particular episode."

Buck Facts

- Duke Danton is named after actor/director Ray Danton.
- Look for Academy Award winning actor/director Tim Robbins as an extra—he's the slave on the left when Ryma urges the slaves to rebel at the climax of Part 2.
- Buck sings "Strangers In The Night," his second Sinatra cover after he warbles "Chicago Chicago" in the pilot.
- Guest Don Marshall starred in the sci fi show Land Of The Giants and guest starred on a great classic Star Trek episode, "Galileo 7."
- This episode was re-made at the end of Season One as "Buck's Duel To The Death."
- Twiki in a starfighter, blowing up living beings violates every law of Isaac Asimov's theories of robotics.
- Having retired pilots brought back to defend Earth is a concept revisited in the later episode "Return Of The Fighting 69th."
- This is the second time someone in the 25th Century calls Buck a "barbarian."

Michael Caffey, photo by Pat Jankiewicz

- Diane Markoff ('Female Pilot'), a Universal contract actress, also appeared on *The Incredible Hulk, The Hardy Boys/Nancy Drew Mysteries, Quincy* and *Cliffhangers.*
- Listen for Danny Dark doing the re-cap at the beginning of Part 2. Besides being the NBC narrator at the time, he was the voice of Superman on the long running cartoon *Super Friends.*
- Roddy McDowall starred in the *Planet Of The Apes'* film series. Having a character named 'Galen' may have been an homage—Galen was Roddy McDowall's name on the *Planet Of The Apes'* TV series.
- David Groh played Valerie Harper's husband on Rhoda and was a Mafia Don on Melrose Place.
- In his fight at The Food Processing Plant, Buck battles legendary stuntmen Gene LeBell and Bob Minor. Minor doubled William Marshall in the *Blacula* movies.
- Buck uses judo again in this episode.

MICHAEL CAFFEY on directing *Buck Rogers* in the 25th Century's "Planet Of The Slave Girls."

One of the most impressive TV genre directors, Michael Caffey has done episodes of *Wild, Wild West, The Amazing Spider-Man, Kolchak The Night Stalker* and *The Adventures Of Brisco County, JR.* with Bruce Campbell. Known to friends and his kids (Including Go Gos' singer/songwriter Charlotte Caffey) as "Big Mike," he helmed *Buck*'s first two ongoing episodes.

"We used to call that show Suck Rogers! I did a two-hour *Buck Rogers*, 'Planet Of The Slave Girls.' I had Jack Palance in that. Jack Palance does Jack Palance and you don't direct Jack Palance! He was a big, powerful man, full of energy. When he played Kaleel on Buck, I would say to Jack, 'Hey, Jack, I want you to make this interesting—I want you to say your lines and keep going around, all the way around this huge circle of a set.' He would say 'Okay,' do it and it would be just amazing.

"Jack was strong, an ex-fighter. At one point, he was supposed to be shaking something out of somebody. Well, Jack scared the guy so much and shook him so hard, the guy fell on his knees! I had to shoot the scene over! I said, 'Jack, take it easy, this guy is one of your own men.'

"During the rehearsals and various takes, Jack was exhorting the populace of his volcano planet, which amounted to 20 people. Finally, his voice went and it became hard for him to speak, so he had to come back and loop it later on. I loved the *Flash Gordon* serials as a kid, so it was a thrill for me to have Buster Crabbe there and actually have a scene between two generations of Buck Rogers.

"Gil Gerard was fine as Buck Rogers, but he's the only actor I can think of where I would watch him do the lines in front of me, and something seemed to be happening, but you would go to see the dailies and *nothing happened!* It's always the other way around, something more comes through. But you would watch, thinking, 'Did I shoot that? Did I print that?' He wasn't bad, just flat, but I never had that happen before."

He remembers Buck's robot sidekick Twiki played by Felix Silla "was a little grumpy. He didn't like being in that suit, it was hot in there. The FX were not that bad on *Buck*."

Pamela Susan Shoop as Tangie

"Vegas in Space"

Season 1, Episode 5

Directed by Sigmund Neufeld Jr.
Written by Anne Collins
Original airdate October 4, 1979

Cast
Buck Rogers...Gil Gerard
Wilma Deering...ErinGray
Dr. Huer... Tim O'Connor
Morgan Velosi...Richard Lynch
Falina Redding...Ana Alicia
Major Marla Landers....Juanin Clay
Tangie...Pamela Susan Shoop
Hood...James Luisi
Amos Armat...Cesar Romero
Morpheus....Joseph Wiseman
Twiki...Felix Silla
Voice of Twiki...Mel Blanc
Rita...Alice Frost
Man...Ted Chapman
Sinaloa Computer Pitboss...Olan Soule (Voice, uncredited)

Falina, an innocent girl, is abducted by Morgan Velosi, inter-planetary mobster. Velosi plans to have information extracted directly from her brain to beat a rival, Amos Armat. Buck is forced to go to Sinaloa, the "Vegas In Space" to get Falina back. Mobster Amos Armat desperately offers to turn himself in, if the Earth Directorate rescues his employee, Falina. Being an expert blackjack player, Buck is the perfect guy to take the mission. Blackjack is now called "10 and 11s."

"Sort of a Las Vegas in Space," says Buck admiringly, when told of the futuristic gambling Mecca. "The idea of traveling to what some people refer to as an orbiting city of moral depravity obviously agrees with you, Buck," says Dr. Theopolis cheerfully. When Buck, accompanied by Major Marla Landers, arrives there, he finds it is also a place of desperation. Cheaters are dealt with harshly by the planet's army of guards.

Meanwhile, Velosi's skilled torturer, Morpheus, plans to extract information from Falina's brain using drugs. As with "Slave Girls" and other first season episodes like "Fighting 69th" and "Flight Of The War Witch," the villains regularly employ torture. Poor Falina is strapped down as Morpheus attempts to painfully pull secrets from her brain.

When he hits a winning streak, Buck is suddenly accompanied by Tangie, a busty casino girl, who latches onto his arm. She is being kept there by Morgan Velosi and wants to get back to Earth by any means necessary. Velosi reminds Tangie that the only way off Sinaloa is through him.

Tangie is essentially a Vegas call girl in one of the most revealing costumes ever seen on the series , sent to keep the casino's high rollers company. "You poor thing, you look absolutely lost," she coos to Buck.

Anne Collins' script is one of the very best of the series, a cool concept, interesting characters and she even got a prostitute in the 'family hour'! Collins even takes the time to invest Buck with depth and character that later episodes never bothered with. It's a perfect way to start the series after the bombastic two parters. We find Amos Armat wants to turn himself in over an employee because he secretly knows he is Falina's father.

The highlight of the episode is a moment Anne Collins Ludwick takes to illustrate Buck's plight, being in a future without any friends or loved ones. We see that because Buck doesn't know what happened to his friends in their personal lives before the apocalypse, he will never have a sense of closure.

She gives Gerard a chance to really act in a key scene, giving the sci fi hero an interesting touch of pathos. It's so good, you wish the series had taken the time to have more moments like this. Hit with melancholy while gambling, Buck remembers being at Edwards Air Force Base, when "Toby, Kaplan and I hopped in a car one Wednesday afternoon and just drove til we hit Vegas... That was just before I left for Houston, the last time I saw Toby, he was bound and determined to head up the Space Aeronautics Board. He could've too. I wonder if he ever did?"

"You won again," Tangie marvels, pulling Buck out of his reverie. *"Yeah, I won,"* he says ruefully, adding "it only took me 500 years to get here."   Easily winning again and again, Buck jokes "I was cheating—I was using my brain."

Although she is meant to be the "B"-story, Tangie quickly steals the episode. Beautiful and in trouble, she also shows a manipulative side when she doesn't get her way. Although a lot of beautiful women guested on the show in auto pilot, this episode features some impressive acting by guest Pamela Susan Shoop

Buck is only concerned with saving Falina, while Tangie pleads with Buck to help her instead.

"He won't let me leave," she says of Morgan. "He says I'm too valuable a commodity." She makes it clear that if Buck bought her freedom, she would be *very* grateful. When he doesn't oblige her (the money he wins is part of the mission), she realizes he's an undercover agent from Earth. Tangie quickly turns on him, attempting blackmail when her feminine wiles don't work.

"If you don't help me buy my way out of this city, security's gonna get a call from me," a scorned Tangie threatens. In the end, Buck finds a way to save Tangie, Falina and even Marla Landers, who Morgan was attempting to seduce. There's a big *Star Wars* influence on the Sinaloa sequences in this episode—Buck dresses in the white shirt and black vest, which unmistakably resembles Han Solo, while the guards are all in black capes and Darth Vader-style helmets. Marla Landers and Buck have good byplay, but the chemistry isn't there—you miss Erin Gray's Wilma.

When Erin Gray originally decided not to do the series, Juanin Clay was brought in as her replacement, "Marla Landers." Notice that she has the exact same number of letters in her name as "Wilma Deering" and a sound-alike first name? The Landers character would have stepped in for Erin Gray on the series, if the actress hadn't changed her mind about not doing the series.

ANNE COLLINS LUDWICK (Writer, "Vegas In Space"): "'Vegas in Space' was the first episode to be shot. Major Marla Landers was the character we'd created to 'replace' the Wilma Deering character, and she had to be cast. It was the first casting session I'd ever sat in on – I remember it as a steady stream of beautiful women trying to sound authoritative. The scene they had to read was one Glen had written for the pilot, and contained big, make-or-break words like 'subterfuge.'

"The woman they ultimately cast, Juanin Clay, was one of the few who came across as an authority figure who also had a soft, vulnerable (i.e. feminine) side. She did a great job in that episode, but at some point during the shoot, Erin finally agreed to do the series, and Major Landers was never heard from again.

"Erin Gray's return was a relief to everyone. Not only did it insure a smooth transition from the movie pilot to the weekly series, but Erin herself was a grand addition to the cast. She always knew her lines, always looked fabulous, was always on time, always good-humored, always accessible, always game for anything, and she always played well with others. *And could that lady tell a dirty joke...*"

ERIN GRAY: "After they did the movie, they told me it was going to be a TV series. I said, 'I don't want to do a TV series,' I almost bailed out of the series a couple times. I was originally told it was a 10-hour miniseries and we shot most of it and then it was put on hold. That's why I was a blonde on *The Rockford Files*, because I was still blonde from *Buck*. I was tired of being a blonde, I worried constantly dyeing my hair would damage it and prevent other commercial work, it also bothered me being away from my child and working 16 hours a day.

"On weekends, I was doing press for the show, so I had no time for my family. They tried to re-cast it and finally came up with Juanin Clay. I don't know if this is true, but I heard (*Buck* casting director) Monique James sent footage of actresses who should be on the show and (Then NBC President) Fred Silverman said, 'Get me that girl!' Monique said, 'That's Erin Gray' and Fred said, 'Then get me her—I keep going back to her!' That's the only time I had a conversation with Bruce Lansbury. I was sort of dazed and surprised they called me back for it. Actors like to be wanted and that's all it took.

"Bruce said, 'We really want (to keep) you for this part.' Juanin actually had the part and did an episode—'Vegas In Space' but they weren't happy and brought me back. She was one of the girls I tested against for the part of Wilma in our original *Buck Rogers* miniseries, which became the movie. Who can blame her? It was a great part."

BUCK Highlight: the show gives another glimpse at the different alien races of the 25th Century. When Buck sees—and wants— a curvaceous blue-skinned girl, Marla quickly warns him that it's actually a male alien.

Buck Facts

- Joseph Wiseman was Dr. No in the first Sean Connery James Bond and Draco in Buck's pilot film.

Pamela Susan Shoop models mirrored dress.

- Buck makes a reference to defeating The Draconians in "Awakening."
- Richard Lynch, with his features scarred from a real life fire, used his scars to a long career playing vampires, cult leaders and bikers.

- The voice of the Sinaloa gaming machine is character actor Olan Soule, best known as the voice of Batman on *Super Friends*
- Both guest actresses Juanin Clay and Pamela Susan Shoop had auditioned to play Wilma Deering when it looked as though Erin Gray wouldn't do the series.
- Buck uses his unique form of clumsily applied judo, 'Buck Fu,' on one of Morgan's henchmen.
- One of the cheaters apprehended in Sinaloa is carrying—and trying to conceal— a hilariously huge '70s-era calculator.
- We see a 25th Century answering machine in Falina's apartment!
- Marla and Tangie are seen via flashback in the later episode 'A Blast For Buck.'
- Buck re-creates golf in this episode, using Twiki as his caddy.
- Cesar Romero, best known as The Joker on the classic Adam West *Batman* TV series, was the first of several of that show's classic rogues gallery to guest on *Buck.* He was joined in later episodes by Fellow Bat Guests Frank Gorshin, Julie Newmar, William Smith and Sid Haig, among others.

BUCK BABE: PAMELA SUSAN SHOOP
Space Hooker With A Heart Of Gold

Although she appeared in numerous episodics like *Fantasy Island* ("I was a wood nymph on that!"), *The Highwayman, Wonder Woman* (as a fellow amazon on Paradise Island), *Magnum P.I.* and *The Incredible Hulk*, vivacious redhead Pamela Susan Shoop made her most vivid impression as Tangie, an alluring but desperate space hooker in the *Buck Rogers* episode 'Vegas In Space.'

Clad in a tight, revealing dress of mirror shards, she tries charm, coercion and finally threats to convince the 500 year old hero to get her off the floating satellite of sin. With her doe-eyes, Shoop plays her sad instead of hard, making the character stand out as sympathetic.

Buck Rogers' Story Editor Anne Collins Ludwick was amazed to see what Shoop did with a minor character from her 'Vegas In Space' script.

"Pamela Shoop played a gorgeous exotically/scantily dressed quasi-hooker named Tangie in my first produced episode. To be

Pamela Susan Shoop, photo by Pat Jankiewicz.

perfectly honest, I had written Tangie as a cliché, a siren trying her best to manipulate Buck into helping her escape the orbiting den of iniquity on which she was trapped. But when I saw dailies, I was floored by the wonderful spin Pamela had put on the character.

"Without changing a word of my dialogue, she'd imbued Tangie with an air of desperation that made the character much more sympathetic and interesting," Anne Collins Ludwick marvels. "It demonstrated a lot of initiative and talent on her part, and I was so impressed with that, I went down to the set to say so in person. But I was even more impressed when I saw that she could not sit down like a normal human being in the thin strips of metallic material they'd literally sewn her into.

"She could only rest between takes by standing on a solid-backed dolly and being slowly tilted into a semi-reclining position, but she accepted this indignity, and my praise, very graciously, and to this day, having watched several decades worth of TV actors mindlessly deliver lines I'd written, I still remember Pamela Shoop as someone who'd added a delightfully unexpected dimension to a character I'd created."

Pamela Susan Shoop smiles. "It's surprising because *Buck Rogers* was considered a family show, yet here's this casino in Outer Space with me as a prostitute who will do anything to get back to Earth. It was fun doing a role like that—I enjoyed playing a Space Hooker With A Heart Of Gold. I played her very ingenuous and sincere.

"Tangie was frightened and very intimidated, instead of being a harsh prostitute doing the hard sell. The writer (Anne Collins) actually came up to me and said 'Thank you so much, you gave this character so much more dimension than what I wrote,' which was a really great thing to hear," the actress says, still moved. "It's one thing to put on a wardrobe like that and play it brassy, but I like to play against my look. Tangie actually wasn't my first hooker, I had played one burned out on drugs on the TV miniseries *79 Park Avenue*. Nothing bothers you if you become the character, even wearing an outfit like the one I wore on *Buck Rogers in the 25th Century*."

Speaking of that outfit, it's jaw-dropping, even for a show like *Buck Rogers*, whose episodes had no shortage of cleavage and spandex. As Tangie, Shoop sported a flashy, skimpy and quite revealing dress. "That costume looked great, but when I first saw it, I said *'ARE YOU INSANE?!?'* The sides were completely nude—except for one little waistband, everything was nude on the sides. It was incredibly uncomfortable because it was literally all mirrors! I couldn't even sit down, so I had to lean against a slant-board between shots. Still, I would love to wear it again!"
Ironically, the actress had auditioned for Wilma Deering on the series, before Erin Gray decided to reprise the role. "I was up for Wilma, before Erin got it. She's really sweet and beautiful,

Buck Rogers joins The Legion Of Death in Plot To Kill A City.

Erin has always been one of the nicest ladies in the business. Gil Gerard was nice to me too, he had a ball doing that show."

"The Plot to Kill a City" Part 1 & 2

Season 1, Episode 6 & 7

Directed by Dick Lowry
Written by Alan Brennert
Original airdates October 11 & 18, 1979

Cast
Buck Rogers...Gil Gerard
Wilma Deering...Erin Gray
Dr. Huer...Tim O'Connor
Argus...Victor Argo
Woman...Sena Black
Twiki...Felix Silla
Voice of Twiki...Mel Blanc
Sherese... Nancy DeCarl
1st Cop...John Furlong
Pirate...Seamon Glass
Seton Kellogg...Frank Gorshin
Varek...Anthony James
Joella Cameron...Markie Post
Jolen Quince...John Quade
1st Rowdy...Richard Reed
Technician...Mitch Reta
Barney...James Sloyan
Hartsteen...Whitney Rydbeck
Ticket Clerk...Gwen Mitchell
Katrina...Nonice Williams

Buck goes undercover with a group of interstellar mercenary assassins known as The Legion of Death. After one of their members
is killed by the Earth Defense Directorate, they vow to destroy New
Chicago and kill Dr. Huer as payback. A bomb rocks the Earth De-

fense Directorate, knocking Twiki off his feet when a wall blows out.

"Why is it the good die young," Twiki wonders, when he thinks he's been 'killed.' The terrorists include pretty but evil empath Charisse, Quince, a fat telepath, their mad leader Kellogg (a fun Frank Gorshin) and his bodyguard, Varek, a radiation scarred mutant who is described as "a wretched, wretched creature." Varek and his people were human once, but post nuclear war, he can become transparent, pass through solid objects and is so deformed, he's forced to wear a mask.

To stop them, Dr. Huer realizes, they will have to infiltrate the group, which will be very dangerous. Worried for Buck's safety, Twiki wonders "Beety Beety Beety, why can't we just phone this in?" Buck poses as "Raphael Argus," after capturing the real Argus and taking over his ship, which talks to Buck in a sexy woman's voice.

When Wilma goes undercover onboard the ship, it tells her "I do the warming up around here, Sweetie, and don't you forget it!" The resourceful Wilma disables her, telling the computer that she's "doing a little home repair, Sweetie!." The computer's voice, running down like HAL in 2001: A Space Odyssey, hisses at Wilma, "You...little...witch!"

Nancy DeCarl stands out as the sexy and cruel Charisse—when they have Buck at their mercy, she pipes in with "I say we kill him now!" She's right, of course. It's Brennert's funny way of acknowledging one of Star Trek's most beloved clichés—where one of the men want to kill Captain Kirk, only to be put off by the sexy alien moll, who falls for him. Buck refers to Quince and Charisse as "Porky and Babydoll." To her credit, DeCarl's femme fatale doesn't reform and is allowed to escape at the end. When the Legion of Death realize Buck is only posing as Argus, he must prevent them from killing him as well as exterminating all life in New Chicago.

Markie Post, pre-Night Court and Evening Shade, is also impressive as Joella, a beautiful barfly at a Space Bar. When Twiki sees her, he immediately declares "What a fox!" Post opts to help Buck because "we've come this far together, we might as well go all the way!" Joella humorously laments of Buck, "Why do all the good-looking ones have to be crazy?" She also expresses a love for futuristic baseball.

Continuing a funny running gag from "Vegas In Space," Buck once again desires a hot alien (Sena Black), only to be put off on talking to her when he sees her nose is an elephant trunk

Brennert's strong writing makes the villains standout. As a writer with a science fiction background, he plays it straight and Gerard's Buck is more clever and resourceful than he is in most episodes. Brennert also has the non-powered Buck up against a legion of aliens with super powers in this two-parter and the fun is seeing how he outwits each of them. Frank Gorshin, who starred on episodes of the original *Batman* and *Star Trek*, seems to relish being a larger-than-life villain again.

Anthony James, always playing hitmen, mafia goons and assassins, gets to show hidden depths to his tormented Varek. Buck urges Varek to stand up to Kellogg, because he knows mass killing is wrong. The villain is moved by Buck's argument. When Kellogg beats Buck and sets up a nuclear device that will wipe New Chicago off the map, Varek betrays him to save both Buck and the people of Earth. Although phasing through the anti-matter plant gives him grevious injuries, Varek sacrifices himself to stop the meltdown at the plant.

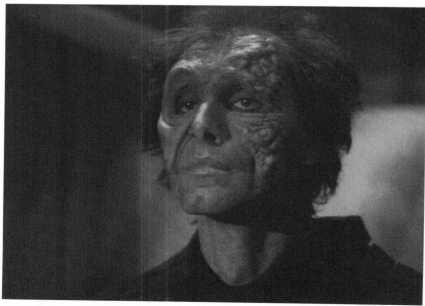

Anthony James as Varek.

He unmasks to show Buck his wrecked face, explaining that he wants our hero to save New Chicago because he doesn't want the residents to suffer like his people did. The ending strongly implies Varek is dying as he asks Buck to take him home. He promises to do so, telling Varek, "It's the least I can do for a fellow survivor." Buck realizes he, like Varek, is the sole survivor of a long dead race, the 20th Century. A great two-part episode that tries to hew closer to the comic strip *Buck Rogers*, "Plot To Kill A City" is fun and not afraid to be grim either.

Buck Facts

- Buck tries to re-create wine. Wilma and Huer hate it. Wilma also has no idea what a grilled cheese sandwich is.
- The anti matter plant is guarded by maintenance androids, who only show up in Brennert scripted episodes. They resemble crash test dummies, but the idea that some jobs are too dangerous for humans in the 25th Century and are performed by androids is a cool one that was worth exploring.
"Don't know why no one else picked up on the maintenance droids, but they were simply another futuristic element I thought added to the 25th century texture," says Alan Brennert.
- Character actor Whitney Rydbeck was in everything from the *Brady Bunch* TV series to the sci fi comedy *Sleeper* with Woody Allen.
- Popular bad guy Anthony James (Varek) had fun with his bad guy image in *The Naked Gun 2½: The Smell of Fear*.
- Originally titled "Flight From The Legion Of Death."
- Nancy DeCarl guest starred on *Buck*'s sister show, *Battlestar Galactica*, and is married Larry Manetti, of *Magnum P.I.*
- More of Varek's people show up in "Flight Of The War Witch" as worker drones. It was probably just a frugal re-use of the costume.
- Barney is based on Black Barney from the *Buck Rogers* comic strip.
- The Public Address system at the spaceport calls for "Arriving passenger Adam Strange from Alpha Centauri, please report to Reservations Desk." Adam Strange was a DC Comics hero with a similar story to Buck...He's an Earthman who winds up on Alpha Centari.

- There's also a reference to "Flight 624 from Thanagar." The planet Thanagar is home to DC Comics' alien heroes, Hawkman and Hawkgirl.
- The P.A. is voiced by Shannon Farnon, Wonder Woman on *Super Friends*.
- Markie Post played Electra Woman in a failed pilot for a '90s revival of *Electra Woman And Dyna Girl*.
- Post's Joella is the only human besides Buck who can tell what Twiki is saying when he does his computer sounds.

25th Century Guest ANTHONY JAMES Varek

In two of the best episodes of *Buck Rogers in the 25th Century*, "The Plot To Kill A City," Buck faces down a team of baddies, all with super powers. The deadliest, Varek, wears a mask through which we can only see his agonized eyes and mouth.

He actually has the power to alter his density to pass through solid walls and has the touch of death. Buck stops the others through his wits and skill, but finds Varek insurmountable. As the moments tick away to a nuclear bomb destroying New Chicago, Buck finds an unexpected ally in Varek, who gained his powers but lost his face and his people in a nuclear war that claimed his planet.

Buck is puzzled why Varek would betray his master and help him, until the tall, hulking villain rasps, "You can't imagine life on my planet...Children afraid to look at their own reflections. Children with the touch of death." In his black cape and mask, the villain saving Buck recalls the death of Darth Vader in *Return Of The Jedi*, which this two-parter predates by five years. Varek is unexpectedly touching and clearly doomed by his actions.

The show's writer/Story Editor Alan Brennert, felt "Anthony James gave a wonderful performance. He delivered the character's big soliloquy beautifully."

To have Varek played by Anthony James, an actor who has been typecast as numerous heavies throughout his career, is all the more impressive. With his bushy eyebrows and high cheekbones, there's something about Anthony James that looks malevolent...Sinister, like he's up to something. The acclaimed painter of Greek descent has used this look, along with his intense eyes, to great effect in his long career as a character actor, playing thieves, criminals, killers and assorted near do wells.

"That's why it's called acting," he explains with a warm laugh

He made his debut in the Oscar winning drama *In The Heat Of The Night* and has menaced everyone from *Charlie's Angels* to Clint Eastwood. He even took his act to Outer Space again after saving Buck, playing a Romulan in the twenty-sixth episode of *Star Trek: The Next Generation*'s first season, "The Neutral Zone." In 2364, he was Sub Commander Thei, serving Commander Tebok on a Romulan Warbird.

"There have been many miracles in the history of the world, from the Burning Bush to the parting of the Red Sea, but to me, there was no bigger miracle than my 'Plot To Kill A City' episodes of *Buck Rogers in the 25th Century*, where I actually got to be the hero," a happy Anthony James declares. "Not just the hero, mind you, but a totally sympathetic good guy! I ended up being the one who saved the day and I get to save Buck Rogers and all his friends. That was a first for me—I saved the day, but had to wear a mask to do it."

"What I also loved about those episodes of *Buck* is that I actually got to do a dramatic scene, instead of just being mean. Varek, My character, has been hideously burned in a nuclear war that killed his people and his planet, that's why he has to wear the mask. It was a sad and tragic history that he had on the planet he came from. That was very important to me, to have a chance to do that kind of character, with that kind of dialogue. It was a very important television episode for me, because I rarely got a chance to do those kind of roles and those kinds of scenes."

The highlight of the episode is Varek's sad soliloquy to Buck. "I loved that—I loved giving that speech and that I actually got to be the good guy, even though I wore a mask and had these terrible powers," he relates. "You have to constantly look to be inventive, even though the producers and director just want you to be a bad person, a bad character. I don't like to leave them like that. I like to bring something that makes them a little more special than the other things I have done or typical bad guys...even if it's the way they walk or the way they sound, just do something to make them a little different. *Anything* to make them a little different."

Did he play an alien differently than he would play a human bad guy? "No, because what's important to me whether it's an alien or a human, is that there's an emotional element to the character. Varek has a lot of emotion and emotional history in his character that are very similar to human feelings. Just tragic, terrible painful feelings happened to that character. So, in some strange way, unless the alien doesn't have feelings, like Mr. Spock or a similar alien character devoid of emotions, I like to make them as emotional as possible.

"Whether they are being mean or sad, the alien takes on a human quality only because there's an emotionality involved. Otherwise, it's a flat character. I always feel the emotional part of a character is the most interesting part and I try to express that emotionality in the most interesting way possible,"

He wanted Varek's plight to resonate with viewers. "What's very helpful when you do a scene like that is a director like Dick Lowry, who did those two shows. Usually in television, they want the regulars to get their close-ups first. I asked permission from the director and Gil Gerard. I said to them, 'Would you mind if I do my close-ups first, because I am emotionally ready for it?' Gil graciously said, 'By all means, do it!' It helps when you have people supportive like that and willing to help in any way they can, it makes difficult scenes easier to do and a collaborative effort.

"Dick Lowry was a terrific guy and a great director to work with. I did a Tom Sawyer/Huck Finn movie with him after that, with a very young Cynthia Nixon in it long before *Sex And The City*, and a very young Anthony Michael Hall played Huckleberry Finn. I have a new autobiography out, *Acting My Face: A Memoir*, where I talk about how important those two *Buck Rogers in the 25th Century* episodes were to me."

On the show, the radiation scarred Varek sports a mask and black Darth Vader like suit. "Remember that mask I had to wear? The day I was going to shoot my first scene, I went to the wardrobe trailer and they gave me the costume and mask. I went back to my trailer and put them on," the actor recalls.

"The eyes on the mask were too small and round, which made the whole mask and face expressionless. So what I did, without ever asking anyone, is decide to make the eyes larger and shape them so they had a sad look to them. I went to the makeup woman and borrowed a razor blade, because they use razor blades to sharpen the eyeliner pencils. She said 'Sure' and I went back into the trailer, and began cutting the eyes on the mask without asking anyone, making them the way I thought they should look.

"I looked at the mask and the eyes really didn't look the way I wanted them to, so I went back and borrowed her razor blade again. I put on the mask and again thought, 'no, it's not exactly what I want with the eyes,' so I went back to the makeup lady to borrow her razor blade a third time and this time she gave me a very strange look and she got very suspicious. She was so polite before, I assumed she had just gotten annoyed that I kept borrowing her razor blade.

"Later, I had told one of the actors what I had done with the mask and how the makeup woman acted the third time. He laughed and said 'No, you didn't annoy her—she thought you were a 'cocaine guy,' using her razor blade to chop up coke in your dressing room! That's why she gave you a funny look. You're gonna get a reputation for doing cocaine on the set.'   I said, 'Oh My God, I could suddenly see myself before a judge, saying 'honest, your honor, I just wanted the eyes to look fatter!'" James chuckles.

"By the way, nobody noticed I had changed the mask! Nobody caught me and honestly, it made the mask and character look a lot better... The mask gave Varek a sad look that fit his background. Something about the mask gave the history of the tragedy of my race. There was a lot of pathos to Varek. Nobody said anything or brought it up, I never brought it up, but it definitely worked better, as far as I was concerned.

"Frank Gorshin played the leader of our Legion Of Death and he was very funny and nice, telling stories, doing impressions. Wonderful, funny guy but he took his acting very seriously. We were out of town on location for a couple days while working on the episode, I can't remember where, but we were all staying at the same hotel. We would all meet for breakfast and got to know each other better, John Quade, Markie Post and Erin Gray, who were all very nice. We'd all go to the location knowing each other, which was fun. When shooting was done, we would hang out at the lobby or restaurant, everyone was wonderful people and wonderful actors, so overall, it was an amazing experience."

Anthony James returned in the second season episode, 'The Golden Man.' "It was a fun part, but not as impressive as Varek— this guy was a greedy bad guy who just wanted to exploit The Golden Man. A typical bad guy role, not layered like Varek."

The actor is now an acclaimed painter. "I have always wanted to live in New England, so when I retired, I moved to Arlington which is right near Boston and haven't worked in 20 years. Haven't been back to California since. My first movie, *In The Heat Of The Night* won best picture, and my last movie, *Unforgiven* won Best Picture. I thought, 'Well, those are nice bookends for a career' and a book on my art was coming out, so I said 'well, I will retire now and go where I want to be.' I love to paint and read about art.

"Mary Woronov, another guest on *Buck Rogers,* is also an artist and painter. We did Mortuary Academy and Charlie's Angels together. It was the first season of Angels and Kim Basinger was in that with us! When we did Mortuary Academy—a Police Academy takeoff, Mary and I went out to see each other's paintings. We both wound up in a book about actors who are artists, which looked at actors who paint. They did a solo book on her and then a solo book on me. Mary is a wonderful person, wonderful actress and a wonderful painter. "

Katherine Wiberg is a resourceful slave girl from Earth.

"Return Of The Fighting 69th"

Season 1, Episode 8

Original airdate: October 25, 1979
Written by David Bennett Carren
Directed by Philip Leacock

Cast
Buck Rogers...Gil Gerard
Col. Wilma Deering...Erin Gray
Dr. Huer...Tim O'Connor
Major Noah Cooper...Peter Graves
Roxanne Trent...Elizabeth Allen
Commander Corliss...Robert Quarry
Sgt 'Big Red' MacMurthy...Woody Strode
Cpl M.K. Schultz...Eddie Firestone
Lt Harriet Twain...K.T. Stevens
Twiki...Felix Silla

Voice of Twiki...Mel Blanc
Alicia...Katherine Wiberg
Clayton...Robert Hardy
Westlake...Duncan McKenzie
War Technician...Clifford Turknett
Eli Twain... Dan Sturkie

Buck and Wilma team up with an over the hill squadron led by Deering's old flight instructor, the legendary Noah Cooper, to participate in what's certain to be a suicide mission—an attack on Necrosis IV(great name), to battle enemies from Wilma's past.

These foes are a twisted couple, scarred, bitter Commander Corliss and his metal-handed moll, Roxanne Trent. The two are using a cache of nerve gas found in the ruins of Washington D.C. to destroy Earth. Can Buck save the planet and rescue Alicia, a young slave girl? Can Wilma trust Noah, after she forced him to retire? It begins when Wilma and Buck chase a stolen freighter hijacked by space pirates. They get away after killing two cadets, Clayton and Westlake, whose deaths Buck blames on Deering.

Buck is so angry, he yells at both Wilma and Dr. Huer. "You gonna try to tell me that lousy stolen freighter was worth the lives of those two cadets? They were just kids! They had no business being out there. I tried telling you that."

"I didn't want them hurt anymore than you did," Wilma replies. When he finds they were after nerve gas from his century, he realizes how dangerous it really is. This is a nice touch—Wilma and Huer have gotten pilots killed since the movie, but this is the first time Buck has actually called them on it... In the feature film, two pilots (one female) are killed when Wilma orders them to ignore Buck's advice on fighting the Draconians, and Buck never brings it up again. Life is cheap in the 25th Century!

Buck learns the freighter was full of 20th Century nerve gas and other bio-weapons that can be used against New Chicago. Since the weapons are over 500 years old, Wilma isn't sure they constitute a threat.

"Those are nerve gas cannisters, Wilma. You drop one of those in our atmosphere, spread around with an air blast, we would all be dead within a week. Yeah, I'd call that a threat," Buck states.

Theo and Huer ponder who should be saved and who will die if they attack with the cannisters. Twiki puts his faith in his best pal. "It's in the bag, everything's copacetic, I trust Buck!"

Noah Cooper is a father figure to Wilma and Huer cautions Buck, "When it comes to Noah Cooper, she doesn't think very clearly." Peter Graves clearly has the gravitas to play somebody that Erin Gray's Wilma Deering would credibly look up to.

Torture and kink are also a big part of *Buck's* first season, despite networks cracking down on action and violence. This is best epitomized in the episode when Alicia, a young slave girl, is being abused by her owner, Roxanne Trent, a cruel master with a cybernetic copper hand. When Roxanne flexes it, she notices the slave give it a curious look.

"You were smiling," she screams, seizing the girl's arm in her metal hand. "You think I'm hideous. You think you're better than me because you have two normal hands! Well, I can rectify that." She crushes the young girl's arm and screams in her face, "What are you doing, Alicia? Your mind is always off somewhere. Five years I've owned you and you always seem to be dreaming with your eyes open. If the market for Terran servants wasn't so depressed, I would sell you in an instant!"

Roxanne begins exerting pressure on the slave's forearm—before she can break the bone, Captain Corliss enters, back from stealing the freighter. Roxanne's torture is even more cruel when we learn that Alicia is deaf. She also crushes Wilma's hand and has a nice fight scene with her. Wilma beats her with judo.

Corliss is a pilot whose face was scarred after a skirmish in space with Wilma. Corliss and Roxanne attacked Earth and were repelled by Wilma's squadron. A fire in the cabin while they were fleeing severely burned Corliss' face and destroyed Roxanne's hand when she doused the flames to save him. Corliss tenderly kisses Roxanne's cybernetic hand.

The space pirates discovered 20th Century weapons, including machine guns. The disfigured duo are gonna disperse the 20th century nerve gas into Earth's atmosphere, just as Buck predicted. Dr. Huer was sending the weapons in a freighter up into space to be destroyed when Corliss hijacked it. Corliss and Roxanne capture Buck and Wilma. They are about to repay Wilma by setting Buck's head on fire so Wilma will burn her hands putting him out—one of the show's more creative deathtraps.

"Have you ever been on fire, Rogers?" Corliss asks our hero. "Can't say I have," Buck replies, before nervously telling Wilma, "Don't worry, we'll get out of this...If you buy that, I have a nice corner lot for you in Anarchia!"

A big episode for Wilma Deering, so Erin Gray gets to display a range of emotions as Wilma. 'Fighting 69th" embraces Buck's pulp roots with a villainess sporting a metal hand, scarred bad guy, space pirates, more slave girls, the ancient ruins of Washington DC, this episode is just plain fun—even if old pilots being called back in to save the day had just been used in "Planet Of The Slave Girls" with Brigadier Gordon.

As noted, one of Erin Gray's biggest opportunities on the show, she seizes it and clearly enjoys playing against living legend Peter Graves. This episode marked a *Mission Impossible* reunion between Peter Graves and *Mission Impossible* producer/creator, Bruce Lansbury, who was now doing *Buck*.

Going through an asteroid belt with the Fighting 69th, Buck jokes, "Watch out for falling rocks!" The thrilling climax has Buck save Wilma and Alicia with a 20th Century artifact—a machine gun!

At the very end, we learn Buck knows sign language, which he uses to communicate with Alicia. "How did you learn sign language," Wilma asks. "Someone taught me in the 20th Century," he says enigmatically. " A female friend who taught handicapped kids." Could this be a reference to Jennifer from 'A Dream Of Jennifer'? Wilma reveals in the 25th Century, deafness is conquered in childhood, with electronic surgery.

Similarly, it's nice to see Robert Quarry, the B movie bad guy who starred in the *Count Yorga: Vampire* films. He chews up every scene he's in as a somewhat sympathetic bad guy.

Wilma and Buck go to a cool space bar—a must for every fantasy show post *Star Wars*— with a couple big-headed aliens. When Wilma tells Buck "Noah's just too old to go into Space again." A disgusted Buck tells her, "Even in the 25th Century, they still throw people on the scrap heap because of their age." She's hurt by this, "Buck, I didn't want to ground him. He wasn't capable anymore." Buck wants Wilma to admit to herself, "You love that old man."

In an amusing aside, Peter Graves introduces the crew to the Fighting 69th's mascot, a scruffy little dog named Lucky—the first dog we ever see in the 25th century. In reality, Lucky was a rescue dog who became famous as tabloid *The National Enquirer's* mascot. In exchange for covering the show, they requested he be in the episode.

Because the episode is so grim, with nerve gas and burned flesh, there's a lot of playful stuff, too, like Wilma seducing several guards so she and Buck can steal their uniforms. "I sure like men in uniforms...You've got the cutest blue eyes—you think there's any way we can get together? When do you get off duty? I'm talking to all three of you, you know," she says seductively.

There's an even funnier bit at the ending celebration, Twiki walks up to Wilma.

TWIKI: "Ya wanna dance, Wilma?"

WILMA: "Thank you, no, Twiki."

TWIKI: "Awww, nuts!"

WILMA (To Buck): "Say, Big Fella, would you like to dance?"

BUCK: "Sure, why not!"

WILMA: 'Great! Twiki, I just found you a dance partner!"

TWIKI: "Buck, can I lead?"

This is the sort of light humor most later episodes are missing, it keeps the jauntiness that the pilot movie and first few episodes excelled in.

DAVID BENNETT CARREN ("Return Of The Fighting 69th" writer, STARLOG Platinum, by Lee Goldberg) "It was a wonderful experience, essentially the over-the-hill gang in Space. All these old pilots had to be brought in for a mission. And they brought in a great cast and had great villains.."

ALAN BRENNERT (From his "Confessions Of A Story Editor"): "For weeks, Anne and I have had one word pounded into our heads by the network: *relatability*. The characters in our show must be ones the audience can relate to, the stories must have mature, adult themes...Return of the Fighting 69th...In our quest for relatability, we have perhaps gone a bit too far with David's script, although this does not occur to us at the moment. Not only do we have a corps of over-the-hill pilots proving their worth after years of retirement...Not only do we have a heart-tugging father/daughter relationship between Wilma and Noah Cooper, the squadron's leader...But in the last draft, we also had David change a minor character (Alicia) into a deaf/mute servant girl who spunkily helps our heroes escape. Taking no chances with this one, boy.

"Shaking his head and smiling, David says 'This one has everything in it but a dog.' We laugh and continue making notes on the script. Not thirty seconds later, Jock Gaynor pops his head into the office. 'Oh Good, you're all here,' he says. 'Listen, I wanted to talk to you about Fighting 69th. We're gonna put a dog into it.' We all start laughing, but Jock goes on: 'Now it seems there's this dog named Lucky. *The National Enquirer* found it a few years ago near death and nursed it back to health. They put it on the cover and it's been on a couple shows since then...' The realization sinks in slowly; he ain't kidding. They really do want to put a dog in the show! Is this real? Am I hallucinating?

"David is slipping into a state of shock. I have my *Springtime For Hitler* face on and Anne is snapping up the phone to call Bruce Lansbury. 'Bruce, you can't be serious...' I can't hear Bruce's end of the conversation, but it's clear that he's adamant; *The Enquirer* will do a photo feature, it'll be good publicity. Anne sputters helplessly on her end: 'Bruce, this is the cheapest thing we've done in—in two or three weeks!' Lucky will be written into the show. 'All right, but I won't put him in the spaceship!' Anne insists, 'He stays on the ground!'"

BUCK Facts

- Robert Hardy (Clayton) went on to play Cornelius Fudge in the *Harry Potter* movies.
- Buck learns in the 25th Century, the mandatory retirement age is 85.
- we learn Wilma's childhood nickname is "Dizzy Dee."
- This episode marks the first Anarchia reference since the pilot.
- This wasn't Peter Graves first sci fi outing in Chicago, He saved the Windy City from giant, sex-starved grasshoppers in Bert I. Gordon's The Beginning Of The End.
- Besides dying in the arena fighting Kirk Douglas in Stanley Kubrick's *Spartacus*, Woody Strode teamed up with William

Shatner to battle *The Kingdom Of The Spiders* and appeared on *Batman*, as henchman to Marsha, Queen of Diamonds..

- Katherine Wiberg (Alicia) also worked with William Shatner on *T.J. Hooker.*

Buck Babe KATHERINE ANN WIBERG: Alicia the helpful Slave Girl!

Usually, Buck rescues alien babes from slavery. In 'Return Of The Fighting 69th,' he actually rescues Alicia, an Earthling—or 'Terran.' Alicia is a resourceful deaf/mute slave girl Buck saves from her alien captors and gets her back to her parents on Earth. Because Alicia is eager to return the favor, she gets Buck and Wilma out of a death trap set by Roxanne, her cruel owner. Played by Katherine Ann Wiberg, an actress who really is deaf, she gives a nice performance and guested on other shows. *Buck Rogers* was one of her first big gigs.

"I'm trying to remember the studio and the cast," she says apologetically. "It's been 35 years since I performed my role as Alicia, a deaf mute, using only expressive communication - no verbal or sign language involved. On the production floor doing our scenes at Universal Studios is how I met with the leads of the *Buck Rogers* series, Gil Gerard and Erin Gray. There were other space characters on the show, I even saw Peter Graves.."

The iconic Graves made a big impression on the young actress. "He really did—Tall, slender, (he was) rumored to be the highest paid actor on set, with his thick white hair. I don't recall talking very much to any of the actors except a few 'Hi's here and there

"Being deaf has it's disadvantages, but I did exchange some small chat. My character and role on *Buck Rogers* was my second professional contract job and I was basically busy absorbing all aspects of the production and more at the NBC/Universal studio.

It was then that I got the head shots and SAG /AFTRA membership all together as a package when I signed on for the job. I was offered a limo ride to and from work, which was exciting, but since my mother joined along to help facilitate and encourage me, the limo unfortunately, wasn't needed.

"As for Twiki the robot, who was played by a well known actor from another show (Felix Silla, 'Cousin Itt' on *The Addams Family*)

- I don't recall having any scenes directly with him, but I believe his voice was computer generated and operated from one of the stage hands. Unfortunately, I misplaced my script otherwise I'd have more details on the other actors.

"As for evil couple who controlled the enemy fighters attacking Buck and Earth, they (Robert Quarry and Elizabeth Allen) were very nice. I did enjoy working on the production and enjoyed everyone that I met and worked with, great people on set and off."

In one of Wiberg's biggest dramatic moments, Elizabeth Allen crushes her arm with her indestructible copper hand. "When Elizabeth is seen grabbing my wrist as if to cause me pain, both of us had been trying out the metal hand device/prop prior to shooting our scene.

"Elizabeth 'tested' her metal hand against my wrist as to get the feel of grabbing my arm in anger," she laughs. "Unfortunately, my mom wasn't allowed to take pictures nor did the idea of doing so ever come up. In those days, people didn't even carry a personal phone—how technology has changed for all of us! Not only that, but privacy laws were more tight.

"I think my drama teacher, Todd Rutherford, who had been instrumental in my career, may have been assisting around the set, too, although his presence was either as a hired ASL (American Sign Language) advocate /interpreter or he may have just visited and helped out. Todd was my drama teacher at California State School for the Deaf, Riverside. I think he may have helped Gil Gerard do the signing to me at the end of the show. "

Jamie Lee Curtis on Buck Rogers.

"Unchained Woman"

Season 1, Episode 7

orig airdate: November 1, 1979
Written by Bill Taylor
Directed by Dick Lowry

Cast
Buck Rogers...Gil Gerard
Col. Wilma Deering...Erin Gray
Dr. Huer...Tim O'Connor
Jen Burton...Jamie Lee Curtis
Malary Pantera ...Michael Delano

Sergio Sanwiler...Bert Rosario
Majel...Tara Buckman
Twiki...Felix Silla
Voice of Twiki...Mel Blanc
Hugo...Walter Hunter
Warwick...Robert Cornthwaite
Gymon...Danny Ades
Shuttle Captain...Jim B. Smith
Lt. Zimmerman ...Charles Walker

Dr. Huer, accompanied by Twiki and Theo, enters negotiations on interstellar diplomacy with Ambassador Warwick, an old friend of Huer's. The scientist hopes to use their friendship to sway diplomacy. Meanwhile, Wilma sneaks Buck aboard a prison shuttle. She knocks out the pilot—an android who will have no memory of the incident—and puts Buck aboard as a convict. His only means of contacting Huer and Wilma for rescue is a necklace.

Buck is posing as a convict to rescue Jen Burton, a woman wrongfully imprisoned in an alien jail for murder on the planet Zeta. Jen is being punished for crimes committed by her pirate boyfriend, Malary Pantera. The Earth Defense Directorate feels she will incriminate him once free. Unfortunately for Buck, Jen truly loves Pantera and refuses to help deter him in any way, even after Buck breaks her out. Worse, Buck has to get her across a hostile alien desert if they want to be rescued. The prison sends Hugo, an unstoppable android guard to recapture or kill the duo.

There's a lot to like in this episode—an outstanding guest turn by a blonde Jamie Lee Curtis, Bill Taylor's script is a playful sci fi take on Victor Hugo's *Les Miserables*, to the point that Buck poses as 'Val Jon"(the hero of *Les Miserables* is 'Valjean') and there's a tip of the hat to the author by the name of the android. "Unchained Woman' also has some funny dialogue, such as when Buck discovers the alien jail is co-ed.

BUCK: When did the penal system go co-ed?

JEN: What?

BUCK: You know, boys and girls together.

JEN: How else would you do it?

BUCK: Men in one place, women in another.

JEN: Do you know the problems *THAT* would cause?

Once imprisoned on the impregnable, inescapable Zeta, Buck hears a Guard say "On Zeta, they do it right!" He quips "You ought to put that on a bumper sticker"—before he realizes the guard has no idea what a bumper sticker is. When Wilma uses another Buck phrase, 'piece of cake,' Huer queries her, "I beg your pardon?" She translates it as "everything went as planned."

Jamie Lee Curtis in blonde hair makes an appealing prisoner for Buck to play off of. Their banter across the desert on foot is quite amusing, as Curtis' character doesn't understand Buck's 20th century slang. When Buck breaks her out of jail, he commands her to 'Hit the deck,' to which she asks 'What's hit the deck?'"

When he tells her it means 'Get Down,' she asks "What's get down?" She doesn't even know what "Fink" means. When he has to rob someone so they can travel incognito, Buck tells her "I never mugged anyone before." Jamie Lee Curtis looks at him, "'mugged'?" "An old 20th Century custom," he explains. "C'mon, I'll give you a demonstration!"

Her faith in Pantera seems to be justified when he comes back for her only to find he's replaced her with a new moll named Majel and he only came back to kill her not rescue her, so she doesn't squeal on him. Buck can't stop the android until Wilma realizes the manacle they wear is a homing signal for Hugo. Not to be outdone by a flashy guest star, Wilma also finds time to judo flip Hugo.

A cut above the usual Buck Babe of the week, Jamie Lee Curtis brings a lot of energy to the stock 'girl on the run' role. She had already done her legendary John Carpenter horror classic *Halloween* at this point, beating out several *Buck Rogers'* guest actresses, reportedly including Anne Lockhart ('A Dream Of Jennifer') , but the movie had not caught on yet. Its word of mouth cult following would not catch on until a re-release of it in 1979. She also played another *Buck* guest, murdered Playboy Playmate Dorothy Stratten in a TV movie. Curtis was shooting *The Fog* the same year she did *Buck*, before becoming the ultimate scream queen of '80s horror.

Like Jamie Lee, Tara Buckman (Majel) was another beautiful Universal contract actress, appearing in stuff like this, *Quincy M.E.* and the unintentionally hilarious *Death Car On The Freeway*, as well as being a regular on Universal's *The Misadventures Of Sheriff Lobo*.

Dr. Huer gets to do more than he usually does, when he exposes his friend, Ambassador Warwick as being in league with the space pirates. While Twiki complains that it's a "bummer" he can't join Buck on Zeta, he does help Huer realize his friend is a traitor. "I smell a rat," Twiki says to Huer about the ambassador.

Walter Hunter's Hugo, with his slow, unstoppable walk and rigid demeanor impressively pre-dates Arnold Schwarzenegger in James Cameron's *Terminator*. It's also creepy and humorous the way he mechanically repeats "Escape is not possible, all prisoners will report to the day room." At the time of this episode, Network Standards and Practices were really cutting down on action as perceived violence, which is why Jen and Buck keep repeating "He's an android, he's an android!" when Hugo attacks, to remind the kids it's not a human being they are beating up, therefore not imitable violence.

The space pirates that Pantera hangs out with are on the Universal Backlot, at The Well of Miracles, where a lot of the classic *Frankenstein* and *Dracula* films were shot. Zeta's alien desert is good ol' Vasquez Rocks, seen as different planets in numerous episodes of the show.

As Buck and Jen cross the desert, a tentacle wraps around Jen's leg. "SAND SQUID," she screams. The sand squid, attracted by the sound vibrations of people walking on the ground above and it's maw resemble the giant worms of Universal's cult classic *Tremors*, which the show predates by 11 years.

William Conrad's wonderfully overheated promo is one of his best on the series. "Buck and a beautiful female prisoner escape across an alien desert, pursued by a murderous android!"

ERIN GRAY: "I loved Jamie Lee Curtis. I didn't get to know her too well on *Buck*, but I did later when she did the show *Anything But Love* with my husband Richard. She threw a baby shower for me on set, when I was pregnant with our daughter, Samantha. "

DENNIS 'DANGER' MADALONE (Stuntman, Sand Squid): "I was some kind of alien creature underneath the sand in the desert for this episode and when someone walked over me, I would reach my arms up through the sand and grab them and pull them under the sand. Shooting it, I felt like a turtle egg below the sand ready to hatch. In other episodes, I was always a guard for Buck to beat up."

ANNE COLLINS LUDWICK: "We had some interesting guest stars like Jamie Lee Curtis, Gary Coleman, Markie Post, Roddy McDowall, Dorothy Stratten—may she rest in peace—and others, but I don't recall spending much time on the set once production really got rolling."

BUCK FACTS

- Robert Cornthwaite is the scientist who tries to communicate with the monster in Howard Hawks' *The Thing*.
- Tara Buckman played the ill-fated Mom in the '80s slasher Santa movie, *Silent Night Deadly Night*.
- Curtis appeared in another classic slasher of that era, *Prom Night*, with fellow *Buck Rogers* guest Eddie Benton.
- Wilma looks pretty amazing in her red cat suit.
- Michael Delano appeared *in Ocean's 11* with Brad Pitt, Julia Roberts and George Clooney.
- Bert Rosario (Sergio) is in *Who's That Girl* with Madonna.
- Bill Taylor also wrote for *Wonder Woman*. with Anne Collins and Alan Brennert.

Amazons Teddi Siddall and LiBerty Godshall prepare to abduct Buck.

"PLANET OF THE AMAZON WOMEN"

Season #1, episode 10

Original airdate: November 8, 1979
Directed by Philip Leacock
Written by "Michael Richards"(a pseudonym for DC Fontana) &
Clayton Richards

Cast
Buck Rogers...Gil Gerard
Wilma Deering...Erin Gray
Dr. Elias Huer...Tim O'Connor
Ariela...Ann Dusenberry
Cassius Throne...Jay Robinson
Prime Minister...Anne Jeffreys

Twiki...Felix Silla

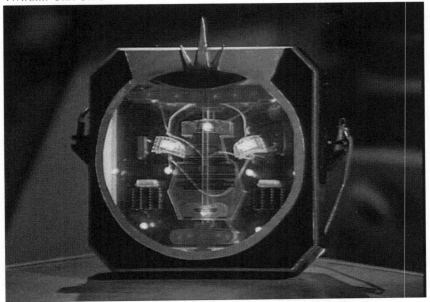

Mr. DeBronin, tough computer negotiator from planet Ruatha.

Voice of Twiki...Mel Blanc
Jayel...Antoinette Stella
Renna...Wendy Oates
Nyree...Liberty Godshall
Macon...Darrell Zwerling
Linnea...Teddi Siddall
Pilot...Wally K. Berns
Kersh...James Fraracci
Mr. DeBronin...Ron Gans (uncredited)

While Earth/Terra negotiates a deal to keep mining on the planet Ruatha, Buck is on patrol to keep the airspace clear. Lured away by a phony distress call, he's beaten up and captured by two beautiful amazon women—twice! Before they ambush him, the two amazons, Linnea and Nyree, are excited to hear from Buck, because "he sounds good-looking!"

In a judo/Buck-fu fight with the two attractive amazons, Buck quips, "You're in this for the kicks!"

He's taken to the planet Zantia, where he and the few men who remain there are being sent into an arena. None of them has any idea what is about to happen to them. "Gladiatorial games," one of the men wonders nervously. "Human sacrifice?" Instead, the men are being sold to the women of Zantia.

Cassius Throne, the slave master who auctions the men off, tears Buck's shirt open, to show his manly chest. "Move around," he instructs Buck, "show them the merchandise!" "This is degrading," Buck mutters.

Being a virile specimen of 20th Century Manhood, Buck triggers a bidding war. Buck is purchased by Ariela, the beautiful, rebellious daughter of the planet's female Prime Minister. Noticing no other men around, Buck realizes the men have been taken by Ruatha and plans to get them back. Wilma tries to find Buck and gets Cassius to reveal his whereabouts by threatening to make him into a "grilled cheese sandwich," a long-extinct food item she learned about from Buck.

The amusing B-story involves negotiating truce and trade deals between the two planets. Dr. Huer and Dr. Theopolis are Terra's main negotiators, while Ruatha has a similar clock-faced computer to Theopolis, an angry one, named Mr. DeBronin. "I have no intention of doing anything but getting back to the company of non-Terrans," DeBronin smugly tells Huer, Theo and Twiki. Saving the day, Buck forces both sides to negotiate, informing DeBronin "all we're gonna do is rap," to which the haughty computer snaps, "I beg your pardon!"

Twiki brings in food and drinks, announcing "Get your red hots," as though he's selling hot dogs at Wrigley Field. A confused Huer wonders, "what on Earth is he talking about now?" "I've stopped asking," deadpans Dr. Theopolis.

When Buck wraps up his main adventure, he joins the negotiations, determined to fix them. Thinking he's going to screw everything up, Huer starts chugging down alcoholic beverages. The rate Huer is downing them makes Twiki exclaim, "Holy Toledo, Doc!"

Thanks to his unique diplomacy, Buck gets Earth it's mining rights, brings the men back from Ruatha and ends slavery on Zantia. At the end of the episode, Buck offers to make Wilma sweetbreads.

Ann Dusenberry is a terrific guest star, with a great line when

Dr. Theopolis.

listening to Buck speaking his long-forgotten 20th century slang. As Buck tells her she has a lot of chutzpah, she retorts "Chutzpah? What is that, a disease?" Anne Jeffreys is good as her Mom, the Prime Minister. Side amazons Nyree (Liberty Godshall) and Linnea (Teddi Siddel) are fun and two of the most beautiful women to ever appear on the show. .

A wry, amusing episode, co-written by D.C. Fontana, one of classic *Star Trek's* best writers, even if she uses a pseudonym. That's obviously why Buck exhibits some of Captain James T. Kirk's panache in forcing the negotiations to continue. A female ruling class oppressing the weaker sex of men was used in the first season of *Star Trek: The Next Generation*, for the episode, "Angel One."

When Wilma excitedly tells Dr. Huer that Buck is making her dinner, he tells her, "Oh, I'm sorry—my, my, my..." Buck is served a drugged alien alcohol known as "Centari Brandy."

Another gleefully sleazy, breathlessly voiced William Conrad promo on this episode: "Buck finds himself the center of attention on a planet of DESPERATE WOMEN with a SHOCKING SECRET!"

Buck Facts

- Mr. DeBronin shows other planets use computer negotiators like Theopolis.
- The first time a horse is seen in the 25th Century, on the amazon planet.
- Jay Robinson (Cassius Throne), guested on the original *Star Trek* and played the evil Dr. Shrinker on the Saturday morning show of the same name and Caligula in both The *Robe & Demetrius And The Gladiators*, a film in which. fellow *Buck* guest Julie Newmar made her screen debut.
- Ann Dusenberry (Ariela) was a very popular actress at Universal, appearing in everything from *Jaws 2* to guest starring on numerous TV series, like *The Incredible Hulk*.
- Ron Gans would voice another character on the show, in the second season's 'Journey To Oasis.'
- Liberty Godshall (Nyree) quit acting after appearing in several of her husband, Edward Zwick's films. She's now a producer.
- Amazon Teddi Siddal was directed by John Huston in *Prizzi's Honor*, became a screenwriter and married actor Gary Cole after she met him while writing for his show, *Midnight Caller*.
- Anne Jeffreys had previously appeared that same year on *Battlestar Galactica*.

MEET DR. THEOPOLIS

Actor Eric Server, was a familiar guest star on many Universal shows, including *Kung Fu*, *The Incredible Hulk* and *Murder She Wrote*, even appearing on the short-lived *Sidekicks*, alongside Gil Gerard. Although he was never seen on *Buck Rogers in the 25th Century*, he was a regular, who provided the voice of super intelligent computer Dr. Theopolis, replacing Howard F. Flynn, who played him in the pilot movie.

"I had fun doing the voice," says Eric Server. "I never, ever met the cast when we did the TV series. I would just go to the looping stage at Universal Studios and the script supervisor would read their dialogue to me flat, no inflection, nothing going on. I was dying, just dying at the flat delivery, because I was being given noth-ing to work with. I was like, 'Please, let me go down there and read (Theo's lines) off camera!' Unfortunately, we didn't have that opportunity, but I think we put on a helluva show anyway. I was excited to know that Twiki was being done by Mel Blanc.

"Once a week, I would go to the dubbing stage and hear Mel tell all these great stories about the old days. It was such a treat, I would have paid them to be able to hear Mel Blanc talk! I was kind of the orphan stepchild, because I came in through the backdoor. An old school casting director named Phil Benjamin brought me in to do Theopolis when Howard didn't do the series."

Theopolis' appearances on the show became fewer and he was gone before the end of the first season.

"We got rid of Dr. Theo because his batteries always died in the shot," laughs Erin Gray. "Either in the master shot, close up, two shot, his batteries always died and he cost us way too much time, money and film. We finally just said, 'Get him the fuck outta here!'"

Twiki and Gary Coleman.

"Cosmic Whiz Kid"

Season 1, Episode 11

Original airdate: November 15, 1979
Directed by Leslie H. Martinson
Written by Alan Brennert & Anne Collins

Cast
Buck Rogers...Gil Gerard
Wilma Deering...Erin Gray
Dr. Elias Huer...Tim O'Connor
Hieronymous Fox...Gary Coleman
Roderick Zale...Ray Walston
Lt. Dia Cytron...Melody Rogers
Koren...Albert Popwell
Selmar...Earl Boen
Twiki...Felix Silla

Voice of Twiki...Mel Blanc
M.D. Toman...Lester Fletcher
Guard...Tobar Mayo
Drunk...Tony Epper

Buck is called to planet Genesia, when their President is kidnapped... He's surprised to learn that their leader, Hieronymous Fox. is a 493-year old child genius from the 20th Century who was thawed out to run their world. He's been abducted by Roderick Zale, a crafty millionaire who specializes in political kidnappings. Buck, curious about meeting another person from his era, teams up with Fox's bodyguard, Lt. Dia Cytron, to get him back.

When NBC's biggest star at the time, Gary Coleman, playing streetwise Arnold Drummond on *Diff'rent Strokes*, wanted to be on *Buck Rogers in the 25th Century*, the ratings-challenged network wasted no time making it happen. William Conrad's opening narration even trumpets that "Gary Coleman rockets into the 25th Century!" Despite this, the episode is not quite as painful as it sounds, although it does make you groan when Coleman calls Twiki "Transistor Face."

Coleman seems eager to fit into the show's universe and even makes a Marvel Comics reference, telling Zale, "Don't give me that Dr. Doom jive!' *My Favorite Martian*'s Ray Walston makes a fine villain and Earl Boen is particularly great as telepathic henchman, Selmar. Lester Fletcher as M.D. Toman has the best scene in the episode and best justification for a villain on the series.

It's a fight scene in a space bar filled with aliens (as noted earlier, these were de rigeur post *Star Wars*—seemingly every sci-fi show and cartoon had to have at least one scene set in a Mos Eisley Cantina-style setting) Because he comes from Lansing-12, a heavy gravity planet, the old, fey Toman has super powers and calls himself 'A Terminator.'

He easily punches Buck around surprised aliens, while boasting "How does one become a Terminator? I realized early in life I could either stay on Lansing-12 and become a librarian or go off planet and put my talents to use." It's a very funny, honest motivation for a henchman to make, and reminds one of the old joke that if Superman stayed on Krypton, he would probably have been a plumber. Ironically, as they talk about Terminators, Earl Boen is best known as psychiatrist Dr. Silberman in the James Cameron *Terminator* movies.

Buck tries to interest his 25th Century friends in 20th Century cooking, serving them "Mexican Chili"—which he has tried to replicate with uncooked lizard meat.

Having two of the show's best writers on 'Cosmic Whiz Kid,' Alan Brennert and Anne Collins, means they adhere to the continuity of previous episodes. There's a Maintenance android, a cool recurring concept that only shows up in Brennert-scripted episodes. Lt. Dia wants Buck to help not only because he is over 500 years old, but because she had heard about how he saved Jamie Lee Curtis' Jen Burton escape from the prison planet in 'Unchained Woman.'

Buck also breaks a date with Tangie from the episode 'Vegas In Space' to save Fox. As Tangie was clearly a hooker in that episode, there is no word on whether or not this is a real date or a paid 'date.'

ALAN BRENNERT (Co-writer): "'Cosmic Whiz Kid' was absolutely written for Gary Coleman. He was a fan of the show and we patterned the character and his speech patterns after Gary. . He wasn't just a fan of the show, but of science fiction in general—I also met with him on the '80s *Twilight Zone*, where he wanted to do a guest appearance. Anne's outline and my script were tailored for him."

ANNE COLLINS (Co-writer): "Afraid I have pretty much no recollections of 'Cosmic Whiz Kid.' It was always wonderful to collaborate with Alan, though, and I don't have any specifically bad memories of that episode, so I guess I was happy with Gary and the way the thing turned out."

FELIX SILLA (Twiki): "We did that episode with Gary Coleman and Oh My God, the kid was great! Gary came on the set and he knew his and everybody else's dialogue! He memorized the whole script. That was really impressive. We only used him for two days, because he had to go back to his own show, *Diff'rent Strokes*, which was a huge hit for NBC. Because he was starring in that, we could only use him for those two days. We brought him back for another episode of the show ('A Blast For Buck'), but I think he only appears in the last scene of the second show. He was a huge star at the time, so that was all they could spare him for."

Buck Facts

- Gary Coleman is depicted as being cryogenically frozen for decades in Mike Myers' comedy, *Austin Powers: International Man Of Mystery*.
- Buck listens to Three Dog Night's song "Shambala," where the lyrics seem to describe his life in the seemingly perfect 25th Century. "Wash away my troubles, wash away my pain...Everyone is helpful, everyone is kind..." The song has been used in many other genre shows since, including *Witchblade, Lost, Supernatural* and Rob Zombie's horror flick, *Devil's Rejects*.
- Earl Boen also voiced godlike alien The Beyonder on the animated *Spider-Man* series and played an alien in *Battle Beyond The Stars*.
- Leslie H. Martinson directed the very first Batman movie in 1966.

Tigerman, Kane Ardala.

"Escape from Wedded Bliss"

Season 1, Episode 12:

Orig airdate: November 29, 1979
Story by Cory Applebaum (Anne Collins' pseudonym)
Written By Cory Applebaum and Michael Bryant (Alan Brennert pseudonym)
Directed by David Moessinger

Cast
Buck Rogers...Gil Gerard
Col. Wilma Deering...Erin Gray
Dr. Huer...Tim O'Connor
Princess Ardala...Pamela Hensley
Kane... Michael Ansara
Garedon...Alfred Ryder

Michael Ansara, photo by Pat Jankiewicz.

Twiki...Felix Silla
Voice of Twiki...Mel Blanc
Tigerman...H.B. Haggerty
Disco Skater...Elaine Nista
Disco Skater...Tracy Miller
Disco Skater...Nancy Morris
Disco Skater...Gary Stang

A glowing, unstoppable flying triangle blasts The Earth Directorate building, rocking Huer's office. He and Theopolis barely survive. Princess Ardala has sent it and will use it to level the planet unless Buck is turned over to her.

Appalled, Huer refuses but has no alternative. Buck sneaks off on an old motorcycle with a sidecar. When Twiki sees him going, he asks "You're not really running, are ya, Buck?" Moved, he invites Twiki along (he rides in the sidecar), telling him to grab his toothbrush, before adding "Lord knows what you use for a toothbrush!"

As he starts the cycle, Buck drops a single pill of concentrated fuel in the tank and smirks, "if only OPEC could see me now." The pair go to see Garedon, an old man in a cave. He's a Draconian who designed Ardala's flagship who Buck hid on Earth when Garedon wanted to get away from it all. Buck enlists his help before Huer finds him again.

Buck is turned over to Ardala,   as his friends worry about his fate. "God only knows what he's going through right now," worries Wilma. Buck learns why The Princess wants him—to be her husband! The saucy Ardala tells him, "I must be won in order to be wed!"

That means a fight to the death with Tigerman. "If you lose, you die," she taunts. He takes her muscular pet out with his Buck fu, but refuses to kill him. When he tries to escape, Kane blasts him with a stun gun. Once Buck's unconscious, Kane tells him admiringly, "You're a stubborn man, Rogers. Maybe that's what the Princess sees in you."

When he revives, Kane is about to marry them. "Those who are about to be wed," he says ominously, "prepare yourselves!" "Talk about shotgun weddings," Buck fumes.

Humorously, Buck would have to wear a collar as Ardala's mate—one that would allow her to kill him whenever she likes.

Suddenly, Tigerman threatens Ardala to save Buck. Tigerman growls to Buck, "I owed you a life. We are now even." Giving Tigerman a surprising character motivation of honor is interesting. Meanwhile, Garedon, Wilma and Huer have come up with a way to stop Ardala's triangle. Buck makes split pea soup which he fakes with a soy bean derivative that even Twiki refuses to try.

"Escape from Wedded Bliss" is the episode where a clash with star Gil Gerard led to the show losing two of its best writers, Anne Collins and Alan Brennert. Despite the use of the show's best guest, the arch femme fatale Princess Ardala, it's also a boring, listless outing.

Buck is glum about being paired with Princess Ardala? He rejects Ardala so indifferently, even suggesting Kane take Ardala for himself and revolt against her father Draco, it's a complete betrayal of the independent, feisty Ardala as played by Pamela Hensley. She's not property to be passed around, she's the show's coolest, campiest guest star and deserved better than this episode. There is a nice beat of Ardala alone, clearly lonely and sad that Buck does not want to be with her, a nice touch in showing a new side to the character deftly played by Hensley.

Humorously, when Ardala brings Buck aboard, she has roller disco performers to entertain them in a way that makes it painfully obvious that this is the way the future looked to filmmakers in the late '70s.

There's many callbacks to the pilot episode/movie, including Buck rendering Ardala unconscious and wandering the ship as well as Twiki disco dancing. The episode also gives usual one note henchman Tigerman a new depth.

As this marked the end of Alan Brennert, it's only fair that Wilma mentions getting in from a Maintenance drone, as they are in all of Brennert's episodes, whether or not his name is on them. His last produced script would be 'A Dream Of Jennifer.'

Buck Facts

- Alfred Ryder (Garedon) appeared in *True Grit* with John Wayne, was an alien on *The Invaders* and was in the first ongoing episode of *Star Trek* under Captain Kirk ("The Man Trap").
- Tigerman H.B. Haggerty was a former pro football player for the Detroit Lions named Donald J. Stansauk. The big, bald Stansauk later became a professional wrestler (which he also played on *The Incredible Hulk*.) His initials "H.B." stood for "Hard Boiled."
- Ardala's desire to have a subservient Buck all to herself is explored in her next episode...when she has him cloned!
- OPEC The Organization Of Petroleum Exporting Countries, is a cartel that attempts to manage the control of oil and set the price on the world market. They were responsible for the gas shortages of the '70s.

Buck Guest: MICHAEL ANSARA: Killer Kane

With his rich voice and unmistakable presence, character actor Michael Ansara made the role of Ardala's right-hand man Kane his own, after being played in the film by Henry Silva. The actor, who also has his own Star on the Hollywood Walk of Fame (6666 Hollywood Boulevard) also appeared on other classic sci-fi shows, including *The Outer Limits, Babylon 5, I Dream Of Jeannie* (with then wife Barbara Eden) and *Star Trek*.("I was Kang the Klingon, which I reprised years later on on *Deep Space Nine*, one of the spinoff shows.")

"I played Kane on *Buck Rogers*, which I always confused with Kang," he laughed. "I really enjoyed working with Pamela Hensley. The relationship between Kane and Ardala was always fun. Pamela and I had a bit of a repartee, but Kane was secondary to Princess Ardala. I was a leading Klingon on *Star Trek*, so to play second in command here was a demotion! I haven't seen Pamela since we did *Buck*, but I liked working with her.

"We did put a little comedy into all our scenes. Pamela and I wanted to carry it on and make a series about our two characters! We talked to Universal about it, but it didn't work out. Pamela and I always thought we deserved a spinoff series, because, even though we were the bad guys, our banter was always pretty funny.

"At the beginning of my career, when I played a lot of bad guys, I never thought of the bad guy as being a bad guy, he was a human being...even if he was from Outer Space. He stretches the rules and regulations a little bit. My feeling was, If you think of yourself as the bad guy, it becomes a caricature, at least that's how I felt as an actor. The bad guy is simply someone doing what he thinks is right. Take it from me, I played Judas and I didn't play him like a bad guy to Jesus—in his mind, he was justified. I played an Indian sometimes, a cowboy sometimes. One day you're the criminal, the next day the sheriff. It's all a part of acting."

"I thought I was typecast at the beginning of my career because I played so many Indians! For awhile, I refused to work because they would only cast me as Indians. Don't get me wrong, I loved playing Indians, but I wanted t do other things. I came from the stage where I got to play everything, so I held off for a little over a year when they started to cast me in other, more diverse roles."

Born in Syria of Lebanese descent, Ansara "was supposed to be a doctor. When I became an actor, my mother was always for it but my father was sort of oblivious to it. My mother backed me up. I went to the Pasadena Playhouse and did many plays. When I became a professional actor, my mother was for it, being the good mother that she was, anything I wanted, she was for it."

Besides *Buck* and *Star Trek*, he appeared in many genre shows. "including *Time Tunnel*, there's a lot of shows like that where I just remember that I did it, same with *Lost In Space*, although I do recall Kurt Russell played my son in that. I occasionally got a movie that would run for two or three months of shooting and then I would go right back to doing television. I can't remember them all! (TV and film producer) Irwin Allen was a personal friend. I was doing *The King And I* onstage and shaved my head for that. I had worked with him before on the movie *Voyage To The Bottom Of The Sea.*

"After that, he did many movies and shows. Irwin saw me with a shaved head and said, 'Mike, you look great like that!' and used me a hundred times! I'm exaggerating, but he used me over and over. He told a reporter 'I like Mike because he can work with hair and without'—but he liked me more without hair...Even when I let it grow out, he put a rubber cap on my head so it would look shaved! I left my hair off ever since. I played a lot of aliens for him, but I didn't enjoy the silver paint.."

"I did love doing *Babylon 5*—a beautiful part, where I played a character named Elric. He was a very mystical, spiritual guy from Outer Space. He comes from a tribe of people from a distant planet, he was very effective, people loved him and I loved doing him. He was powerful, mystically, an interesting role. It's always fun to play aliens."

Wilma in disguise, Buck and Kimberly Beck in Cruise Ship To The Stars.

"Cruise Ship To The Stars"

Season 1, Episode 13:
Original Airdate: Dec 17, 1979
Written by
"Michael Bryant"(Alan Brennert) and
"Cory Applebaum" (AKA, Anne Collins)
Story by Alan Brennert (as "Michael Bryant")
Directed by Sigmund Neufeld Jr.

Cast
Buck Rogers...Gil Gerard
Wilma Deering...Erin Gray
Dr. Huer...Tim O'Connor
Jalor Davin...Leigh McCloskey

Sabrina...Trisha Noble
Cruise Ship Captain...Brett Halsey
Alison...Kimberly Beck
Twiki...Felix Silla
Voice Of Twiki...Mel Blanc
Tina...Patty Maloney
Voice of Tina...Grace Gaynor (uncredited)
Young Man...Timothy O'Hagan
Miss Cosmos...Dorothy R. Stratten

Undercover, Buck, Wilma and Twiki all board The Lyran Queen, a luxury space-liner, to guard Miss Cosmos, a genetically perfect beauty queen. Because of her perfection, she's worth millions... They can freeze her body tissue and sell her organs on the black market across the universe. There's reports of an attempt on Miss Cosmos' life, so the three are assigned to protect her.

The stunning Miss Cosmos is being repeatedly stalked by a savage, super powered woman. This mystery woman, Sabrina, fires powerful blasts out of her hands and stuns The Captain

When he meets Miss Cosmos, even womanizer Buck is truly impressed. He admits that "the prospect of meeting the perfect woman is fascinating." Tara, Miss Cosmos, played by the late Playboy Playmate Dorothy R. Stratten, is equally impressed with Buck.

"You'll have to forgive me for staring," Miss Cosmos says to him, "I have never met a 500 year old man before."

"That's alright," Buck quips, "I've never met a genetically perfect woman before either." Miss Cosmos then suggests "Think of the permutations." "I love to think of the permutations," Buck blurts. "Maybe later, after the danger's over..."

Buck meets Allison, a cute fellow passenger who is on board for relaxation because she suffers from hypertension (so she claims) and blackouts. She's with her boyfriend Jalor, who patronizes her.

Unbeknownst to Allison herself, she changes into Sabrina—a completely different personality and appearance, a super strong psychokinetic beauty. In a kinky twist, Jalor is secretly romancing the Sabrina personality too. Sabrina attacks Wilma.

Allison is a transmute, an innocent mutant, but her alter-ego, Sabrina, helps Jalor abduct Miss Cosmos, who is going to be carved

Tina, Twiki's robot girlfriend.

up while alive and awake with a laser scalpel to auction her genes to the highest bidder. As reward for her her help, Sabrina thinks Jalor will help her purge Allison so she can retain the body permanently.

Buck, Wilma and Twiki use sonic guns to subdue Sabrina. In the end, Jalor is taken away and Allison is going to be helped with her Sabrina personality.

Dorothy Stratten, the Playboy Playmate usually called "Star 80" because that was the year she was Playmate of the year , 1980, is one of the most beautiful women to ever appear on the series. She has a strong posthumous popularity after being murdered at age 20 by her estranged husband. Dorothy Stratten's voice was dubbed by fellow *Buck Rogers* guest actress Anne Lockhart.

ABC's *The Love Boat* was a ratings juggernaut at the time of "Cruise Ship To The Stars," which is why *Buck* did this playful parody. *The Love Boat* format usually told three stories of love on the high seas. *Buck* does the same, with our hero flirting with Miss Cosmos, while Wilma and Twiki both have their own dalliances.

There's a lot to like in the episode, especially the Wilma and Twiki subplots. Wilma goes undercover as heiress "Wilma Durant," looking striking in a wig and swimsuit. Twiki, who appears to be sexually active on The Lyran Queen, opines that "Wilma's lookin' real foxy!"

Poolside in disguise, undercover in a curly black wig, Wilma is immediately hit on by a spoiled trust fund type named Guerney Langston, JR.(a funny Timothy O'Hagan). When Wilma tells him her family owned Rygel 2, he excitedly says "Your family owned Rygel 2? My family owns Rygel 3—we're practically neighbors!"

Robot Sex

Even better is the Twiki story. Buck's little pal falls for a gold female ambuquad waitress named Tina. "Hold the phone," he says when he sees her. She has big lips to show she's a girl and says 'Booty, booty, booty.' Seeing Twiki disco dancing with a female version of himself is quite surreal. "Now I've seen everything," Buck says.

Talking to Twiki, Huer is shocked when the little robot abruptly walks away to chase Tina. "Twiki? Twiki? Where are you going?" "DON'T ask," cautions Buck.

Twiki calls Tina "Babe" and tells her that "Buck taught me all I know." When Huer asks Buck if he's enjoying the cruise, he says "if living my life vicariously through Twiki counts, I'm enjoying myself...I'm afraid he's developed a very active libido."

When Twiki teaches Tina "The Bump," Dr. Theopolis frets "Her name is Tina and I think her interest in Twiki is purely physical." "You'd better believe it," adds Twiki.

This actually leads to the unpleasant idea of robot sex in the 25th Century. Twiki actually tells Tina at the episode's end "Now we can get it on" as he kisses Tina. Buck jokes to Huer, "If I were you, I'd prepare for the patter of little metal feet!" Maybe the urban legend of Twiki being modeled after a penis isn't that far off.

This is obviously the episode Gil Gerard was thinking of when he told the press in 1980, "I'll be damned if I'm going to do Charlie's Angels In Space with a guy, a girl and a robot."

Despite his misgivings and that Alan Brennert and Anne Collins hid behind their pseudonyms, this episode is cheesy fun, an extremely entertaining guilty favorite displaying the humor that Gerard so despised at its best.

ERIN GRAY: "I remember Dorothy Stratten coming to the set and every guy eyeing her. No one had ever had quite that impression on the set before!"

Despite her jaw-dropping beauty, Dorothy Stratten's voice was deemed too soft and looping was required. Reportedly, producers and writers chanted "Loop her! Loop her!" during dailies. Her replacement voice was reportedly *Battlestar Galactica* regular Anne Lockhart, a frequent guest on Universal genre shows like *Buck* and *The Incredible Hulk*.

ANNE LOCKHART (Miss Cosmos' voice): "Honestly, I have no memory of doing the actual dubbing on Dorothy Stratten's voice at all, but then, I haven't seen the thing in 30 years!"

ANNE COLLINS (co-writer, "Cruise Ship To The Stars"): "At one point, we were pitched the idea —it came to us unsolicited, from an alleged writer we had no intention of ever hiring—of an intergalactic beauty pageant culminating in some dire predicament requiring Buck to rescue some requisite scantily dressed woman. Alan and I summarily rejected the premise, deeming it a far too obvious, and rather sophomoric, attempt to pander to the audience's appetite for T & A. So we were aghast when Bruce informed Alan and me a short time later that the network wanted us to write an episode involving an intergalactic beauty pageant winner. 'But… but we can't,' we stuttered, 'we just turned down that idea. The guy who submitted it will think we stole it from him.' Bruce just shrugged. 'So let him sue.' And, ultimately, that's exactly what the guy did. And to our further chagrin, the studio simply paid him off as if his claim was legitimate, adding insult to the injury of our having to write 'Cruise Ship to the Stars' in the first place."

Buck Facts

- *Buck Rogers'* guest Trisha Noble (Sabrina) appeared in the conclusion of George Lucas' *Star Wars* prequels, playing Jobal Naberrie in deleted scenes of *Revenge Of The Sith*.
- Grace Gaynor (Voice of Tina) was a popular guest actress, and married to *Buck* producer Jock Gaynor.
- Buck eats with a gravity fork!
- Alison wears a two-toned outfit to hint at her split personality.
- Alison is going to New Phoenix, a Phoenix is also something that rises from the ashes of a previous form, which cleverly hints at her psychotic secret identity.
- Clips from the episode appear in 'A Blast for Buck.'

Dorothy Stratten as Miss Cosmos.

- Tina, Twiki's robot girlfriend, is mentioned in other episodes

Buck Babe: Dorothy Stratten/ Miss Cosmos

Canadian Dorothy Ruth Hoogstraten had re-christened herself "Dorothy Stratten" after meeting an angry, wannabe celebrity named Paul Snider while she was working at Dairy Queen. When the pretty girl became a Playboy Playmate in August '79, they married shortly after. Stratten's Playmate status led to her appearing in several movies including *Galaxina*, where she played the sexy robot of the title and shows like *Fantasy Island*, as well as *Buck Rogers'* 'Cruise Ship To The Stars' at age 19.

In 1980, her pictorial proved so popular, she learned that she was going to be named Playmate Of The Year.

A jealous Snider found out that Stratten (who he was separated from at the time) had started a relationship with Oscar-winning film director Peter Bogdanovich after appearing in his film, *They All Laughed*. Snider lured her back to their West Los Angeles apartment, where she was bound, sexually assaulted and killed by a shotgun blast to the face on August 14, 1980. Snider then turned the gun on himself in a classic murder/suicide.

Ironically, her death led to a job for another *Buck Rogers'* guest actress. In *Death Of A Centerfold: The Dorothy Stratten Story*, a TV movie based on her short life, Stratten was played by Jamie Lee Curtis from "Unchained Woman." In Bob Fosse's 1983 feature film *Star 80*, she was played by Mariel Hemingway, who was one year younger than Stratten while Eric Roberts played Paul Snider In questionable taste, *Star 80* actually shot in her apartment, the murder scene, even recreating the bloody finish.

"Dorothy Stratten was murdered almost immediately after doing our series," Gil Gerard recalls. "She was a very sweet girl. I was saddened when it happened. I don't know if she had a great career as an actress ahead of her, I'm trying to be charitable, but as a human being, she was a very sweet, nice girl and I was really horrified when it happened. I thought, 'My God, what a tragic way to go...'

"The whole thing that (director Peter) Bogdanovich did (writing a book on what a great actress she was), I thought, 'I don't know if she would have had that kind of career, unless she really trained and worked at it, but when she did our show, she had a hard time talking and hitting her mark. They may have looped her. To get her to walk up to a spot was hard on that episode.

Kimberly Beck closeup talking to Buck in Cruise Ship To The Stars.

Kimberly Beck from Cruise Ship To The Stars.

"Usually, you just put a piece of tape on the floor, and walk up and stop. She would keep looking down in the scene to see her mark.

"To help her out, they put a sandbag here and she literally tripped on the sandbag. I was like, *'Oh, girl...'*" Gerard winces sym-

Twiki girlfriend Grace Gaynor

pathetically. "But she was a very sweet person and it was a horrible thing to happen to anybody but especially when it's someone you worked with who you know is very sweet and nice."

"When I think of Dorothy, I get sad," says Erin Gray. "She was a nice girl, and to die so horribly by someone who purported to love her, was just tragic. When she was on set, it was the only time I came to work and no one noticed me—and I was wearing my spandex! That had never happened to me before, so I decided to check out the competition.

"Dorothy had this Marilyn Monroe quality, where men were just captivated by her. She was doing a scene with Gil and she had this low, whispery voice. I thought she wasn't doing anything in the scene until I went to dailies and was as captivated by her as everyone else in the screening room was; her every gesture toward Gil which I hardly noticed when she did them on set, was stunning on film. Seeing the dailies of it, I thought, *'I see what she's doing there!'* Whenever I think of her, I just get sad and I feel bad for what happened to her."

Buck Babe: Kimberly Beck:

A busy genre actress, Kimberly Beck helped Corey Feldman kill goalie masked maniac Jason Voorhees in *Friday The 13th: The Final Chapter,* save the local roller disco rink in *Roller Boogie,* appeared in Luc Besson's *The Big Blue,* was protected by William Shatner on *TJ Hooker* and her friend, writer/producer Dean Devlin named Will Smith's son and dog after her son and dog (Dylan & Boomer) in the alien invasion blockbuster, *Independence Day!*

As the sweet passenger Allison, Kimberly Beck seems to be a nice girl when Buck first meets her. That's before he realizes she harbors a dark secret.

"I played a woman with a split personality, a real split personality, which turns me into Trisha Noble," Kimberly Beck laughs. "I did all of the Universal Shows on at the time—*BJ & The Bear* with Greg Evigan, *The Misadventures Of Sheriff Lobo,* with Claude Akins, who was a great guy and that was a fun show, too, and *Buck Rogers in the 25th Century.* Gil and Erin were nice people, and of course, I remember Twiki the robot! You can't forget Twiki! My episode was famous because the girl my split personality is trying to kill was played by Dorothy Stratten."

She has fond memories of the Playboy Playmate. "Dorothy Stratten was sooo sweet—I do remember she had a very soft voice, almost a whisper. My main memory of her was of an extremely sweet girl. I didn't really have any big conversations with her because I didn't really talk to anyone. I was just happy to be there."

"On the set of *Buck Rogers* at Universal Studios, I met Dan Aykroyd and John Belushi, because they were making *The Blues Brothers* next door. They came over to look at The Playmate Of

The Year when they heard that Dorothy Stratton was filming *Buck Rogers* next door to them! They had their suits on with their hats and their sunglasses, literally in their full *Blues Brothers* outfits. They said hi to me and all that, but it was pretty clear they basically came to look at Dorothy Stratten!"

Robot Buck Babe: Grace Gaynor

A perennial bad girl on classic genre shows like Adam West's *Batman* (as a sexy moll who helps Burgess Meredith's Penguin capture Batman, Robin and Chief O'Hara), *Wild Wild West* (where she's kept in a giant bird cage) and *The Man From Uncle*, Grace Gaynor uses a loopy Judy Holliday voice as Twiki's girlfriend Tina.

"My husband Jock Gaynor produced both *Buck Rogers* and *Wonder Woman*," says Grace Gaynor. "I was an on camera guest actress on *Wonder Woman* as Lynda Carter's friend, but for *Buck Rogers*, Jock brought me in to do a voiceover for this robot and it's really the best voiceover I ever did. It was on *Buck*, where I played the voice of the love interest of Buck's little robot sidekick...Twiki's robot girlfriend," she giggles. "I loved doing that, it was a lot of fun!

"I dubbed it by myself, alone in a sound booth, Mel Blanc wasn't there or anything. My girl robot would say 'Booty! Booty! Booty!' instead of Twiki's 'Beety Beety beety.' That was funny, I was this cute robot who hooks up with Twiki on this Love Boat in Outer Space. I also did the voice of a transvestite on Buck or *Wonder Woman*—his voice was too masculine, so they brought me in to do it. If I kept my voice down, I could pull it off. That was a fun thing to do, acting-wise, because you don't have to put on any makeup or outfits, you just stand there and do your thing!"

Space Vampire brooding.

"Space Vampire"

Season 1, Episode 14

Original Airdate: Jan 3, 1980
Written by Kathleen Barnes & David Wise
Directed by Larry Stewart

Cast
Buck Rogers...Gil Gerard
Wilma Deering...Erin Gray
Dr. Huer... Tim O'Connor
Space Station Commander Royko...Christopher Stone
Vorvon...Nicholas Hormann
Dr. Ecbar...Lincoln Kilpatrick
Twiki...Patty Maloney
Voice Of Twiki...Mel Blanc

Space Vampire and Wilma.

Technician...David Moses
Helson...Phil Hoover
The Captain...Jeannie
Fitzsimmons

This cool high-concept episode had one of the show's more melodramatic promos by William Conrad: "A Space Age Vampire stalks a lonely space station and Buck must race to prevent Wilma from joining the ranks of the undead!"

When the freighter Demeter slams into Space Station Theta with its pilot and crew all dead, the entire base is put under quarantine by Commander Royko, an old flame of Wilma's. He fears it may be some kind of airborne virus, when casualties start mounting at the station. Because Wilma and Buck were dropping Twiki off there for routine repairs on their way to the planet Genesia (where they are going to visit Hieronymous Fox from "Cosmic Whiz Kid"), they're stuck there, too.

The pair and Twiki decide to help Royko find out what happened to the ship's crew. Royko isn't really interested in their help and Theta Station is plagued by more mysterious deaths that Buck is determined to solve.

After seeing unusual marks on the victims and watching the Captain's Log from The Demeter, where the terrified female Captain is killed off camera by an unseen attacker, Buck and Twiki are convinced it's the work of a vampire. With Theta Station under quarantine, Buck deduces the source of deaths is an energy-draining space vampire, a Vorvon, who plans on making Wilma Deering his next victim. Only Buck is convinced that the Vorvon exists.

Buck may believe it's the 25th Century space vampire of the title, but Royko doesn't. He's skeptical of Buck's Vorvon theory and doesn't want Buck or Twiki's help. "Be cool, Big Daddy," Twiki tells

Royko. While they are investigating, a ball of light sweeps through the station and takes a particular interest in Wilma.

Eventually, that ball changes into a glowing eyed vampire (er, "Vorvon."..) With his pale skin, red eyes, giant bulbous head, pointed ears, super long fingernails, sharp fangs and purple lips, he's one of the show's most striking visuals. Despite his giant fangs, The Space Vampire drains his victims through his fingers.

He begins seducing Wilma, whispering things only she can hear. Buck notices the abrupt change in her behavior. The Vorvon tells Rogers, "You stand between me and something I want very much," Wilma Deering. He hypnotizes and almost kills Buck, who breaks the spell and burns the undead creature with a religious item called a power lock.

"Feels like I went the distance with Muhammad Ali," Buck groans to Twiki. "If my hunch is right, this (powerlock) is the 25th Century equivalent of a cross." The Cross, which remained unchanged for 2,000 years, now resembles cheap Indian jewelry.

Buck can't prove to Royko that The Vorvon exists because it doesn't photograph on the station's security cameras. Even Twiki can't see it—since he's a robot, his eyes are cameras, so he's under the same rules, an interesting detail. Wilma becomes distant, moody, withdrawn and scared. Until the creature finally summons her, telling her "I've come for you...You may come to me now." She does and is drained. She becomes his slave. He sends her to kill Buck.

Meanwhile, Dr. Ecbar suspects the space vampire has put all its victims into a state of cellular suspension. Buck deduces that the monster drains peoples' souls and makes them his puppets. If Buck can destroy the Vorvon, the people would come back to life. This is also how the show could circumvent trouble with broadcast standards and practices, with so many deaths in 'The Family Hour,' the 8:00 time slot.

"A space age vampire," Buck says, astonished. The Vorvon claims Royko and the rest of the station, all of whom come after our hero. A vampirized Dr. Ecbar attacks Buck, who lays him out with his own brand of judo.

Pretty soon, a hot, vampirized Wilma Deering arrives, draining the guards as she then tries to seduce and destroy Buck. He burns her with the power lock and knocks a vampirized Royko out.

The station's undead crew move George Romero-zombie style, with The Demeter's Captain and her crew. To further spread his vampirism, the Vorvon takes a shuttle to escape...Only to find, too late, that Buck has booby trapped the ship to fly into the nearest star. The bright light kills The Vorvon and frees all of his victims, including Wilma.

At the end, Dr. Ecbar says "I feel like that Lazarus person you told me about, Buck." Royko thanks Buck, Wilma and Twiki. Returning to New Chicago, a grim Dr. Huer has bad news for Buck: He killed his rubber tree plant.

One of the most popular, best remembered episodes of the entire series, "Space Vampire" is truly entertaining. The storyline of Buck, Wilma & Twiki chasing a vampire plays like a futuristic episode of *Kolchak: The Night Stalker* with some humor and some scares. Nicholas Hormann is gleefully evil as the Vorvon and establishes menace, despite his   pickle shaped head. Director Larry Stewart throws in a lot of clever touches, like putting red-tinted lenses on the camera whenever it's from the Vorvon's point of view.

Reportedly, Gil Gerard tried to prevent Wilma Deering from being the star of the episode and Erin Gray fought for it. She was right to do so—it's a great Wilma Deering show—we see her character vulnerable, emotionally entranced and then sinister and seductive once she's become a vamp—er, "Vorvon,"

She's unnerving (and let's be honest, unnervingly hot) in vampire form, rocking spandex and a midriff. Wilma Deering does more in this one episode than she does in the entire second season and Erin Gray makes the most of it, eager to show other sides to her character. Writers Kathleen Barnes & David Wise were primarily animation people, who contributed to such cartoons as *The Godzilla Power Hour*, *Tarzan* and *Batman: The Animated Series*. Their imaginative story for this live-action series is more ambitious than most *Buck Rogers* episodes—and it really pays off. Turning this week's Buck into a horror movie is an impressive change of pace in Space.

Having the freighter that brings The Vorvon to Theta Station be called The Demeter is a cool nod to Bram Stoker's Dracula, where The Demeter is the ghost ship that brings The Count to England, after he's killed everyone on board in the classic novel.

Other cool, horrific touches include Wilma having her life force—and will—drained, which gave a lot of younger *Buck Rogers* viewers nightmares (and made The Vorvon the envy of teenage boys everywhere), Jeannie Fitzsimmons' terrified Captain's Log, the dead crewmembers rising from the morgue once The Vorvon arrives and shuffling after Buck are all impressively eerie. The Vorvon going down the halls as a glowing ball of energy is very similar to the classic Star Trek episode "Day Of The Dove," which starred Buck's Kane, Michael Ansara.

"Space Vampire" came six months after Hollywood's 'scary summer,' where over 30 horror films opened, including *Alien, The Amityville Horror* and *Dawn Of The Dead.* Dracula himself made a big comeback that summer. John Badham directed Universal's *Dracula*, starring Frank Langella and Laurence Olivier, Werner Herzog helmed Nosferatu, with Klaus Kinski as a bald, rat like creature of the night, while Stan Dragoti's *Love At First Bite*, a comedy with George Hamilton as The Count was the biggest Dracula hit of the year. Stephen King's vampire story *Salem's Lot* also became the first of his books adapted as a miniseries ever that same year. Barlow, the lead *Salem's Lot* TV vampire was imagined as a Nosferatu-type vampire, which the Vorvon is clearly intended to be as well.

Christopher Stone makes a great antagonist as the no nonsense head of Theta Station. Jeannie Fitzsimmons has the scariest scene in the show, with her ship's log account of her crew being picked off one by one, while Nicholas Hormann plays The Vorvon with a wonderfully creepy attitude.

DAVID WISE ("Space Vampire" co-writer, In STARLOG Platinum Magazine #1, "Scribe Of the serpent god," by Bill Florence): " *Buck Rogers* was really just another dopey action-adventure show, only set in Space, but 'Space Vampire' had some (sci fi) elements in it, including a space station with a self-healing hull and a sick bay, so it was very pleasant to do. It did go through it's little twists and turns, as most TV shows do."

Wise and writing partner Kathleen Barnes pitched 'Space Vampire' to *Buck Rogers'* producers on Halloween day. "That's a good time to pitch a horror story, because people are halfway thinking in that direction. So we came up with the idea of a science fiction vampire who steals souls instead of drinking blood, which is very old and very new. The producers liked it."

In their original draft—as in the final show—Wilma was The Vor-von's primary target. "Erin Gray is a fine actress who had been given nothing to do on that show, because Gil Gerard wanted all the glory, so we wrote 'Space Vampire' for her...Word came back from the producers that we had to make it some girl Buck was dat-ing. (The producers) said Gil didn't want Erin to do it! We thought 'That stinks,' but we wrote the whole script that way. Then, at the last minute, Erin must have threatened some dire action, because suddenly, when they went to shoot the script, the female lead was Wilma again. This only meant changing a couple lines and chang-ing the name to 'Wilma,' because we had written it for her, but put another name on it."

The writer wished he could have given a specific reason why the Space Vampire chose Wilma "other than that she's the leading lady. The vampire had been wiping out people left and right, and he tells Wilma he'll destroy them all if she doesn't give herself to him willingly.

"She agrees, in order to save Buck and everybody else. She must allow him to do his little thing with his index finger and pinky, which was sort of our fang substitute, since he's a soul vampire. That was a neat moment, where she has to stand there and let this happen to her. Erin played it very well. She was crying, but her expression was one of terror and resolve. Tears started coming out of her eyes, almost of their own accord, because she wouldn't allow herself to show anything to the vampire. It was a great moment. I spoke to her later and she said she was thrilled with the role."

The Space Vampire's name was "Vorvolica" in their original script (after the Boris Karloff/Val Lewton horror film, *Isle Of The Dead*), but the producers changed it to Vorvon. "For some reason, whenever they wanted to futurize something on that series, they simply added the suffix '-on,' so the vampire became a vorvon."

ERIN GRAY (Wilma): "That's my favorite episode and the one fans always ask me about. It was also the second time my son Kevan was ever on a set, when I was shooting the 'Space Vam-pire' episode. I told the nanny 'Bring Kevan to the set because I want him to know where Mommy goes to work every day'—except Mommy forgot to read the call sheet on what we were shooting

Space Vampire closeup.

that day! Right at the moment where The Vorvon has me pinned against the wall and is sucking my essence, there's a tear coming down my cheek when I suddenly look over The Vorvon's shoulder and see a terrified Kevan going 'AAAAAAAA!'

"I don't remember any drama about 'Space Vampire' or that the writers had to do a non Wilma draft. I was just thrilled with the 'Space Vampire' episode and I was thrilled to do the episode because it was directed by Larry Stewart, who was always hugely supportive of me. It was the only episode of any *Buck* season where I had a part I really got to sink my teeth into it, no pun intended."

DEE WALLACE STONE (Actress/Christopher Stone's Widow): "The great thing about Chris is whatever he was hired for, he would throw himself into it. If *Buck Rogers* needed him to be a Space Station Commander, he was the best damn Space Station Commander they ever saw!"

Buck Facts

- Since *Buck Rogers* is set in Chicago, the irascible "Royko" has to be an homage to legendarily irascible Chicago columnist, Mike Royko.

Nicholas Hormann today.

Lincoln Kilpatrick (Dr. Ecbar) knew all about mutated vampire zombies—he played one attacking Charlton Heston in *The Omega Man*, a '70s take on Richard Matheson's classic sci fi/horror hybrid *I Am Legend*. which had fellow *Buck* guest Paul Koslo in it.

• Space Vampire Nicholas Hormann was present for *The Trial Of The Incredible Hulk* as The Kingpin's lawyer.

• Within a year of meeting a Space Vampire, Christopher Stone (Royko) would transform into a werewolf alongside his wife Dee Wallace in *The Howling*.

- The movie *Dracula 3000*, made decades after "Space Vampire," also uses the conceit of making The Demeter a space freighter.

25th Century Guest: Nicholas Hormann
Interview With A Space Vampire!

A distinguished, handsome Yale-Trained dramatic actor who has performed on both Broadway and the American Conservatory Theater, Nicholas Hormann appeared in many films and TV shows. He's been seen alongside the likes of Michael Caine, Denzel Washington, Dustin Hoffman, Martin Sheen, Halle Berry, Pierce Brosnan and Kelsey Grammar in diverse projects, where he's worked for Oscar-winners like Oliver Stone, Aaron Sorkin and Robert Benton.

He even played Calvin Klein on *Seinfeld* ("All my scenes as Calvin were with Kramer. When my scenes were being shot, Jerry Seinfeld would sit on the floor like a kid and watch. He'd tell me, 'That was great, Nick!' Jerry was cool It was the one job where I kept cracking up with laughter! The Calvin Klein office did call my agent to ask who played him. It was a great experience.").

Hormann is still surprised and bemused to find himself known as The Vorvon, a bulbous-headed 'Space Vampire' who preys on Wilma Deering in the *Buck Rogers in the 25th Century* episode of the same name. Erin Gray calls it as her favorite episode, adding, "I had a lot of fun with Nicholas as The Vorvon. I kept wondering, 'what does he look like under all this?' I want to read this book just to see what his real face looks like!'"

Besides turning a space station into his new base of operations, Hormann's vampire feeds on the helpless humans trapped there, building his army of the undead. Just as his plan to spread his vampirism across the universe is about to be unleashed, he pits his supernatural strength against Buck and Twiki.

"To this day, I'm not sure how I wound up as the Space Vampire," Hormann confesses with a hearty laugh. "It's become a cult thing. Several years ago, some twentysomething kids in Seattle called me in California just to tell me how I scared the daylights out of them when they were little! That was a nice compliment. It was a clever episode—Dracula in Outer Space."

His Vorvon sports massive fangs. "I still have the fangs that I wore in it," he confides. "They did a dental mold of my teeth and made me an appliance from it. I still trot them out occasionally on Halloween. That was the only thing I was able to keep, as prosthetic makeup isn't made to last, it rots away. They gave those fangs to me. I think there was a big story problem, because I had these great big fangs even though I drained my victims through my fingers. You never see me sucking blood with my teeth, I drain my victims' essence with a fingernail. Maybe they were vestigial fangs, as the Vorvon found this new space age way of using his hands...?"

"My son, Matthew Hormann, found an old VHS tape of my *Buck* episode and gave it to me. Watching it again, I realized it was pretty funny. All that ridiculous spandex everybody is wearing tells me more about when the series was shot than about the 25th Century, but that's always true with sci-fi. The appearance of my 'Space Vampire' looks so cheesy today, with my green and purple faced vampirized minions...I mean, as The Vorvon, I have this obvious Halloween eyebrow that's clearly been glued on, maybe that's why kids loved it, because it's so cheesy!

"For an actor, there's safety in being behind some sort of a mask, it gives you a freedom . I remember delighting in that costume while deciding how I would get my blood lust up. I would feel it in my veins, especially when I got into proximity of Erin Gray!"

As The Space Vampire, he spends most of his time on the show seducing Erin Gray into becoming his willing slave. "To be a contract actor on the West Coast whose first gig is to vampirize Erin— it doesn't get any better than that," he proudly proclaims. "Again, because I was hidden so completely by the makeup, playing this extravagant, outrageous character, I could sort of take liberties a little bit with her; I was hypnotizing and seducing her and could be with her intimately in the scene. Of course, my vampire doesn't do anything too indecent, because it was a family show. If I did, I blame I on my vampire costume—give a guy fangs and he goes crazy!"

"The director, Larry Stewart, was nice. I remember him telling me, 'When you speak, make him as lower a register as you can.' Even still, they modified my voice with a filter in post to make him sound even more creepy. I address the camera when I call Wilma to me.

"Erin Gray was such a pro; she always hit her marks and was pleasant to work with. I didn't know that she had a toddler at home, she just looked stunning. We had some pretty late days on *Buck Rogers*, because of all the special effects. The main thing I remember about Erin is that she was funny. The director (Larry Stewart) said to her, "I want you to walk down the hall like you mean business—' and she said, 'Oh, you want the 57th Street New York Strut!' I don't know if she remembers that, but it made me laugh because I was fresh off the boat from New York. Gil Gerard was fine, a decent guy, but I don't remember him or the robot too well, because most of my scenes were with Erin. When we shot the episode, I didn't know Erin was a contract player like me."

Buck Rogers in the 25th Century came to him in a unique way. "I am first, foremost and shall always be a stage actor. I was performing in New York in an off-Broadway play, when a woman called Eleanor Kilgallen who was Vice-President of Contract Players for Universal Studios in New York City, saw this production in a little walk-up theater on the East side of New York. I was in it with Amanda Plummer (*Pulp Fiction*), who was still unknown at the time.

"Eleanor asked my agent if I would be willing to fly out to Los Angeles to test for a TV pilot. I flew out and did the screen test in one day, flying back that same Monday, because that's the one night the play was dark. She told my agent, 'After seeing his screen test, we're not offering him the pilot, but we would like to know if Nicholas would be interested in being a contract player for Universal Studios?'

"I said 'well, sure,' because I was young and looking for adventure—it was Hollywood! My wife Ann and I came out to California the summer of '79, where I met Monique James, Eleanor Kilgallen's counterpart in Hollywood—she was head of contract players at Universal Studios on the West Coast. She would call me up and tell me, 'This week you're going to be on *Quincy, M.E.* with Jack Klugman.' Universal was the last studio to do a contract system like that. They wanted to muscle it up with actors who were a little older, not kids off the farm in Kansas, so they had a little stage experience.

"Time went by and I wasn't getting any work. Monique calls me one day and says, 'There's a show here, *Buck Rogers in the 25th Century*, would you have any interest in playing a...Space Vampire?' I said, 'a—what?!?' Monique goes, 'Darling, you need not worry! You will be under such heavy makeup, no one will ever recognize you'—even Erin Gray, apparently, who says in your book that she still has no idea what I really look like! Happily, I know what Erin Gray looks like and I assume she looks as good as ever.

Space Vampire and vampirized Demeter Captain Jeannie Fitzsimmons.

"I was such a boy scout, I did what I was told. Monique James wants me to be a Space Vampire? I said sure! I showed up and 'Space Vampire' was the very first contract work I did for the studio. I seem to recall that my makeup was designed and applied by one of the famous Westmore brothers, which one I cannot recall. I had to go in at five in the morning for three hours of makeup a day. I was in that makeup chair at five a.m. for all my days on *Buck*, before Gil or Erin got there.

"It was a one hour show, so I believe it was a seven day shoot—a five day week, the weekend off and we came back for two more days. My part only took five days, the rest of the scenes were Buck and Wilma trying to find a way to stop me. I spend the first part of the episode as a ball of light. After it aired, nobody recognized me, just as Monique predicted. I kind of wish they brought back The Vorvon—he was already dead, so it wouldn't have been too much work to bring him back."

"I do remember going to the Universal commissary with Monique as I was wearing my full Space Vampire drag, this crazy costume. I was feeling a little self-conscious in the big head and the giant fangs, but when we got there, no one batted an eye! People were dressed as everything in the commissary, cowboys, baseball players, soldiers.

"Eleanor and Monique told me that Lew Wasserman was terminating the contract program at the end of my first year. I said, 'Was I that bad? Did I single handedly close down the contract department," 'he jokes. "They called the contract players 'contract babies' and I was one of the last ones. Lew Wasserman was ending it because the strike was coming. "

Besides acting in the occasional movie and TV show and teaching acting and theater, Hormann "also narrates a lot of audiobooks now. I take each book and decide how I am going to do the narration. It took five days to do one by Henry Kissinger. It's fun, but not as fun as being a Space Vampire!."

"*Buck Rogers* was campy in the best sense....I also sensed that Erin knew how campy it was. As far as I was concerned, it was just a job, a one-off, as Buck kills me by sabotaging my escape, so I am pleased that so many kids remember my Space Vampire so vividly. It's a big conversation piece in my career," he grins.

25th Century Guest: JEANNIE FITZSIMMONS
"The Demeter Captain"

One of the most unnerving moments in the above average "Space Vampire" is when Buck sees the Captain's Log. Jeannie Fitzsimmons' Captain expresses her increasing anxiety and terror as her crew on the doomed Demeter is picked off one by one.

This sequence is very effective. She details daily each terrible death, before whatever did it comes for her. Later in the episode, Fitzsimmons returns as one of The Vorvon's undead army, trying to attack Buck.

"It was interesting to play someone who is so scared and then comes back as a vampire," the actress says. "She was this ship

Captain, but now that she's 'dead,' she's a bad person who creates havoc for Buck, Wilma and their little robot friend."

"As The Captain, I have to be more and more frightened in the scene where I talk about what was happening to my people. Because it's The future, it's on a spaceship instead of a boat—the episode is about a space vampire, after all."

Becoming a vampire, "I was green—I was literally painted green for the scene where I come back as a vampire," Fitzsimmons titters. "It wasn't a huge scene, but I thought it was quite fun to come back as this cartoonish nemesis.

"Even though the whole episode was about vampires and zombies, the whole show was not dark stuff. It wasn't negative, it was playful—it's *Buck Rogers in the 25th Century*, y'know?"

Religion In The 25th Century

After seeing the future's version of a Cross wielded against the Vorvon, one wonders what the 25th Century views of God are. The show had several self-proclaimed gods, like Kaleel in 'Planet Of The Slave Girls' and The Traybor in 'Buck's Duel To The Death,' but they were simply cults on their planet of origin. The fact that Mardi Gras is celebrated (in 'A Dream Of Jennifer') implies there may be a season of Lent, or, with the generic name change ('Festival of the Masks') suggests that the ritual is carried on without meaning.

Of course, since Earth went through social upheaval and nuclear war in the 500 years that Buck Rogers has been frozen, he may be the last Judeo-Christian left in the future. Meeting Dr. Huer in the pilot, he observes, "If I'm dead, I obviously didn't make it to Heaven!"

In 'Slave Girls,' Major Duke Danton references Buck had told him about Lazarus and Buck himself mentions Moses in 'Cosmic Whiz Kid.' Dr. Huer exclaims "Good Lord" in the same episode. Huer mentions Heaven in 'A Dream Of Jennifer."

During 'Space Vampire,' Dr. Ecbar tells Buck "I feel like that Lazarus person you told me about, Buck" and Wilma says "I can only hope and pray they're still alive," so there's apparently some sort of Belief system, or Buck preaches to his friends between episodes when not running around with the guest babe of the week...

Morgan Brittany and Gil Gerard in Happy Birthday Buck.

"Happy Birthday, Buck"

Season 1, Episode 15

Original airdate: Jan 15, 1980
Directed by Sigmund Neufeld, JR
Written by Martin Pasko

Cast
Buck Rogers...Gil Gerard
Wilma Deering...Erin Gray
Dr. Elias Huer...Tim O'Connor
Raylyn Merritt...Morgan Brittany
Dr. Delora Bayliss...Tamara Dobson
Col. Cornell Traegar...Peter Mac Lean

Twiki...Felix Silla
Voice of Twiki...Mel Blanc
Carew...Chip Johnson
Rorvik...Bruce Wright
Lt. Garth...Eric
Mason'/'Security Agent...Abe Alvarez
Alien Squadron Leader...Harry Gold
Niles...Tom Gagen
Marsden...Clay Alexander

As his 534th birthday approaches, Buck is irritable while some-one from Dr. Huer's past is coming to kill him.

Noticing Buck's been restless and angry lately, his friends are concerned. "Buck's been moping around like that for days," Wilma observes. "His birthday is making him more homesick than ever for the 20th Century."

Getting even more moody the closer he gets to his birthday, Buck yells at Wilma and Huer, "I feel sorry for you people. You will never know the joy of a sunset that just happens." This is a direct callback to the pilot, where we learn that Theopolis and the computer council program the planet's sunsets.

"Buck's been moping around like that for days," Wilma observes. "His birthday is making him more homesick than ever for the 20th Century." Twiki suggests a surprise party for his best pal, Buck. The others think it's a great idea. Wilma and Dr. Huer plan on boosting Buck's spirits by throwing him that party. Planning on inviting all of Buck's 25th Century friends proves to be a challenge. "Jen, Joella, Marla, Allison, Tangie, Felina, Miss Cosmos," she says preparing the guest list, "I do believe there's a pattern forming here!" Jen is from 'Unchained Women,' Joella from 'Plot To Kill A City," Marla, Tangie and Felina from 'Vegas In Space,' while Allison and Miss Cosmos are from 'Cruise Ship To The Stars.'

Meanwhile, brutal albino Colonel Cornell Traegar, embittered killer, overpowers an alien guard and escapes from a prison planet that has been his unhappy home for 15 years. Bitter about his incarceration, Traegar heads for Earth to punish the man he holds responsible: Dr. Elias Huer. Traegar's hand turns everything he touches into lifeless silicon.

Traegar seeks revenge on Dr. Huer for sending him there. Traegar brainwashes beautiful courier Raylyn Merritt and Dr. Delora Bayliss to make this happen. He also has plans to touch Huer and turn him into solid silicone.

Huer asks Buck to accompany Raylyn to New Detroit, unaware that she is a pawn in a revenge plot against him. Buck goes up against the evil Colonel and has to find a way to thwart his dangerous hand.

There's a lot to like in this episode, scripted by DC Comics writer Martin Pasko. Traeger is pretty clearly a supervillain, and would have easily fit in with The Legion Of Death from the "Plot To Kill A City." The guard in the *Planet Of The Apes'* style makeup once again hints at the different alien species that live in Buck's universe.

The show's main plot is borrowed from the Gregory Peck/Robert Mitchum classic *Cape Fear,* about a jailed man from the past coming back for revenge. With his white hair and sensitivity to light from his imprisonment, Traegar is almost albino in appearance, a fact Buck uses to defeat him. Like The Vorvon in 'Space Vampire,' he is overpowered by light. Buck uses judo to battle Traegar, knocking the villain back, when he falls onto his own hand, transforming himself into silicon.

At the end, Buck opens his birthday gift, which the viewer is cleverly not allowed to see.

One of the show's running jokes is that Twiki picks up Buck's 20th Century attitudes. That includes good ol' fashioned sexism. When the little ambuquad is getting supplies for Buck's party, Twiki casually asks Wilma, "where do I put these, babe?" Surprised, Wilma says "Babe? Thank you, Twiki—I take that as a compliment!"

ERIN GRAY: "I stand by Wilma's response to Twiki. As a woman, I had no problem being viewed as a sexual object—and my uniform had an armband flag with rainbow colors, which you see in that episode. I had no idea what it meant. I only found out what it meant many Moons later, when somebody told me at a convention that it was used by gay groups. I was honored by that, Wilma was ahead of her time.

"I did learn from a fan that the first *Buck Rogers* comic strip came out January 7th, 1929—my birthday is January 7th, but not in 1929." (1950)

Morgan Brittany tied up.

Buck Facts

- Buck's birthday in the episode is cleverly established as January 7th. As noted above, The *Buck Rogers in the 25th Century* comic strip made its debut on January 7, 1929.
- In the 25th Century, Keys are now called 'de-locking discs.' Wouldn't just keeping the word 'key' be so much simpler?
- Harry Gold (Alien Squadron Leader), the ape pilot/guard, is the father of actresses Tracy Gold *(Growing Pains)*and Missy Gold *(Benson)*. He became an agent and started The Gold/Marshak Agency.
- The villain dies, a rarity on the show—unless their ship is blown up.
- Tamara Dobson was blaxploitation goddess *Cleopatra Jones* in two hit films and starred on "Jason Of Star Command" with Buck guests Sid Haig and Julie Newmar.
- Morgan Brittany co-starred with Haig in the hilariously kitschy *Death Car On The Freeway.*
- Brittany met her stuntman husband when she guest starred on *The Dukes Of Hazzard.*

BUCK BABE: MORGAN BRITTANY

With her translucent blue eyes and impressive presence, Morgan Brittany pretty much owns the episode "Happy Birthday, Buck." Although her character complicates things for Buck, the soap opera siren enjoyed guest starring in the 25th Century.

Her character is an enthusiast of 20th Century culture who immediately gets Benny Goodman's name wrong and humorously gets other facts wrong about Buck's time.

"I think they wanted me to appear on the show because I had just started on *Dallas*, but I had a lot of fun...I would actually watch the *Buck Rogers in the 25th Century* show occasionally, before I did an episode of it. I'm a huge sci-fi fan! That's why I did the original *Twilight Zone* with Rod Serling and *The Outer Limits* ('The Inheritors') I'm the little blind girl in that with Robert Duvall and Alfred Hitchcock's *The Birds*, where I'm one of the kids the birds attack at the schoolhouse.

"So I love sci fi and was thrilled to be on *Buck Rogers in the 25th Century*," she reveals. "I was actually offered a role in the original *Battlestar Galactica*—the daughter role that Maren Jensen played. I was offered that role first. I turned that down because I was getting ready to do The Scarlett O'Hara War and my agents said 'You don't want to get typecast in sci-fi' and I thought, 'Battlestar Galactica looks like it's gonna be really big,' but I made the decision to go the other way and it worked out fine. I went in a different direction; The Scarlett O'Hara War got me Moviola and then Moviola led to Dallas. But it worked out, because it also got me on *Buck Rogers in the 25th Century*!

"It was a really interesting experience for me. The hardest thing about doing that show when they gave me the script was that I played Raylyn Merritt," she says, impressively remembering her character's full name, "I had to learn all of these technical speeches that made no sense to me at all! It didn't connect. When you learn dialogue as an actor, you have to associate the word association! In a space or futuristic-oriented show, nothing makes any sense to you, but you have to learn it over and over and over so it comes out naturally. That was one of the hardest things I ever had to do, but I enjoyed working on *Buck Rogers* a lot! I really wanted to do *Buck Rogers* because I really liked Gil Gerard, after meeting him at different events. He was a great guy, the show was doing very well at the time and I thought 'Wow, this will be fun!' It could be really good, doing a guest shot on a hit show. It turned out very cool."

She found the futuristic technology left a lot to be desired. "I smile just thinking of Twiki, Buck's robot sidekick. I liked the little guy who played Twiki (Felix Silla), but the thing with him was he had to be in this hot costume and he would always complain 'Oh no, I gotta be in the suit again?' Anybody would complain wearing that heavy costume under those hot lights. He was great, Felix was very personable, but every single time they would take his head off, you would hear about how much he didn't like it... I remember when they took his helmet off, I thought 'Here we go again—' and sure enough, Felix let us all know how much he hated his Twiki costume!

"Then, Gil and I had to do a scene in the spaceship. We were sitting in his ship and he's reaching to make the spaceship do something AND THE CONTROLS FELL OFF," she laughs.

"We had to cut camera and Gil says 'Okay, we're gonna need Props over here! We lost our whole control panel, we lost the knobs!' We were trying hard not to laugh, but it was quite hilarious. There was also a scene where Gil and I are drinking this blue stuff. I have no idea what it was, I'm looking at it thinking 'This looks awful—I'm not really gonna drink this stuff!' Everything was so weird and bizarre, because it was set in this far future."

She looks amazing in her array of outfits. "Holy cow, my spandex outfits," Morgan Brittany giggles. "There's a gold spandex outfit I wear in that episode that was so tight, I literally could not breathe—it was so tight, it pushed my boobs right under my chin! I said 'What are you guys doing to me?' They said 'You have to be this space alien' The only way I could sit down in that costume was sideways.

"The costume department made all of those spandex outfits for us. It was literally body fitted to your type—it was so tight, these goofy spandex clothes. My outfit was fitted so tight, I could literally not breathe! You had to sit carefully in those outfits. They tied me up to the chair and I was pleading to be untied between shots. Nobody was coming around to rescue me, so I finally said, 'Are you guys ever gonna let me out of this chair?!?'

"Gil, Erin and everybody wanted the show to be good. They knew that it was campy, but they wanted it to be good. Also in my episode was (*Cleopatra Jones*' star) Tamara Dobson. She was great, very professional, knew her lines, always knew where to go but she was quiet and tall. I didn't work all that much with Tamara Dobson. but she took it very seriously. I remember we both had a lot of technical dialogue, and we would both mess up!"

Peter Mac Lean played the villain, whose mere touch turned people into silicon. "I don't have that much memory of him, except that his character wore sunglasses. I remember, we had so much fun doing the birthday party for Buck at the end. We had a blast—it was like a real party. I think Buck's birthday was one of the very last shots of the show, so it was fun. Erin and I had a scene together at the birthday party—but Erin and I knew each other for years, from commercials and various TV shows, it was great, I loved working with her and wished we had more scenes together."

Her favorite scene in the episode "is probably when Buck and I are having dinner together. That was it, a good conversation, it was flirty, and I'm manipulating him, which is what I am known for, from *Dallas* and other evening soaps, where I'm always manipulating people. It was fun to take my femme fatale routine to Outer Space. You can be a femme fatale anywhere; future, past, even the old west..Trust me, I have been a femme fatale everywhere in different movies and TV shows."

"I enjoyed my whole *Buck Rogers* experience, because I was not used to going on sets like that—I usually did stuff like *Dallas*, so walking down futuristic hallways, getting to climb inside a spaceship or being dressed like that or wearing boots like I wore in that was exciting to me. As a sci fi fan, I was thrilled that I even got to do a stunt sequence and have a fight in a hallway," Morgan Brittany says with a gleam in her bright blue eye. "I never got a chance to do stuff like that, so it was very fun for me to work with a talking robot, even if he was constantly complaining!"

Buck Wilma and Twiki use the mind probe in A Blast For Buck.

"A Blast for Buck"

Season 1, Episode 16

Story by John Gaynor
Teleplay by Richard Nelson
Directed by David G. Phinney
Original airdate: January 17, 1980

Cast
Buck Rogers...Gil Gerard
Col. Wilma Deering...Erin Gray
Dr. Huer...Tim O'Connor
Hieronymous Fox...Gary Coleman
Twiki...Patty Maloney
Voice of Twiki...Mel Blanc

When a mysterious 'gift' enters Earth airspace with a limerick message for Buck that seems to imply a threat, an alarmed Buck, Wilma, Twiki and Dr. Huer get together to figure out who in their rogues gallery sent it. Dr. Huer wheels in a "Mind Probe" that allows each character (including Twiki!) to remember past events in their lives. They use the device on each other in a desperate attempt to find out who sent the 'threat.'

In other words, it's a cost-cutting hour filled with stock footage! With a story provided by budget-conscious producer John Gaynor that utilizes Buck and his friends staying inexpensively in one room watching reruns of past episodes, it's pretty clear that "A Blast for Buck" is a 'bottle' show—one to save money by having all the characters on one standing set (no new costly space battles or laser blasts in this episode!) puzzling over a 'mystery' that can only be solved by Buck reliving his first 15 episodes.

To its credit, "A Blast For Buck" cherry picks from the best of Season One, re-using uncredited clips from various old episodes, featuring Ana Alicia, Elizabeth Allen, Pamela Hensley, Jamie Lee Curtis, Robert Quarry, Woody Strode, Pamela Susan Shoop, Michael Ansara, Victor Argo, Kimberly Beck, Tara Buckman, Karen Carlson, Jack Palance, Buster Crabbe and Juanin Clay, among many others. No beautiful guest actress is forgotten, with long clips of Ardala, Tangie, the amazons, Dorothy Stratten's Miss Cosmos and even Twiki's girlfriend Tina (when Twiki is wearing the mind probe, he immediately flashes back to his romantic escapades on The Lyran Queen.)

Wilma eliminates Princess Ardala from suspicion, by observing "She's ruthless, arrogant and power hungry, but even Princess Ardala wouldn't slaughter innocent people without a reason."

They stall out the hour guessing who sent the satellite, before we discover it's Buck's old friend, the fellow 500 year old Hieronymous Fox, who wanted to give Buck a surprise for New Year's Eve. He sends hamburgers, French fries, milk shakes and champagne (The hamburgers are actually "Rigellian lizard burgers," as cows didn't make it to the 25th Century.) The glib, annoying Fox, played by NBC's superstar sitcom kid Gary Coleman is even more annoying here, because having two 500 year old people cheapens Buck. It makes him less special.

Having a fighter pilot/astronaut make it 504 years is cool—having a pint size child star/comedian do it is one buy too many. That said, when this episode aired, NBC was dead last in the ratings and embattled network head Fred Silverman was trying to keep the ratings up. Having the star of one of the network's few hits, *Diff'rent Strokes*, take another trip to the 25th Century was an example of network synchronicity.

While writing the episode, producer Jock Gaynor asked Coleman if he'd be available for the one scene at the end. The star enthusiastically agreed to reprise his role as President Fox.

Buck remembers limericks as "an old and honorable form of literature."

Ardala and her Buck clones in Ardala Returns.

"Ardala Returns."

Season 1, Episode 17

Original airdate: Jan 24, 1980
Written By Chris Bunch & Allan Cole
Directed by Larry Stewart

Cast
Buck Rogers...Gil Gerard
Wilma Deering...Erin Gray
Dr. Huer... Tim O'Connor
Princess Ardala...Pamela Hensley
Kane...Michael Ansara
Twiki...Felix Silla
Voice of Twiki...Mel Blanc
Tigerman...H.B. Haggerty
Pilot...James Emery

Technician...Betty Bridges
Guard...Bob Minor

When 7 Draconian pilots die trying to fly a hatchet fighter of Kane's design, Princess Ardala realizes the only one who can fly it successfully is Buck Rogers.   Meanwhile, back in New Chicago, Buck, Wilma and Dr. Huer gather as Twiki unveils a "ping pool table"(He misread Buck's pool table design).

A spacecraft labeled "USA 1996 A.D." floats into Terran airspace, with a frozen astronaut inside. Curious about a possible kindred spirit, Buck takes Twiki aboard to investigate...where they are immediately captured and taken to Ardala, Kane and Tigerman. Twiki makes a wisecrack, so Kane asks Ardala, "Shall I order the ambuquad immediately disassembled?"

Buck references almost marrying Ardala in her previous appearance ("We have irreconcilable differences"), as the guards take him by force and Ardala has him cloned in Lab 23.

His neural memories are downloaded and recorded for the clone to study. She unveils the clone to Buck and Twiki—even Buck's loyal ambuquad is impressed..

"It's you, Buck," Twiki exclaims when he sees the clone that Ardala calls "Zygot Mark One." Zygot One is uncommonly cheerful. He returns to Earth and impersonates Buck as Ardala has him cloned two more times in Lab 23. The cloning process is a neat shot of Buck's arm, all by itself, , slowly growing into his whole body.

The Buck duplicate is sent racing back to Earth, claiming to have escaped The Draconians. He also reports that Twiki was destroyed in the escape attempt. Buck and Twiki are stuck in the brig of Ardala's ship, helpless to warn his friends.

Buck's Zygot has a nuclear bomb in him that will detonate when he's back in New Chicago with Earth's three top defense leaders Dr, Huer, Wilma and Theopolis. Wilma vaporizes Buck's double before he can explode. She refers to him as "a robot."

The climax pits Buck against his three zygot duplicates. "What can one Buck Rogers possibly do against three," gloats Kane, while Princess Ardala cautions him, "We shall see, Kane."

Buck has Twiki give him a powerful shock to screw up his Zygots' reaction time. The results on his duplicates mimic drunkenness.

Chris Bunch & Allan Cole had written great episodes of *The Incredible Hulk* and here, they brought forth a terrific Princess Ardala episode, full of double entendres and a new spin on the evil twin concept.

"The Zygots go to my chambers," Princess Ardala proclaims at one point, "I wish to inspect them personally!" The best line is when Kane frets outside Ardala's chambers, "What could she conceivably be doing with three Buck Rogers for almost an hour and a half?"

One nifty bit has Buck in a dogfight, only to reveal he's dreaming in a chair, an image put in his head by The Draconians, who are using it to measure and copy his abilities and reaction time.

There's also a cool fight with a Draconian guard (Bob Minor), wielding a stun-stick, who refers to Buck as "Earth trash."

As always, Pamela Hensley shows why she's the show's best villainess and most popular recurring guest. Hensley is amusing as the campy Princess, complaining to Buck about "that stuffy Dr. Huer and detestable Col. Deering!" Michael Ansara is equally fun as her sycophantic straight man, Kane.

Gerard is witty playing his own clones. When Zygot Buck reports that Twiki was destroyed, Wilma cautions Huer and Theo that Buck must be devastated, because "Twiki wasn't just another ambuquad, he was Buck's best friend!"

Wilma tries to console Buck over Twiki, but the zygot double smiles and says "Twiki? Oh yeah, I'm really down in the dumps about him." She thinks Buck's strange reaction is grief over Twiki. Keenly noticing Buck's odd, nonchalant behavior, she says "It's almost as if his spirit was missing!"

In the wrap up of the episode, Buck playfully pretends to be a zygot, freaking out Wilma, Huer and Twiki. A great first season episode. Gerard had been cutting the humor out of previous scripts, but he clearly appreciated it in 'Ardala Returns' and is really funny as the Zygot Bucks.

Episode Highlight: Wilma kills Buck! Even though it's only Buck's double, it's still disturbing to see.

ALLAN COLE: "We were so happy when they asked us to add Pamela Hensley's Princess Ardala into the script. They wanted her to do a second appearance but none of the scripts they came up with did anything for her. It was our script that convinced her to take the gig. Heck, we were so young and dumb that we didn't know when we pitched the Buck clone idea that we solved a big problem for the show and the Network. I mean, she had a pay or play deal. If we had known, our agent could have held them up for a helluva lot more money."

"Meeting her, Pam Hensley left us both tongue-tied. That she was a beauty goes without saying. But when you spoke to her, she had that incredible ability actors have of tuning into you like you are the only person in the world!"

The writers called the Buck clones 'zygots,' "because each clone was basically the embryo produced by the original. Under the circumstances, it seemed like the perfect SF word. It's like in *The Far Kingdoms* Series, where we coined the word 'Evocator' for wizard. A natural fantasy-type creation."

Cole (from his blog, "BUCK ROGERS IS A FATTY") remembers he and his writing partner, pitched Bruce Lansbury *Buck Rogers* plots. "Chris said, matter-of-factly, 'Oh, we want to clone Buck Rogers three times and put him in aerial combat against himself.' A slight pause, then - "We call it Buck Times Three." "Bloody hell," blurted Lansbury - momentarily losing his British cool... The *Buck Rogers* episode, as it turned out, everybody was so impressed with the story, that it underwent a major change, including the title. "Buck Times Three" became, "Ardala Returns."The character of Ardala was played by Pamela Hensley, as talented as she was beautiful.

"Pamela had co-starred in the pilot and was lured back to do our episode with promises of lots of money and a great script. The idea of the story was that Ardala, who always had a sweet spot for the hunky Buck (played by Gil Gerard) planned to capture Rogers, then clone him and create an invincible armada of fighter pilots. She'd also have an endless supply of willing lovers in Rogers' clones.

"We decided on an amusing trap - a mysterious antique ship, seemingly shot forward in time - just like the Rogers character. It was a ghost ship, the only cargo, a treasure-trove of 20th Century junk food. Rogers, slavering at the sight of all those burgers and fries, Twinkies and Ding Dongs, can't help but visit the craft. And wham! The trap would slam down and Ardala would have him in her clutches. Lansbury called us into his office for our second draft notes.

"As we sat down, both of us realized that he did not appear to be a supremely happy man. My stomach did flip flops, thinking that maybe our script had fallen from favor and was doomed. That we'd be thrown out and told never to darken Mr. Lansbury's door again. And then maybe he'd call some other guys - like Peter Thompson - and tell them never to hire two guys named Bunch and Cole. Bruce said, "Lads, I fear I am the bearer of ill tidings." Chris and I nodded. I also gulped - Chris probably did the same.

"Lansbury slid a small glossy magazine across his desk. It was *TV Guide*. We looked at the cover and saw a picture of Gil Gerard, dressed up in his tight-fitting Buck Rogers costume. We puzzled at it. "OKaaayyyyy?" I said. 'If you look to the article inside,' Lansbury went on, "you'll see that the essayist - a writer well known for his insensitivity - said our Gil looked like an overstuffed sausage in his costume."Chris and I both examined the cover again. We sort of agreed with the writer's description, although we didn't say so. To show you that it really was a problem in the making, Gerard underwent gastric bypass surgery not long ago.

"I looked at Bruce. "What does that have to do with our script?" Lansbury sighed, saying: "The word has come down from Gil. We are to never mention food on the show for the duration of the series. As for your script, obviously you'll have to come up with something other than the junk food trap. And Gil said to lose all the food jokes."

"Chris and I were relieved. Screw a bunch of food jokes. "So, we still have a job?" I asked Bruce. 'Absolutely,' he said. "You've turned in a marvelous script - food references and all. In fact, boys, when you are done with this one, I'd like to have you do another.' The next one was called, "Space Rockers."

Eddie Benton and her space sirens in Twiki Is Missing.

"Twiki Is Missing"

Season 1, Episode 18

31 January 1980
Written by Jaron Summers
Directed by Sigmund Neufeld, JR.

Cast
Buck Rogers...Gil Gerard
Col. Wilma Deering...Erin Gray
Dr. Huer...Tim O'Connor
Stella...Eddie Benton
Kurt Belzack...John P. Ryan
Twiki...Felix Silla
Voice of Twiki...Mel Blanc
Pinchas...David Darlow

Clare...Janet Bebe Louie
Dawn...Eugenia Wright
Oto Anad...Ken Letner

Greedy space mine tycoon Kurt Belzack captures Twiki so he can see why the ambuquad acts the way he does. He feels Twiki's unique thinking will make him different from the other drones who work in his Mines. He is going to open Twiki to see what makes him tick, then he plans to mass produce Twiki duplicates as cheap labor.

Although ambuquads have failed in his mines previously, Belzack notes that Buck "has endowed the drone with many extraordinary features; resourcefulness, courage, loyalty and imagination."

When Buck tries to save Twiki, Belzack uses his space sirens Stella, Clare and Dawn to deter him. Once their eyes glow, they are able to hurl people aside with concussive force. Meanwhile, Wilma Deering is escorting a massive Spaceberg—a huge floating chunk of frozen oxygen—that would mean immediate destruction should it crash.

When Stella, the lead of Belzack's mutant powered Charlie's Angels(they call themselves 'The Omniguard'), first offers to buy Twiki, Buck turns her down, with the excuse "I'm sorry, Stella, he's not for sale. Twiki's a little more than that, it would be like selling family."

He tries to dissuade her, "Twiki is chronically lazy" and "a ham." When they fail to make a deal, Stella and her friends simply power up and knock Buck out. Taking him away, Twiki protests, ' Hey—I'm private property...You're trespassing!"

Waking up, Buck realizes the three women have psychokinetic powers. Despite their powers, he's not gonna let anyone steal his "little buddy."

Stella is serving Belzack with her mutant abilities because he is holding her young son hostage. We never hear any sad stories on what Belzack has on the other two sirens because, as any casual *Buck Rogers in the 25th Century* viewer knows, only the hottest girl's problems matter!

Buck must confront Belzack, free Stella and get Twiki back("I thought you deserted me," Twiki tells Buck, "Are you a sight for sore circuits!"), while poor Wilma babysits the Spaceberg for the whole hour.

While Twiki is the most popular character on the show, very few episodes are actually about him. "Twiki Is Missing" gives him the spotlight and is a goofy, amusing episode with goofy, amusing imagery, including poor Twiki getting lost in space—but still making wisecracks.

Seeing Twiki floating and flailing in Outer Space is odd enough, but when he quips "Some may like to hang loose, but not this 'quad!," the episode reaches full blown absurdity.

Seeing John P. Ryan, who has worked with Jack Nicholson, Charles Bronson and others, given so little to do is disappointing. Ryan's not so much a bad guy than an overburdened CEO implementing cost-cutting measures.

"Eddie Benton" is one of the most beautiful women to ever appear on the show. After this, the stunning actress changed her name to "Anne-Marie Martin" and starred on the cult comedy *Sledge Hammer*. She changed her name to Anne-Marie Crichton, when she married the novelist/screenwriter/director, Michael Crichton. She also co-wrote and conceived the story for one of his biggest hits, the film *Twister*.

The Spaceberg sequence was obviously inspired by *Meteor*, a big-budget Sean Connery/Natalie Wood movie that hit theaters Christmas '79. It was a surprise flop. Whoever thought it was a good idea to put Wilma in a cockpit and shoot only her head and shoulders in this episode should have been fired.

It is clever, the way Buck finds the solution to Wilma's Spaceberg dilemma in a way that helps him, too.

Buck Facts

- Twiki's serial number is 22-23-T, Ambuquad Facility in New Chicago.
- Watch for the wire used to lift the miner when he's blasted by the Omniguard.
- A robot named after Eddie Benton's future husband would be added in Season Two.
- Crichton's blockbuster novel *Jurassic Park* is dedicated to Benton and their daughter.
- Benton (and her real-life Mom) joined fellow *Buck* guest Jamie Lee Curtis for the slasher flick *Prom Night* the same year they did the show.

- John P. Ryan did the killer baby classic, *It's Alive*, with Buck guest Michael Ansara.

Judith Chapman as Lara in Olympiad.

"Olympiad"

Season 1, Episode 19

First aired: February 7, 1980
Written By Craig Buck
Directed by Larry Stewart

Cast
Buck Rogers...Gil Gerard
Col. Wilma Deering...Erin Gray
Dr. Huer...Tim O'Connor
Allerick...Nicolas Coster
Lara Teasian...Judith Chapman
Jorex Leet... Barney McFadden
Karl...Paul Mantee
Olympian...Elgin Baylor
Olympian...Anthony Davis
Olympian...Thomas 'Hollywood' Henderson
Olympian...Carlos Palomino
Quarod...Jerry Quarry
Rand Sorgon...Bob Seagren
Twiki...Felix Silla
Voice of Twiki...Mel Blanc
Zogan...Paul Coufos
Satrap...John Zee

Buck attends the 2492 Olympics on planet Mikos and finds himself immersed in a tense political situation as Jorex, an alien athlete tries to defect to Earth, where he's fallen in love with a talented terran athlete, Lara.

Buck is there to present the Olympic flag from his century, when he meets Lara. She runs the Astro Sled, the 25th Century equivalent of the bobsled. Lara is secretly seeing Jorex, an athlete from Losira, a cold, oppressive planet that is forcing Jorex to do as they wish. This includes taking steroids to give them an edge in the competition. Lara wants Buck to help Jorex defect to Earth. Jorex' handler, Karl Alaric, has a Disharmonizer, a device that can cause Jorex to suffer headaches, painful shocks and even make him explode.

Wilma and Dr. Huer consult a defector from Losira on how to offer help to Jorex. When Karl realizes Earth is helping Jorex, he kidnaps Lara. Buck rescues her and realizes Lara's astrosledding skill—with timely intervention by Wilma—will be the only way to save him. As Buck, Wilma and Twiki reunite the star-crossed couple, Losira's Deputy Minister kills himself immediately on orders from his leader.

An obvious Cold War metaphor, with Losira standing in for The Soviet Union who were famous for doping their athletes with anabolic steroids, keeping them from defecting and spying on other countries, the timing of the episode was no accident. In the episode, Losira is even spying on Buck and athletes from other planets. 'Olympiad' is an interesting artifact of its time. The 1980 Olympics, XXII Olympiad, was held in Moscow. US President Jimmy Carter boycotted America's involvement to protest Russia's invasion of Afghanistan. This episode clearly reflects the fear and suspicion in the air at that time.

There's also some lighthearted stuff, too. Buck and Twiki walk around the workout room of the Olympic Village, where the little robot can't get round all the muscular, bulky athletes. Twiki complains he "can't see the forest for the knees!" As two athletes are about to fight, Twiki cuts between them, telling the two "Don't let me come between you guys!" The Amiable Ambuquad isn't just there to provide comedy relief—Twiki also breaks into different rooms later to help Buck out. Losiran steroids turn women into love slaves. Humorously, a lot of the Olympians seen are stuntmen who work on the show, including the giant Gene LeBell. There are now Sonic Boxers, whose gloves make the sounds of The Viper ships on the original *Battlestar Galactica*.

Being budget conscious, the show finds a way to show fans from a dozen planets without bringing in thousands of expensive extras. The athletes compete in a workout room while metal boxes, "Responders," play the sound of cheering crowds. "Used to be a thousand people jammed in a stadium—now this," Buck says sadly. They use a similar tactic to avoid showing crowds in 'Space Rockers.'

The highlight of the episode is the beautiful Judith Chapman, as the wonderfully earnest Lara. Chapman went on to become a Soap Star *Doing over 750 episodes of *The Young And The Restless*), and guest starred on numerous genre shows like *The Incredible Hulk, Darkroom, Knight Rider, Fantasy Island* and *Galactica 1980* (On the episode 'The Return Of Starbuck,' considered the best episode of that series).

Buck Facts

- Barney McFadden co-starred in TV's first Stephen King miniseries, *Salem's Lot*.
- Nicolas Coster played Blair's dad on *The Facts Of Life*, which came on after *Buck* on Thursday nights on NBC.
- Real life boxer Jerry Quarry guested on *Batman*.
- The Weightlifter's equipment makes the same sound as the killer military robot from the "Mr. Ring" episode of Universal's *Kolchak: The Night Stalker*.
- Paul Mantee was a Klingon on *Star Trek*, one of Catwoman Julie Newmar's henchman on *Batman* (as was producer John "Jock" Gaynor) and in *Day Of The Animals* with Michael Ansara.
- The star-crossed couple, Jorex and Lara, appear to be named after Superman's parents, Jor El and Lara.

BUCK BABE: JUDITH CHAPMAN (Lara)

As Earth athlete Lara, Judith Chapman turns to Earth hero Buck to keep her and lover Jorex from being separated by his cruel, fascistic planet and Soviet-style handlers. 'Olympiad' was one of her first acting gigs.

"Every new show for a young actor, is exciting with one more new thing to learn about the business," Judith Chapman states. "One of my favorite memories of appearing on *Buck Rogers in the 25th Century* was meeting the actor, Nicolas Coster (who plays Allerick in the episode). Nicolas taught scuba diving, which is something I had always wanted to to do.

"After the shoot, I got certified, and continue diving to this day. Just saw Nicolas Coster a few months ago, at an audition in L.A. We immediately started talking to each other about our latest diving adventures."

Other Buck guests like Morgan Brittany remember having their breasts and bodies pushed into tight spandex costumes. "I loved the little Olympic outfits they always stuck me in for the episode—very intergalactic style! Also liked being in that little tube with Buck, on the slalom course, that 'Astrosled'... I used that clip when NATAS, honored me with an award for 25 Years in the business... It looked so funny, in a good way... Special effects have come so far since Way Back When," Judith Chapman laughs. "Unlike Morgan and those other actresses, large breasts have never been an issue for me, but skimpy outfits? Yes! Seeing all of these shows these days, all I can say is WOW!!... I looked pretty cute, skimpy, skimpy outfit and all."

As for the regulars on *Buck*, Chapman says "Series stars—And I've worked with many—have a really tough time working with new guest stars every week or so. To be gracious, professional and welcoming while preparing their own new script? Gil and Erin could not have been more welcoming, gracious and pro... That is why a book is being written about this 80's icon of T.V... I Had been working nonstop in episodics at the time. If Producers knew you, they offered you the job... Unlike today. When everyone auditions, even if it's only for a few lines... Different world now, where you even have Oscar winners on TV.....

"I feel so lucky to have worked so much back when network episodic TV ruled. I watched the show when I was putting together a reel, when NATAS honored me with an award for longevity in the biz. Just laughed and enjoyed my episode," she says triumphantly. "Used the piece of me and Buck in the slalom course.. Working with little people like Twiki? That was like being on *The Wizard Of Oz* or *Star Wars*. *Buck Rogers* was a fun show, how lucky were we, Morgan Brittany and I, being able to do it! Just saw Morgan in Atlanta last month when I was there to perform *Vivien* at the 75th anniversary of *Gone With The Wind*... Lovely to see her again, she's so gracious and came to my play—and we were both space girls on *Buck Rogers in the 25th Century*! Small world."

Writer CRAIG BUCK (In Starlog Magazine): "I pitched this story to Bruce Lansbury. I really didn't know much about *Buck Rogers*. It wasn't my kind of show, but in my career, I've often written for shows I've never seen before. Lansbury gave me some scripts to read so I could get an idea of who the characters were and I watched a couple episodes. I always tune in to The Olympics, but I don't get really excited about them. I was just imaging what the Olympics would be like in the future. I write many futuristic things and it always amuses me to try to figure out where things will go.

"Because it was a Glen Larson show, there was no one more formulaic in TV than Larson. *Buck Rogers* was very formulaic, although Bruce Lansbury added a bit of character to it...They were more concerned with plot than with character and it seemed like many issues on that show were purely structural.

"When I wrote for *The Incredible Hulk*, even though it was a big cartoon show, the producers were very concerned with character. They felt it was very important to remember that David Banner was a man fighting his own inner demons. It was really a heavy character show. They never did anything close to that on *Buck Rogers* and I think that's one reason the show didn't last. One of the reasons *Star Trek* is so popular and *Hulk* did so well is that those shows were character based. *Buck Rogers*, on the other hand, was really hardware based. There's only so much emotional investment you can make in a robot. It was more hardware than heart."

Anne Lockhart and Mary Woronov in A Dream Of Jennifer.

"A Dream Of Jennifer"

Season One, Episode 20

Directed by David G. Phinney
Written by "Michael Bryant" (Pseudonym for Alan Brennert)
Original Airdate: Feb 14, 1980

Cast
Buck Rogers...Gil Gerard
Wilma Deering...Erin Gray
Dr. Elias Huer...
Tim O'Connor
Commander Reeve...Paul Koslo
Sylvie...Gino Conforti
Nola...Mary Woronov
Jennifer/Leila...Anne Lockhart
Twiki...Felix Silla

Voice of Twiki...Mel Blanc
Lt. Rekoff...Jessie Lawrence Ferguson
Toby Kaplan...Cameron Young
Supervisor...Shawn Michaels
Guard...Dennis Haysbert
Clerk...Marsha Mercant
Mime...Mitchell Young-Evans

After spotting a woman in a crowd, Buck is stunned and obsessed with catching up to her. He meets and falls for the woman who is a dead ringer for his 20th century girlfriend Jennifer, but it may be a deliberate hoax to lead him into a trap.

"A Dream Of Jennifer" opens at what looks like a then modern late '70s outdoor shopping mall, albeit one filled with colorfully dressed people. A sign humorously reads that it's the "Old Chicago Shopping Mall," sponsored by the Earth Preservation Society. Buck has taken Twiki with him to gather parts to build a hot tub, when he spots what he believes to be his girlfriend Jennifer in the crowd. He drops everything to give chase, while Twiki observes "Uh Oh—a pretty girl and it's off to the races!." She loses him in the crowd.

We flashback to the 20th century—the very first one on the series—where Jennifer comes by while Buck is talking with Toby, his best friend. Jennifer has come to give Buck a "going away and come back to me soon" present. Buck remembers that this is their last date before the flight that led to him being frozen.

Wilma notices that he's been lost in reverie and asks "Buck, are you alright? You've seemed kind of upset all day." While Buck's friends are troubled by his obsessive quest to find the woman, Dr. Huer reveals to him that he had been married and also had dreams and nightmares about his wife after she died. In the pilot, when Wilma visits Buck's 25th Century apartment, she picks up her picture (which he carried with him in the shuttle) but we never saw her face—probably because they hadn't cast her yet.

Buck sees Jennifer again at a spaceport and finds out that she's actually Leila Markeson, on her way to enjoy Mardi Gras in New Orleans. This being the 25th Century, New Orleans is now "City-on-the-sea" and Mardi Gras is "The Festival Of The Masks."

Buck asks the employee for her name and is told it's against the rules. Another employee recognizes the famous Captain Rogers and gives him the information. Buck decides to follow her to City-On-The-Sea. "Why not," he muses, "I've never been to a 25th Century Mardi Gras before." Once there, he befriends a magician named Silby as he searches for Leila.

He finally finds Leila and pursues her romantically. We find out that she is a 25th Century woman who has sold Buck out to aliens—red skinned Koluan warriors, who recognize Buck as a threat should Earth involve itself in their affairs. They plan to kill both Buck and Wilma, as well as a freighter full of cadets that they are training. They feel Buck is the bigger threat, so he will die first. Leila, who underwent cosmetic surgery to resemble Buck's deceased girlfriend, has many debts, which is why she reluctantly agreed to help the aliens betray her race.

She starts to fall for Buck and begs her Koluan handlers Reeve and Nola to spare him. "You told me he could live," she pleads. Nola is attracted to Buck, who spurns her. The red skinned warrior woman tells our hero, that it's "fortunate for us that you care so much for the Terran female, although I can hardly see why. She's so weak...And soft. You deserve someone much smarter, stronger..." Buck replies, "I'm sure you have someone in mind." "Perhaps," coos Nola. "Thanks for the thought," Buck says defiantly, "but I'm not your type!"

Meanwhile, dating Buck and getting to know him, Leila has grown protective of Buck and when he comes into Reeve and Nola's trap hoping to save her, Leila takes the fatal blast meant for Buck. She tells him, "I'm just an image of someone you lost a long, long time ago," and dies in Buck's arms.

When Buck returns to New Chicago, Dr. Huer tries to cheer him up with what he thinks is an 'aquatic documentary' that Dr. Julius found in the vaults from the 20th Century...*Jaws!* Twiki quips, "Just when you thought it was safe in the 25th Century!"

The Koluan warriors are an exciting addition to Buck's rogues gallery. Casting two of the greatest cult movie stars of all time, Paul Koslo (*Vanishing Point, Omega Man, Robot Jox*) and Mary Woronov (*Death Race 2000, Rock & Roll High School, House Of The Devil*) makes them indelible.

Koslo adopts an interesting clipped speaking style as Reeve, while Woronov is especially stunning with red skin, which makes her brutally efficient alien even more impressive. Most of the alien baddies Buck encounters have normal skin pigments, so it's nice to see the show actually attempt to make the aliens look alien in this episode.

Anne Lockhart was a Universal contract actress who appeared in many of their genre shows like *Battlestar Galactica* and *The Incredible Hulk*. She is also the daughter of *Lost In Space* star June Lockhart. Anne specialized in crying on cue, an ability she puts to good use here.

In Brennert's original draft, the space port employee recognizes that Buck is a man in pain over a woman and bends the rules to help him. A universal bond between people and their common interest in a lost love. Having him do it because he recognizes Buck defeats the show's conceit that no one in the future knows who Buck is—making him the perfect spy/freelance agent. This was one of the unwanted changes that made Brennert remove his name from the script.

Even with Brennert's dissatisfaction with creative meddling to the dumbing down of his script, it's still one of the better episodes of the series and plays like a third season episode of the original *Star Trek. Tim O'Connor talking quietly and sadly about the way he, as Dr. Huer, dealt with the death of his wife, is the strongest scene he got on the show. It displays how O'Connor's Huer is so much more than comic relief or deliverer of exposition.*

ALAN BRENNERT: "I am pleased we got to kill Jennifer in the end, considering that we were on in what was known as 'The Family Hour,' but 'A Dream of Jennifer' is not worth another look, not to me—I see only the ways it could have been better."

GIL GERARD (In Starlog Magazine): "('Jennifer' is) The fourth in a series of the worst scripts I've ever read. It was supposed to be a love story about when Buck sees this girl who looks exactly like the girl he left behind 500 years before which sounds good, but it was badly done. So I read it and said, 'That's it! I'm tired of rewriting these scripts as we shoot. "

ERIN GRAY: "I remember Dennis Haysbert's face being very familiar when his shows and commercials took off, so I wasn't

Anne Lockhart, photo by Pat Jankiewicz.

surprised to find out that he started on our show. I don't think I had any scenes with him, but when his work took off, I thought he looked familiar."

Buck Facts

- As noted above, look for a baby-faced Dennis Haysbert (*24, The Unit*) with a short '80s afro as a space port employee. ("I had no idea Haysbert had one of his first roles on that," marvels Brennert.)
- Brennert's script originally opened with Buck having a nightmare, where he wakes up next to Jennifer, whose face is a skull.
- Mary Woronov was a member of Andy Warhol's Factory and guest starred *on Charlie's Angels* with fellow Buck guest Anthony James.

Mary Woronov, photo by Pat Jankiewicz.

- Maintenance androids resurface in this episode, last seen in Brennert's "Plot To Kill A City." They only show up in Brennert-scripted episodes.
- This was Buck's big Valentine's Day episode.
- At the mall in the opening, Buck is wearing a hilariously '70s open shirt to expose his hairy, manly chest hair.
- Buck uses a lot of judo in this episode.
- Like Nola, another alien woman with great cheekbones who wants Buck as a mate but rejects his fondness for protecting the weak will be seen in Julie Newmar, during the season finale, "Flight Of The War Witch."

- Jessie Lawrence Ferguson (Lt. Ricktoff) went on to star as Sam Raimi's *Darkman* and *John Carpenter's Prince Of Darkness.*
- In the 20th Century flashback, Toby calls him "Rip Van Winkle"—another famous sleeper who missed his own era.
- Overheard on the Space Port P.A. "Captain Christopher Pike, please report to the Veteran Affairs Office at once!" "That's the best joke I ever got on the show," boasts Brennert.
- When Woronov's Nola attacks Buck at 'The Festival Of The Masks,' she isn't wearing her red skin color.
- As the episode is set in New Orleans, it's probably no accident that 'Nola' is also a slang name for the town.
- Buck's friend Toby was first mentioned in the 'Vegas in Space' episode.

25th Century Guest/Buck babe: ANNE LOCKHART (Jennifer/ Leila)

"Appearing on *Buck Rogers* was a very lovely, fun experience with much of the same crew that I had worked with previously on *Battlestar Galactica.* It was a pleasure to work with Gil Gerard and Erin (Gray). Erin and I are still buddies to this day," says Anne Lockhart.

"Being Buck's long lost girlfriend was a nice job, fun to do and completely shot on the backlot. because it was set in the future, we didn't go on location.

"I have a fun death scene in it—I actually get laser beamed to death and die in Buck's arms! I loved my killers, Mary Woronov and Paul Koslo. We laughed so hard making it, Paul and Mary had tears streaming down their red makeup covered faces. We got the giggles so badly one day, the director had to break us for lunch at 11:30 in the morning! We were just too gone with laughter to shoot, so we all went to lunch."

"I haven't seen the thing in 30 years, so I barely remember it. I have better things to do than sit and watch my own work. I never watch my old reruns, but I remember it as a fun job!"

Buck Babe MARY WORONOV (Nola)

Tall and sexy, with high cheekbones, arched eyebrows and bright red skin, Mary Woronov was one of the more alluring and memorable alien vixens on *Buck Rogers in the 25th Century.*

"To be honest, I didn't really feel sexy or alluring in all that red paint," Woronov laughs. "I was this alien helping my male alien counterpart, Paul Koslo, use Earthwoman Anne Lockhart to set up Buck. I think we did it all on the Universal backlot.

"It was supposed to be really serious, but I remember laughing a lot. It was a gig, but I kind of enjoyed being this big red amazon.. I had a few scenes with Gil and Anne, but most of my time was spent with Paul, as we would scheme together. We had a lot of laughs on that and I think I hit on Buck who rebuffs me...It's always fun to be the villainess!"

Judy Landers' discovers music is dangerous in Space Rockers.

"Space Rockers"

Season 1, Episode 19

Original airdate: Feb 21, 1980
Written by Chris Bunch & Allan Cole
Directed by Guy Magar

Cast
Buck Rogers...Gil Gerard
Col. Wilma Deering...Erin Gray
Dr. Huer...Tim O'Connor
Lars Mangros...Jerry Orbach
Karana...Nancy Frangione
Joanna...Judy Landers
Yarat...Richard Moll
Twiki...Felix Silla
Voice of Twiki...Mel Blanc

Rambeau....Jesse Goins
Cirus...Leonard Lightfoot
Mark...Jeff Harlan
Elaine...Cynthia Leake
Technician... Mitch Reta
Security Man...Joseph Taggart
Tarkas...Paul LeClair

As William Conrad's hyperventilating promo declares, "a sinister musical mastermind uses 25th century rock & roll to plot a youth rebellion that threatens the entire galaxy!"

The music of rock band Andromeda turns teens violent, so Buck must stop the concert and defeat their evil producer, Lars Mangros (a slumming Jerry Orbach). He sneaks hypnotic signals into Andromeda's music to get kids to riot because he wants to put "everyone under 30" under his sway.

"Space Rockers" is typical fun cheese from Buck's goofy and enjoyable first season. Andromeda look hilarious in their beads, tights, glitter and day-glow makeup, as do their 'teenage' fans, who all look to be in their late 20s. The rioting is all very tame, including the kids who steal Buck's ship for a joyride.

When the young thieves insist the music compelled them to, Buck tells them that the excuse "'The Devil made me do it' was obsolete even in the 20th Century!"

It's also funny to see serious dramatic thespian Orbach paired up with '70s TV sexpot Judy Landers. Landers, with her sister Audrey, were a '70s & '80s TV sensation in the golden era of jigglevision The big eyed blondes appeared on such shows as *Fantasy Island* and *Vega$*. To see her doing scenes with Jerry Orbach as her evil music producer boyfriend, are truly surreal.

"Don't you find me attractive," she whimpers to him, as he improbably ignores her while trying to weaponize rock & roll—well the 25th Century synthesizer elevator music that Andromeda plays that we are told is future rock & roll. At least Twiki notices her, hailing Landers with, "See ya, babe!"

Bunch & Cole, who wrote several better than average episodes of *The Incredible Hulk*, did two cool episodes of *Buck*—this and "Ardala Returns." They have fun with Buck's man out of time milieu, when Wilma and Huer discuss 'modern' music.

Dr. Huer: "Andromeda, the most popular group in the galaxy today."

Wilma: "They have an incredible influence over young people, Buck."

Buck: "Sounds like The Beatles..."

Wilma: "The who?"

Buck: "Not The Who, The Beatles...It was a group that was popular around my time."

In the happy ending, Lars is defeated and we see Twiki dancing, as he declares "Beety Beety Beety, Long live rock & roll!" The episode aired after an infamous Who concert in 1978, where 11 people in Cincinnati were crushed to death as the crowd rushed to their seats. Could this have been an inspiration for the *Buck* plot where rock music turns kids wild episode?

The most amazing part of 'Space Rockers' occurred behind the scenes. It was the last episode shot of *Buck*'s first season, which marked the end of producer Bruce Lansbury's involvement with the series. For his last act on the show, he hired a recent graduate of The American Film Institute, Guy Magar, who had no professional experience whatsoever to helm the episode.

GUY MAGAR: "For the record, I had never worked on the show—any show— or on any backlot before I directed my episode. I was not the Production Assistant or an AD on the show, as has occasionally been reported...I was just a film student with an American Film Institute(AFI) film that I was showing everyone in town hoping to open doors and Bruce Lansbury was one I had hustled to see it, but nothing came of it at the time. It is almost impossible for any producer to hire a first-timer to direct any network episode, especially a complicated, special effects-laden action show like *Buck Rogers in the 25th Century*, as they are responsible for each and every episode which I believe was on the high side at the time of around $1.5 million per show.

"It is almost unheard of for any showrunner to risk their high-paying job and back a random film student with only a $500 short student film to show and get him approved to direct through the ranks of a never-take-a-chance studio and TV network execs. I think at that point, the show was cancelled—or a new producer was taking over."

The director pauses thoughtfully. "In a nutshell, I was in the right place at the right time with amazing luck. Bruce had just been fired or quit and was literally packing to leave Universal Studios that very day. There was ONE open director spot left for the very last show of the season, which turned out to be 'Space Rockers,' which they were contracted to deliver but obviously was no longer of great importance to Bruce...

"When I randomly walked into his office that very day to just say Hello—as I mentioned, Bruce had seen my $500 student film a few weeks earlier and was NOT impressed. But today, when I walked in, Bruce had a big smile when he saw me and Bruce was not the smiley type—because here was the greenest least-experienced, zero-hirable student director whom he could hire immediately as his last act before leaving. Obviously, that would 'mess it all up' because he hated the star, Gil Gerard, he hated the studio, and the network and wished to somehow sabotage the show and screw everybody—with a very green ME directing the last episode! And that's how my career started!"

"When he hired me I obviously had no idea why, I was just ecstatic to have the job and I'm sure he would have officially said he 'did it to help a young director with promise to break in' on a very unique/rare opportunity of a last episode of a canceled series,' but I never saw him again after that day. I heard enough on set during production to realize why I had had the great fortune to be hired for my first network series job...which allowed me to join the Directors Guild of America(DGA) and quite literally change my life.

"I obviously did not 'screw it up' and with that show, it brought others and I never needed to show my AFI student film again. I will forever be gratefully indebted to Bruce Lansbury for giving me my break, regardless of whatever motives were involved and please include that thanks to Bruce if you do use this story.

"Interestingly, my guest star was Jerry Orbach on his first TV job. Jerry played the evil agent of the band who was making all the trouble for the band and Buck Rogers. He was a big Broadway star and lived in New York, who told me he needed to make better 'real' money in TV, but he was so shocked at the low level of campy-acting acceptable in that world that he ran back to New York after the show. Jerry told me when we finished, he was going back to the stage 'for his sanity.' He later did make it in TV a decade later as the original detective star of *Law And Order,* shot in his beloved New York. That delivered the money and fame he was looking for and was more worthy of his talents than *Buck Rogers.* My other guest star was Richard Moll also on one of his first TV jobs...he went on to find fame as the lanky bald bailiff on *Night Court.* (Where he co-starred with first season *Buck Rogers* guest Markie Post.)

"Because they hired me for the episode, I was also the only young director hopeful I know about that received what was then obscurely known as the 'Steven Spielberg deal,' as he was ob-viously the first to get one like this. It meant a seven-year deal where Universal paid $250 a week...in case you turned out to be a dud, their investment was nil since my secretary was getting $375 a week...and if you turned out to be talented, they had you for seven years. "

In his autobiography Kiss *Me Quick Before I Shoot,* Magar re-members directing the episode that would change his life and give him a career. "(Bruce Lansbury) explained to me that his *Buck Rog-ers* series had just been cancelled and he was leaving the show. There was only one episode left to shoot, and the other produc-ers could handle it...

"Amazingly, he said, 'The directing slot is still open for the very last episode. Would you like to direct it?.'..I am absolutely con-vinced that if my 80-year old Egyptian grandma who didn't speak English and was bedridden, had somehow wheeled into Bruce's office that day, he would have hired her, I just got lucky

"I later discovered that Bruce was not a fan of this series. I heard through production team whispers that he wasn't fond of the net-work, the studio, and most especially, the star. Bruce had either been fired or had just quit when the series got cancelled that day, and with the last directing slot open, the rumor was he was going to hire the greenest, most unproven, most inexperienced, most sure-to-fail director he could find, and stick it to everybody on his way out, heading to vacation.

"*Buck Rogers* was a technical show because of the many spe-cial effects, and doing science fiction was not an easy assignment in those pre digital days. There were plenty of reasons to be over-whelmed and screw up, especially for a first-time director...The most fun I had was working with art and wardrobe departments, designing futuristic (musical) instruments and super-techie hand outfits."

ERIN GRAY: That's hilarious! I remember when we were shooting the show, Gil was worried that Guy was so young and the crew was griping that 'the kid wasn't getting the coverage he needed.' I said to Gil, 'Do you really think the studio would bring in someone who didn't know what they were doing?' I had no idea! I'm pleased Guy started out on our show and that his career has gone so far."

ALLAN COLE ('Space Rockers' co-writer): "On Space Rockers," The idea just popped into being. I don't recall whose it was. But it had nothing to do with any incident that I'm aware of like the tragic Who concert. When you are getting ready to pitch a show, you run through scads and scads of ideas. Sometimes, something that doesn't work will have the germ of something that will lead to another thought, then another, and another, until - voila! Bruce Lansbury said the Network wanted to do something about rock stars.

"Chris (Bunch, co-writer) had once worked for one of the big music PR firms (as the self-described 'worst PR hack in music history') And over the years , I freelanced on the side doing concert reviews to help stretch the meager wages they pay news people. I mean, we both had backgrounds in the field, some of which went way back. For example: when I was in college I interviewed Brian Wilson for the school newspaper. The Beach Boys' first hit was on the juke box at the joint we had lunch in, but they hadn't made a dime yet.

"I paid for the salad Brian had for lunch, he was so broke. People are always asking writers where their ideas come from and frankly there really isn't a real answer. All attempts to explain are just fumbles around in the dark. Ideas are what you do. The more you think up ideas, the more swarm into being. It's like words - the more you work with words the bigger your internal thesaurus becomes. But it isn't just the number of words you know - it's that they come unbidden when you are writing. It's not a yesno, yesno, yesno bio computer process. But something natural. Like odors bring flashes of memories into being. Or, touch, or sound.

"Chris and I were on set for both of our *Buck Rogers* episodes. Jerry Orbach and Judy Landers were great. The two of them were incredibly easy to work with. The crew just loved them. Orbach was one of the nicest people you'd ever want to meet and Ms Landers was incredibly charming. A calm presence in the chaos that is a TV shoot. I can't say much about working with Twiki the robot, because all of Twiki's dialogue was done in post production."

Buck Facts

- Judy Landers appeared in *Hellhole*, a women-in-prison melo-drama with fellow *Buck* babe, Mary Woronov.
- As noted, Jerry Orbach starred in one of the longest running TV franchises of all time, the Dick Wolf criminal justice show, *Law And Order*.
- Richard Moll became a TV star in his own right on *Night Court*.
- Jesse Goins is one of the murderous criminals who turn Peter Weller into *RoboCop*.
- Guy Magar directed the demonic revenge movie *Retribution*.
- Leonard Lightfoot played an android on *Star Trek: The Next Generation*.
- Cynthia Leake was Teegra in Ralph Bakshi's Frazetta inspired sword & sorcery cartoon, *Fire And Ice*.

BUCK BABE: JUDY LANDERS-NIEDENFUER

Usually cast as pretty damsels in distress, Judy Landers' IMDB is a treasure trove of the most popular genre shows of the '70s and '80s. Sometimes with her sister Audrey, sometimes alone, Landers landed on *The Love Boat, Charlie's Angels, Happy Days, ALF, The A-Team, Night Court* and *Knight Rider*, so it was no surprise that she was sent to The 25th Century.

Appearing in one of the crazier episodes, she plays Jerry Orbach's innocent girlfriend and is relieved when Buck and Twiki defeat her evil boyfriend. The actress was happy to do the show.

"*Buck Rogers in the 25th Century* was actually the first job I got without having to audition and I was thrilled when my agent called with the offer to guest star on the show! But I was thrilled mostly because I had a huge crush on Gil Gerard," she giggles sheepishly.

"I was always perfect in learning my lines and almost never forgot a line, but on this set? I became so distracted when Gil was around, I actually needed two takes! Gil was a gentleman, but so flirtatious, I loved every minute of it!"

"Buck's Duel to the Death"

Season 1, Episode 22

Original airdate: March 20, 1980
Written by Robert W. Gilmer
Directed by Bob Bender

Cast
Buck Rogers...Gil Gerard
Col. Wilma Deering...Erin Gray
Dr. Huer...Tim O'Connor
The Trebor...William Smith
Darius...Keith Andes
Vionne...Elizabeth Stack
Kelan...Fred Sadoff
Twiki...Felix Silla
Voice of Twiki...Mel Blanc
Dr. Albert...Robert Lussier
Greta...Stephanie Blackmore
Maya...Heidi Bohay
Karem...Francisco Lagueruela
Young Officer...Douglas R. Bruce

When Buck accepts an invitation to take Twiki to the planet Katar (He was told they would find him "enchanting"), he finds it's not a social visit at all, but a desperate 'Hail Mary' pass to get him to battle The Trebor on their behalf.

On Katar, The Trebor is a warlord abducting young women into his harem and hunting the best warriors for sport. He has the planet in a grip of fear. The Katarans want Buck because it was prophesized that The Trebor's reign would be toppled by The Roshan, a 500-year-old man.

The Trebor is also reported to have supernatural powers no ordinary man can overcome—beams literally shoot out of his hands and electrocute his enemies. Buck can't find any rational explanation for the ruler's supernatural abilities until he realizes The Trebor is a cyborg. Dr. Huer tells Buck that electricity has not been used in 400 years. Huer and Wilma realize that The Trebor has circuitry implanted under his skin and Twiki is able to help Buck thwart being killed by it.

Twiki actually saves the day by finding a way to short circuit The Trebor. With the little ambuquad backing him up, Buck topples The Trebor. To add insult to injury, Twiki calls him 'a turkey.' Once The Trebor is stopped and the girls freed, Buck says "To quote The Beatles, I'm getting a little help from my friends."

William Smith plays The Trebor and certainly looks physically imposing with his muscles and sounds tough with his wonderfully gravelly voice, but it's impossible not to notice that "Buck's Duel to the Death" is a warmed over remake of "Planet Of The Slave Girls." Smith even uses the same delivery as Jack Palance did as Kaleel and fires beams out of his hands just like Palance did. The set up, of a peaceful planet tricking Buck into their conflict to defeat an evil warlord would be used again in Season One's finale, "Flight Of The War Witch."

There's a hilarious sequence where ADR has been clumsily added where it looks like several people have been killed. To clear up that they are okay, we now hear "Get these stunned men to the med techs."

As with "Space Rockers" and "Olympiad," Buck has to address the entire planet to rise up against The Trebor without showing large crowds. This is accomplished by having Gil Gerard simply talk into a TV screen, which we are assured all of Katar is watching. Buck also wears a hilarious '70s futuristic outfit with a wide angels flight collar.

Buck freeing William Smith's slave girl harem gives the show a chance to display the slowest, most lingering ass shots of girls' tightly clad butts ever seen on the series. And that's saying something, as this show knew lingering ass shots. This is blatant even by the early '80s standards it was made in.

When the gorgeous Maya asks Twiki, "Do you always travel with Buck?" "He'd be lost without me," Twiki asserts. Buck tells his little robot pal, "Twiki, you and I are gonna have to have a little talk..."

It's quite humorous that Robert W. Gilmer would write a script about a godlike being who can kill any man and has a harem of beautiful women, who just happens to be named 'The Trebor,' as it's his first name, Robert, spelled backwards. That must have pleased another Robert, the episode's director, Bob Bender.

Buck Facts

- Director Bob Bender was *Buck Rogers'* First A.D.
- Buck describes Trebor as "a shogun," probably because of the then recent blockbuster Richard Chamberlin miniseries based on James Clavell's *Shogun.*
- Fred Sadoff was in the pilot *International Airport,* Gil Gerard's follow up to *Buck Rogers* and Gene Roddenberry's legendary pilot, *The Questor Tapes.*
- Stephanie Blackmore became a regular on *Dallas.*
- Elizabeth Stack is *Untouchables* star Robert Stack's daughter
- William Smith played Arnold Schwarzenegger's father in *Conan The Barbarian,* as well as the hero in the classic B movies *Invasion Of The Bee Girls* and *Grave Of The Vampire.*
- Keith Andes played an orange alien on the classic *Star Trek* episode "The Apple" and did the TV movie "The Ultimate Imposter" with Erin Gray.

"Flight Of The War Witch"

Season 1, Episodes 23 & 24
Original airdates March 27 & April 4, 1980
Directed by Larry Stewart
Written by Robert W. Gilmer & "Walter Mageean" (Pseudonym for producer Bruce Lansbury)
Story by David Chomsky

Cast
Buck Rogers...Gil Gerard
Wilma Deering...Erin Gray
Dr. Elias Huer...Tim O'Connor
Princess Ardala...Pamela Hensley
Chandar...Kelley Miles
Kodus...Donald Petrie
Spirot...Sid Haig
Kane...Michael Ansara
Zarina...Julie Newmar
Tora...Vera Miles
Council Leader...Sam Jaffe
Twiki...Felix Silla
Voice of Twiki...Mel Blanc
Pantherman...Tony Carroll
Goneril...Brent Davis

A messenger beacon arrives on Earth and fascinates Dr. Huer. It simply reads "PENDAR." Upon further investigation, Huer learns that it's from another universe (coming through a black hole), that would like to establish contact with Earth. Buck and Twiki volunteer to undertake the mission.

After a disorienting trip, they arrive in the other universe, where they find the peaceful planet Pendar is being ravaged by the cruel, merciless War Witch Zarina. She leads a warrior race, in her impe-

Julie Newmar and Sid Haig torture Donald Petrie.

rial battlecruiser, on behalf of The Planet Zaad. Although Pendar, like Earth, has a protective defense shield, Kodus, the brave young scientist who created the shield has been captured by The Zaads. Zarina tortures him with her brutal alien assistant Spirot and he's reluctantly giving her information.

She enjoys tormenting him on a daily basis, telling Spirot "Bring my dear Kodus to me...That is, if there's anything left of him." The grim Spirot answers, "Of course, Princess—more than enough." Kodus' fiancée Chandar grieves back on Pendar, when she notices his life signs are weakening from what Zarina is doing to him. Her mother Tora, thinking of Buck, asks her to have hope.

Zarina's forces have been making strikes against Pendar's command center. Buck learns that Pendar has also contacted The Draconians to help them battle the Zaads. Ardala likes the idea of ruling a new universe and tricks Wilma and Dr. Huer into joining her, as she takes her flagship, The Draconia, to the other universe.

Zarina is both ruthless and smart—an older, darker version of Ardala. When The Princess tries to negotiate with the wily War Witch, the more experienced woman only uses her information to capture Buck.

She's excited to have he-man Buck in her clutches, finding him even more attractive than the weak, compliant Kodus. Telling him that she finds him brave "but I can make you a great and powerful man," Buck rebuffs her with "A 'great and powerful man' doesn't wage war on peaceful people." Zarina sneers, "Captain Rogers, you shall not die. When all this is over, I shall make you my personal slave...*And you will wish you had died!*" "Oh no, Zarina," Buck says defiantly, "Then you'll wish that you had killed me." The confrontation echoes back to the pilot film, where Buck and Ardala had a similar discussion. He realizes the only way he can stop Zarina and her battlecruiser is by forming an alliance with Princess Ardala.

The two-part episode, the highest rated of the series, had an amazing guest cast—Sam Jaffe of *Gunga Din*, Vera Miles of Alfred Hitchcock's *Psycho* (whose real-life daughter Kelley plays Chandar, Kodus' fiancée and Tora's daughter), cool character actor Sid Haig (whose career was re-invigorated years later when he starred in Rob Zombie's *House Of 1,000 Corpses* as the twisted Captain Spaulding), Michael Ansara and Pamela Hensley, returning as sycophant Kane and the commanding Princess Ardala, but the real star here is Julie Newmar. Best known for being the slinky, seductive Catwoman on the 1966 Adam West *Batman* TV series, Newmar knew Zarina had to be bigger than life and she is.

In a cone-shaped headpiece, cape, stiletto heels and a perpetual scowl or sneer, Julie Newmar runs away with the episode—even though she readily admits that she was embarrassed by it (see her section)—but she's the best thing about it. She holds the screen in scenes with Ardala, even though Ardala is wearing spandex and a midriff! Almost 20 years older than Pamela Hensley (the script describes Zarina as being in her mid to late twenties), Newmar holds her own, with a sexy, full bodied performance.

As she concentrates on trying to destroy The Pendarans in a two-parter full of robots, space battles and classic character actors, while torturing and seducing Kodus—she is impossible to ignore, a female Darth Vader with a very active libido. As Kodus is being tormented by her, Zarina suddenly strokes his hair and purrs *"Don't be afraid, Kodus—your pain may be over...After I have eliminated The Pendarans, perhaps you will decide to stay here... with me?"*

Julie Newmar angry as Zarina the War Witch

She's like a lioness toying with her prey, an over the top, campy alien lioness maybe, but it works. When Buck, Ardala and Kodus escape, she tells Spirot, "The guards who allowed this to happen? Put them to death." "It's already been done," he re-assures her. On the Adam West *Batman* TV show, one of the playfully kinky aspects was the way Julie Newmar's Catwoman would target Batman's younger, naive sidekick Robin the Boy Wonder for capture as a way to stop Batman from coming after her. She would snare the teenage crime fighter (Burt Ward) and torment him until Batman could free him, which is the same strategy used here with Kodus and Buck.

Buck rescues Kodus, defeats the Zaad fighters and mocks Zarina until she pursues him to Pendar in her battlecruiser. As it enters Pendaran airspace, Twiki and Kodus close the shield, causing the ship to be torn asunder and explode, killing Zarina and all her minions. Kodus and Chandar prepare to marry, as Buck, Wilma, Huer, Twiki and The Draconians celebrate and then return to their own universe.

All the regulars get special business—Wilma has a nice scene tearfully saying goodbye to Buck, Dr. Huer gets to fight and "officially protest" being abducted to the new universe by Ardala, while Twiki helps Kodus close the defense shield in the climax. The little ambuquad even gets to trade insults with another robot, who he tells "Stop talkin' and start walkin'!"

Pamela Hensley also has a lot of fun in the show—it's one of the best ones to use Princess Ardala, showing different sides to her character. Dressed down by Zarina, who tells her "In your universe, they call you 'Princess'? *In mine, we call you a child—a spoiled, arrogant child. I have earned my position, Ardala—while you've been given yours!*," Ardala is emotionally vulnerable. When Buck tries to console her, she tell him brusquely "I'm fine" until she breaks down and admits "Buck? *I'm not fine!*" She has great scenes with Ansara, interrupting his motivational speech to his Draconian pilots with "Shut up Kane! Just give them my best wishes and send them on their way. I don't want them to be late for the war!"

The lack of continuity in *Buck Rogers in the 25th Century* shows here when we learn from Zarina that her chief enforcer, Spirot, is a transmute—able to de-stabilize any part of the composition of a person's body and cause great torment to whoever he touches. This is a completely different definition of "transmute" from "Cruise Ship To The Stars," where we see it's someone with a split personality that turns you into a brutal alter ego. Obviously, it's meant as a generic name for an alien that they re-apply as a sci-fi type word.

When Pendar Council Leader Sam Jaffe explains that they are light creatures—made completely of light and able to de-materialize at any time—it doesn't explain why he's wearing a hearing aid or why Kodus can't transform into light and escape Zarina, like the way the council does before Buck and Twiki.

The "Plot To Kill A City"'s costume for Varek shows up, but it's on a number of guys used to fill Zarina's ship and no mention is made by Buck of the resemblance. It's probably just costume recycling from a fantasy show on a tight budget, but one thing the original *Star Trek* did that helped it's cult following grow is continuity between characters, alien races and episodes. Despite the huge ratings for 'War Witch,' the ratings bounce was not going to help the series, because the show was going with a lower budget and a completely different concept for Season Two.

TIM O'CONNOR (Dr. Huer): "I really liked doing that two-parter with Julie Newmar! I remember seeing her in New York City, when I lived there. She was walking across 46th Street and 8th Avenue, about 11:00 in the morning. She lived down there—and taxi cabs would screech to a halt, cabbies would get out of the car and drop to their knees and bow to her because she would be in shorts—Julie literally stopped traffic! That happened every day in New York when Julie would walk by. I witnessed this and actually saw it happen about three times. I told her that when I saw her on 'War Witch'! She knew it, too, of course—she was there! I got a big kick out of her, she was absolutely stunning, I can still see her in New York City, in those shorts and high heels."

Buck Facts

- Last appearance of Princess Ardala, Kane, Dr, Huer, Dr. Theopolis or New Chicago. They will be missed.
- The Pendar beacon lands at Vasquez Rocks, the setting for classic *Star Trek* episodes (most notably Captain Kirk fighting the Gorn in "Arena"), but was used as another planet on previous *Buck Rogers* episodes.
- Donald Petrie became a successful director, helming the Sandra Bullock hit, *Miss Congeniality* and introducing Julia Roberts to the world in his film *Mystic Pizza*.
- The Zaad battlecruiser wasn't finished, so it was shot upside down to give it a futuristic look.

- We hear "Suspension," the *Buck Rogers* movie theme song with its full lyrics for the first time since the feature film.
- Costume Designer Al Lehman was nominated for an Emmy in Outstanding Costume Design for a Series for "Flight Of The War Witch," part II.
- Newmar changed one of Zarina's lines from "Bring that pretty boy Kodus to me" to "Bring that dear Kodus to me."

BUCK BABE: JULIE NEWMAR (Zarina The War Witch)

Tall, sleek and striking, Julie Newmar has an almost regal presence. She's a genuine pop culture icon, having appeared in such classics as *Seven Brides For Seven Brothers Li'l Abner*, TV series like *Batman*(where TV Guide named her first appearance as Catwoman one of TV's 100 Greatest Episodes), *The Twilight Zone, Get Smart, The Monkees,* and onscreen with stars like Kirk Douglas, Gregory Peck, Bing Crosby and Susan Hayward, Hollywood preferred putting the statuesque Swede in fantasy roles.

Besides playing Catwoman, the beautiful Newmar has been aliens, witches, robots, angels and devils. If you were going to meet an alien queen from another universe, you would be disappointed if it didn't look like Julie Newmar!

"I like playing larger than life characters because I am larger than life," she declares. "I'm good at it and I'm very physical." She put that to good use as Zarina The War Witch of the planet Zaad on the highest rated episodes of *Buck Rogers in the 25th Century with her* Season One finale, "The Flight Of The War Witch."

Her sexy alien queen stalks her warship and lords over her captive, innocent alien scientist Kodus (Donald Petrie), who she has strapped up for interrogation in her private quarters.

"That costume was very strange—I had a giant cone on my head," she laughs.

"UGH," she groans playfully, "I don't remember that part with love. With a costume like that, the character disappears inside all that fluffery. I'm not one for big, heavy costumes. I felt immobilized by the costume on that. I don't like it when the costume is bigger than I am!"

Julie Newmar playfully knits her eyebrows and theatrically strokes her chin. "I am in the two highest rated episodes of *Buck Rogers* and I can't understand why! I had no idea why it was popu-

Julie Newmar as The War Witch. Conquering the Universe for a car payment.

lar. I was also boggled as to why my *Star Trek* was popular either (in the classic episode, 'Friday's Child,' Newmar plays a young alien mother marked for death and defended by Captain Kirk, Mr. Spock and Dr. McCoy). To me, both shows were wearing heavy headpieces, saying a lot of lugubrious dialogue with a lot more lugubrious acting. I mean, what is a pregnant alien princess or an

Julie Newmar, photo by Pat Jankiewicz.

intergalactic War Witch supposed to sound like?

"I did enjoy working with Sid Haig on that and (Saturday morning kids show) *Jason Of Star Command*-we wear practically the same costumes that we wore on *Jason*, except on that show, he was my boss and on *Buck*, Sid was my assistant."

Zarina spends most of the two-parter tormenting Donald Petrie before he became a director. "I tortured him? Shame on me—if

I knew at the time that he was gonna become such a big director, I would have gone easier on him," she jokes.

"The role of Zarina The War Witch is what I call 'serious stuff'— you come in, say the weirdest stuff and you have to be very serious about it. It wasn't my cup of tea, I like to dance and be silly!

"My problem with science fiction is that it doesn't translate well to the human condition as I learned it at The Actors Studio," Newmar notes. "As an actor, you work from the inside out. In sci-fi, it seems that you just put on prosthetics, which is why most Hollywood aliens look and sound as if they're from The Valley. Although I didn't wear a rubber prosthetic face as Zarina, I probably should have!

"I think I got roles like The War Witch because the rules (for actresses) are once you're over 25, you have to play the villainess. They do that to women with certain looks—if they appear mean or dangerous. It's tough for women because we like to be liked."

"With Zarina, I feel 'less is more.' You don't need to be big. The less you see of me, the more you like me in it—like I said, Science fiction is difficult. I somehow feel people who portray aliens are play acting. Playing aliens is kind of a lark. I can't believe it, when I see people playing aliens, I just don't believe it.

"Maybe I should pay more attention to the story when I watch a sci fi thing, but I look at the costumes, the sets, the acting. When I watch something, I view it as a technician—is the scenery believable, is the acting coming from a place that could be someone 500 or 40,000 years from now in space? Those things trip me up. I watch them for that.

"While I'm not a big fan of playing big sci-fi characters like this, I am grateful to Zarina for one thing—she handled my car payment that month!"

25th Century Guest: SID HAIG, (Spirot)

Bald, bearded and intense looking, the likable Sid Haig has made a long career out of playing heavies. As Julie Newmar's henchman on "The Flight Of The War Witch," Haig helped her attempt to conquer the planet Pendar.

"*Buck Rogers in the 25th Century* was actually the second time I had worked with Julie Newmar," he says. "We had done a Filmation show called *Jason Of Star Command*, where I played her boss

Sid Haig, photo by Pat Jankiewicz.

and on *Buck Rogers*, she was mine!. Before she accepted the job, she wanted to know who she was working with. She came down, we met and because I was that much taller than her, the deal was on! She is a very tall woman, 6'4. I remember that Julie was awesome to work with, extremely professional, and the most alarmingly beautiful woman that I have ever seen in my life!

"We were on the set and she went over to the craft service table to get some coffee. As she walked across the soundstage, everything stopped. EVERYTHING—even the guys hammering, just to watch her elegantly walk across the soundstage and get her coffee. Once she sat down again, work resumed. I have been in a lot of cool films with extremely beautiful women, Pam Grier, Bridget Fonda, Ann Margaret, but Julie Newmar topped them all!

"My wardrobe on *Buck Rogers* is almost the exact same one I wore in *Jason Of Star Command*, with the exact same colors, red and black. I didn't really work with Gil Gerard and Erin Gray on that, because all my scenes were with Julie and the guy we were torturing. I did that episode, which was a two parter at the end of the season and I did the next season opener, 'Time of The Hawk,' like 'War Witch,' it was another two parter and it was the very next episode—even though you saw me and Julie blown up at the end of 'War Witch'!"

Donald Petrie, the 'guy he's torturing,' became a big director. "Strange shit happens like that in this industry all the time," Haig smiles. "Some guy there, just doing a job, turns out to be a director who does really great things!"

25th Century Guest: DONALD PETRIE (Kodus)

Before he became a film director and cast Julia Roberts in her first important film, *Mystic Pizza* as well as Sandra Bullock in *Ms. Congeniality*, Donald Petrie was an alien. Guest starring on *Buck Rogers in the 25th Century* 's first season finale, 'Flight Of The War Witch,' as Kodus, a dedicated young scientist from the peaceful planet Pendar. He's abducted by the cruel War Witch Zarina. She grabs him for his knowledge of Pendar's defenses, as a prelude to invasion by her race, The Zaads.

Zarina keeps Kodus strapped to a futuristic torture rack, where she alternately hurts and hits on him at her leisure. He's being held in her warship, which resembles a '70s disco. He spends the two-parter waking up dazed and sweaty in every scene, before Zarina torments him back to unconsciousness for some minor transgression.

The show is a gender flip of *Star Wars*, with the caped, helmet-wearing Julie Newmar as a buxom Darth Vader and Donald Petrie in the Princess Leia part. In the show, Newmar has her hulking assistant Spirot (Sid Haig) put him in agony by merely touching him with one finger.

"That's true," Petrie says with a smile. "Sid is a transmute, who can disrupt any part of my body by simply touching it with his finger, which is pretty painful...It was hysterical! Just hysterically em-

Zarina puts the moves on Donald Petrie.

barrassing with those costumes and robots. Even funnier: Gene LeBell was my stunt double, even though he's twice my size!

"I didn't really see myself as Princess Leia, but I was imprisoned and tortured by Sid and Julie, I loved it. It made me really appreciate and understand how tough it is for science fiction actors—they have to use their imaginations so much more than in the everyday TV world. If you are shooting a scene in a pizza parlor, you're actually there, but when you have your proton gun and it's supposed to do something, it's all in your imagination... even the sound isn't there!

"In my case, I had to really imagine it was truly painful when Sid put a finger on me. I had to writhe in agony and make it believable."

He has nothing but praise for his interstellar Catwoman. "Julie Newmar was a hoot, an absolute hoot. She was just a blast to spend time with, as I spent most of the episodes tied up in her room or in her spaceship's jail."

Gil Gerard notes that "Donald Petrie became a director, his father was also a director, too—Daniel Petrie. I remember he was a terrific guy and I was happy to see his career take off."

Erin Gray remembers Petrie with great fondness. "Donald was wonderful. The Petries are the best Hollywood family. They have hearts of gold and are very creative, while still being real people. His father, Daniel Petrie, even directed me in a film. (*Six Pack*, with Kenny Rogers). Don and I became friends after he did *Buck Rogers*, and he just did the show to get an understanding of what it's like to be an actor, to make him a more effective director. I wish more directors would do that."

"Erin was at the house for Christmas not too long ago," Petrie states. "You remember the old game, *Mastermind*? We played that on the *Buck Rogers* set, just her and me. I asked her for her phone number way back when—I guess it was wishful thinking at the time—and she gave it to me! I still have it, written by her on the top of the *Mastermind* box. I was able to show it to her 20 years later and we just laughed."

Of course, even noble alien scientists have their off days. "I remember, after we had been saved by Buck, I take my onscreen fiancée's hand (Kelley Miles) and we go running to the doors, which are supposed to 'shoosh' open *Star Trek* style. It's the happy ending where we are supposed to go into the hall joyfully because Zarina has been defeated. On take one, the doors didn't open and I slammed right into them!"

Despite this mishap, Petrie enjoyed working with a talented cast that included Sam Jaffe, Vera Miles and Twiki. "The hardest part of the whole two-parter was playing dramatic scenes with Twiki the robot," he laughs. "It was rough keeping a straight face with that robot, but Twiki and I just had to re-build that force field to stop Zarina!"

Ironically, the biggest impression of doing the show came from Princess Ardala. "My favorite scene in the show was with Pamela Hensley. What I remember most is that she was in the tightest leather pants I had ever seen on a woman, practically spandex, and I had to crawl behind her through a tunnel," Donald Petrie marvels. "You know, sometimes acting is a great job!"

Season 2

The TV season started late due to a devastating Screen Actors Guild Theatrical/Television strike in 1980, which lasted from July to October. Because of the hold up, production didn't resume filming until late in the fall. *Buck Rogers in the 25th Century* didn't premiere its second season until mid January 1981. That's not the only reason *Buck Rogers* Season Two is so jarring. Gone are all the familiar trappings of Season One—without any explanation at all.

There is no more New Chicago, Dr. Huer, Princess Ardala, Killer Kane, Dr. Theopolis, Earth Defense Directorate, the war with the Draconians—all are missing and unaccounted for. Even the white jumpsuits are gone. The tone is a bit more dour and while Wilma Deering still looks great, her IQ and personality have been drastically lowered.

Buck, Wilma and Twiki (now with a new stupid, childlike voice) are aboard The Searcher, a deep space vessel looking for the lost colonies of Earth, who left the planet after the nuclear holocaust. This is strange, as that was pretty much the plot to Glen Larson's other sci fi show, the original, heavily hyped *Battlestar Galactica*, which was cancelled after a single season. There are interesting new characters, like Hawk—a bird man whose character is a cross between Mr. Spock and an Apache Chief. He's interesting, mainly because Thom Christopher is an interesting actor doing the best with what he has to work with, and brings an alien element to the series. Usually, Buck met aliens, helped them and sometimes made out with one but never hung out with or befriended one before.

On the downside, losing Tim O'Connor's Huer meant his character was split into two—Admiral Asimov, the cranky top man on The Searcher and the doddering Dr. Goodfellow, who is meant to both deliver expository and provide what little comic relief there is. They both drag it out and don't bring half the charm or gravitas O'Connor invested Season One with. His eccentric, fatherly Dr. Huer is very missed. Even worse, Wilma seems to be a flight attendant, there to babysit Goodfellow. In some episodes, she

Twiki, Wilma in Dairy Queen outfit, Buck in Season Two.

essentially operates as Goodfellow's Seeing-eye dog, towing him through scenes. Wilma was dumbed down between seasons.

The tone is completely different from Season One—it's literally a different show, as John Mantley took over. It's a generic western in Outer Space. Instead of the jumpsuit uniforms, Buck wears windbreakers and Han Solo vests and is dialed way down from Season One. To add to the joyless season is Crichton, a prissy robot that resembles a giant bottle opener. Named after Michael Crichton (whose future wife, Eddie Benton/Anne Marie Martin,

Voyage of the Damned: Admiral Asimov, Crichton, Hawk and Buck rearrange the deck chairs in the doomed second season.

guest starred on Season One's "Twiki Is Missing"), he certainly isn't interesting like a Crichton character. There are some good episodes, but the concept seems drained.

This marked the transition of Season One's producer Bruce Lansbury to Season Two's John Mantley. Unlike Lansbury, Mantley had no history with genre shows and this season is rigidly recycled western plots. Not to say some episodes aren't interesting('The Satyr' being the best example), but the quirkiness of the characters was one of the strengths of the first season and they are stripped of that. Buck is stoic, Wilma is fretful, Hawk is...also stoic. You get the idea.

First season writer David Carren told *STARLOG Platinum* he felt the fall of the show came from handing it to new producer Mantley. "I think they gave it over to John Mantley and did (13) episodes. It was a strike year. I think they cut the budget and I don't think they ever got it going. They were trying to do *Star Trek*. It was similar to a *Buck Rogers* concept that Andrew J. Fenady had in development at one point—a ship crossing the galaxy, going on a mission. Glen Larson came in after Fenady, and his take was the out-of-time concept, which, by the way, was so dissimilar to the original *Buck Rogers*."

He show's budget had also been slashed. David Jones, art director of miniatures at Hartland, remembers "On the second season, I was visual FX supervisor with Peter Anderson and we only had half the budget for a week at a time! It got even tougher. "

"Time Of The Hawk"

Season 2, Episodes 25 & 26

Original Airdate Jan 15, 1981
Written by Norman Hudis
Directed by Vincent McEveety

Cast
Buck Rogers...Gil Gerard
Wilma Deering...Erin Gray
Hawk...Thom Christopher
Admiral Asimov...Jay Garner
Dr. Goodfellow... Wilfrid Hyde-White
Koori...BarBara Luna
Flagg...Lance Le Gault
Llamajuna...David Opatoshu
Pratt...Sid Haig
Captain...Kenneth O'Brien
Twiki...Felix Silla
Voice of Twiki...Bob Elyea
Communication-Probe Officer...Dennis Haysbert
Thromis...Lavelle Roby
High Judge...Michael Fox
Thordis...Andre Harvey

Searching for humans who have escaped post-nuclear holocaust Earth, Buck, Wilma and Twiki are now on The Searcher.
There, they serve with crusty, by-the-book Admiral Asimov, dotty
scientist Dr. Goodfellow and a snippy robot named Crichton in
exploring planets and looking for lost Earthlings.

On a world below, bird people Hawk and Koori go to join Koori's
parents and the rest of their tribe in a bucolic valley. Instead, they
find their entire species has been slaughtered. Finding a dead
man among the ruins, Hawk realizes what has happened—drunken

Koori dies in Hawk's arms in Time Of The Hawk.

humans hunted their people for sport and killed them all. They considered it 'bird hunting.'

"Humans—HUMANS," shouts Hawk. "I shall kill them all—all humans who cross my path!" Going up in his cool bird-shaped fighter ship, Hawk attacks any human craft in his section of Space.

True to his word, he creates so many problems in that sector, Buck is sent to deal with him. Seeing the totems on Hawk's planet, Dr. Goodfellow theorizes that Hawk and Koori's people originated on Earth. Their bird god resembles "Maqui Maqui, the great god of the bird people...Hawk's people must have come from Old Earth!" Goodfellow thinks The bird people are from Easter Island

Landing on Hawk's planet at Vasquez Rocks, which played Earth in the previous episode (and will play another planet in the next episode, "Journey To Oasis"), Buck begins hunting Hawk because it will simultaneously stop attacks on space lanes in this quadrant and fulfill The Searcher's goal of finding humans of Earthly origin.

Hawk's rage even unnerves his wife Koori, who begs him to end his futile quest of vengeance. "You are changing, Hawk, and it frightens me." Unmoved, he refuses to stop.

Hawk and Buck.

Buck captures Koori. When she calls him 'Human,' he tells her that she and Hawk are too, as they are descended from Earthlings. "'Human'? If he heard you call him that, he would tear you to pieces."

Koori gives a sonic cry that Hawk hears in his own craft and engages Buck in a dogfight between their starfighters. Koori takes off her seatbelt to attack Buck, while Hawk uses the talons of his landing gear to rend Buck's ship apart. Instead, it accidentally impales Koori.

Landing carefully, Buck and Hawk form an uneasy truce to get Koori to a healer. By the time they reach the old man in a cave who will try to heal her, Koori has died of her injuries. Buck and Hawk have a furious fight, before Buck falls off a high rock and is knocked unconscious.

Going down to finish Buck off, Hawk is stunned to find he's gone. Buck jumps Hawk and knocks him out, before Wilma picks them up. Hawk is put on trial before The Galactic Court where he offers no defense and is immediately sentenced to death.

Buck appeals this sentence, because "Hawk is NOT a man, he is not a human and that is the most crucial point in these entire proceedings." He feels "Hawk once had one of the greatest gifts that God could give—the gift of flight." Rogers feels kinship to Hawk, as each are respectively the last of their species, "as God is my judge."

Impressed, The Galactic Court agrees to spare Hawk, but only if he goes into Buck's custody and joins him on The Searcher. Moved that Buck eloquently saved his life, Hawk agrees to the terms.

BarBara Luna, who starred in one of the greatest episodes of the original *Star Trek*, "Mirror Mirror," makes a very sexy birdwoman. She appears as a ghost of Koori in "The Guardians" episode.

Thom Christopher is a great addition to the show. As Hawk, he is always interesting.

Unfortunately, he is the only one of the new cast members that works. Stuffy Admiral Asimov (Jay Garner) and nutty professor Dr. Goodfellow (Wilfrid Hyde-White) make you miss Tim O'Connor's warm, eccentric Elias Huer, who they are poor substitutes for. Having the elderly scientist double as comic relief is both annoying and boring.

The Searcher's crew is uniformly generic, anonymous day players and there is not one colorful crewman along the lines of Mr. Scott or "Bones" McCoy among them.

Worst of all is Crichton, a preening, whining robot who refuses to believe he was built by a flawed human like Dr. Goodfellow. An unbilled Jeff David provides his unremarkable voice. In several episodes, you can see a wire guiding one of his limbs. The computers are also early '80s variety, which makes The Searcher look even more cheesy.

None of the villains come anywhere close to Pamela Hensley's Princess Ardala.

The show's budget is showing in this season, with the iconic Mel Blanc replaced by Bob Elyea's cloying new voice as Twiki. Obviously, the loss of Mel Blanc is why Twiki is silent in this episode and the next one, "Journey To Oasis." There's also endless (but inexpensive) scenes of Buck and his friends sitting around talking.

Gil Gerard looks very Lee Majors this season, and seems as stoic and wooden. John Mantley, having produced *Gunsmoke* so long, plays *Buck Rogers* as a joyless, humorless space western.

Buck Rogers in the 25th Century Season Two's biggest tragedy is Wilma Deering. The producers of Season Two were bragging about how Erin Gray's Wilma was "softened" this season. Lobotomized is more like it. Gone is the commanding woman of action of the first season, now Wilma's IQ has been lowered to make her a compliant, squealing damsel-in-distress who can't open a door without Buck's manly help.

This is best epitomized in a scene where the new, dumbed-down Wilma is unable to even get out of a spider web without Buck's assistance, which she and the doddering Dr. Goodfellow stupidly blundered into.

ERIN GRAY: "Basically, we had a new producer for the second season. It was John Mantley, who had come from *Gunsmoke*. The two-part movie that started our second season , 'Time Of The Hawk,' was the exact same script of a *Gunsmoke* episode that he had written. He was quite proud of the fact that he had hired BarBara Luna to play the exact same part that she had played in the original *Gunsmoke* episode it was based on.

"I must say, most of us in the cast missed the tongue-in-cheek humor. We lost a lot of that in the second season. I personally missed Tim, he was my rock. In the first season, most of my scenes were with Tim, and I really enjoyed working with someone so professional. I was very new in the business and he really showed me the way. I could always count on him to anchor the scene for me and to help me get through it and understand it. Mantley had his own idea—he wanted to bring in more mythology, he wanted more mythological stories in the series, which we saw with the satyr and stuff like that. It definitely changed the feeling of the entire show.

"I know Gil personally wanted us off The Searcher and back on Earth, he didn't really like us in Outer Space. I missed losing some of my power as The Colonel, I found myself being a little bit more like 'Coffee, tea or me!' I felt like 'Dairy Queen in Space' that second season. My new outfit made me look like a waitress. I wanted Colonel Wilma to evolve into something more panther-like, with her sexual energy, be a little stronger as she found her womanly power. It never happened! "

GIL GERARD: "I knew we were dead when the first episode of the second season, 'Time Of The Hawk,' went on the air and we lost 10 ratings points within the first half hour. I just knew we were dead. We lost the audience that was interested in us in the first place. Instead of going up in ratings, which would have been a good sign, it went down and it was over. The series was dead."

SID HAIG (Pratt): "Lance Le Gault and I played these two guys who have hunted the bird people to extinction. Gil Gerard and I got along pretty well when I did 'Flight Of The War Witch,' so he brought me back for the next episode, which happened to be the season opener and another two-parter, 'Time Of The Hawk.' That meant, even though you saw me die as one character at the end of Season One, I returned as a brand new character in the very next show!"

Buck Facts

• Character actor Michael Fox (High Judge) is why the *Back To The Future* star of the same name had to add a middle initial.

Thom Christopher, Hawk!

Emmy winning character actor Thom Christopher was one of the only bright spots of the second season, with his noble, driven alien, Hawk.

First introduced, he goes on a misguided crusade to kill all humans, before Buck brings him to justice. Buck intervenes again to keep Hawk from getting the death penalty for his homicidal actions and brings the birdman along with him on The Searcher to have him help look for the lost colonies of Earth.

Thom Christopher is thoughtful about his avian anti hero. "From my very first read of the script and the Executive Producer John Mantley's discussions on the intent with the character, I felt that Hawk was the outsider, the loner, the different one. It is an element I tried to keep going for my period in the show.

"The costumes for both Koori and Hawk really made for the great statement for an 'alien quality.' BarBara Luna, by just her natural persona, makes a very exotic visual statement. I worked on body movement and much research on birds—In flight, attack, stillness on a tree limb...It all coalesced into an 'outer being.'"

When Koori is injured, "I actually carried BarBara Luna...and I can truthfully say that she is really light as feather," he laughs.

Hawk looking concerned.

He never ventured back into science fiction after *Buck Rogers.* "My daytime work on a contractual basis with *One Life To Live* and *Guiding Light* came after playing the Hawk...but my years in theatre did give me the creative imagination to take the larger than life character and give him a believability, or constantly hope I did."

His debut made a big impression on the actor. "The first episode 'Time of The Hawk' was so complete and exciting a creative and professional adventure," he enthuses. "This is all due to the Producers, John Mantley and John Stephens and the very wonderful director, Vincent McEveety.

"As I continue to relish in memory, it was that very special chemistry that takes place on a set between actor and director. It doesn't happen all the time. Vincent didn't just introduce a new perception of the show with this first episode of the new season with new additional characters and this other being, a half bird/half man...He presented' the character...and as our work went on, I knew he was doing this for me. Vincent was a really gifted director who I worked with often in the following years."

Another one of his *Buck Rogers* directors was Jack Arnold, maker of classic *films Creature From The Black Lagoon, Tarantula* and *It Came From Outer Space.*

Hawk and Koori.

"Of course I knew of the legend of Jack Arnold, so I felt a great deal of anticipation in working with him, which was exciting for me. He liked the character of Hawk and was very generous in his appreciation of my work. He was a professional to the very core and very, very funny. I feel it an honor to have him in my 'professional memory bank.'"

Thom Christopher's favorite episodes of the series are "'Time of the Hawk,' 'Hand Of The Goral' and 'Shgoratchx!.' "The writers were very good to my character in all of the shows that he appeared."

His saddest day on the show came "when I was in my dressing room and the Unit Manager called to tell me that the show would be going off the air—cancelled—I would need to return my dressing room key at my convenience."

The role "really was a fantasy journey for me," he says happily. "I felt like all the childhood dreams of science fiction had opened to me and I was in this 'land of dreams,' right in the middle of it and up till its cancellation!"

Appearing in a number of his episodes is Dennis Haysbert, who later became a breakout star in his own right on *24, Heat* with Robert DeNiro and *The Unit.*

"Would you believe I *do* remember Dennis Haysbert," Thom Christopher enthuses. "It was a sequence in the control room of The Searcher and he was in an officers' Blue Uniform, in several episodes, if I remember correctly."

Joining the cast for Season Two was a warm experience for him. "We had a good time together Gil, Erin, Felix and me...In particular, Gil and Erin were very generous in their support of this character in a feathered head piece, spandex and knee high boots and wearing a laser gun. It's like the old theatrical adage, 'don't do scenes with babies and children—they do tend to steal the scene.'"

The Hawk costume "was incredible in concept and design. Once I was confirmed for the role, the first item to be made was a multi layered polyurethane mold of my body from neck to lower stomach," he explains.

"This was done by the studio so beautifully. The curvature of my body was applied in several layers of the polyurethane, so when getting suited up for shooting, my beautiful dresser Jack Tack would just slip the front chest on me and it would fit my body sculpture very nicely. Jack would then have the back piece pre laced on one side and lace the second side while I held it in place.

"Jack was wonderful; patient and always there to make sure all was working correctly in this very comfortable costume. He would also help me into what was a full body black spandex jumpsuit before the breast plate went on. For me, a very dramatic and memorable costume. I have very fond memories of *Buck Rogers in the 25th Century.*"

BUCK BABE: Beautiful Bird Woman, BarBara Luna (Koori)

With her exotic appearance and sultry voice, BarBara Luna has played everything from Indian Maidens, slave girls, immigrants, criminals and even a Jungle Queen on *Fantasy Island*. "That was great," she states, "I actually got to sit on a throne and say the words 'Guards—seize them!'"

BarBara Luna as the birdlike Koori.

She has been particularly popular in sci fi, where she specialized in sexy aliens. Her Italian, Hungarian, Spanish, Portuguese and Filipino background gave her a unique look, her striking, almost otherworldly appearance made her a perfect extraterrestrial.

"I had played so many Indians, slaves and señoritas, I was genuinely surprised when I got a part of an alien with absolutely no ethnicity to it! In the sci-fi world, it doesn't matter what nationality you are... I mean, on *Buck Rogers in the 25th Century*, I was a bird!

"When you're a guest star on a TV show, you're simply trying to learn your lines and go on to the next show. Being a neurotic actress, I was so self-absorbed; I was really surprised when *Star Trek* fans knew who I was!"

Luna enchanted Captain Kirk in the classic *Star Trek* episode 'Mirror Mirror.' (Her character was so popular, she was even made into a doll). She matched wits with everyone from The Six Million Dollar Man to The Amazing Spider-Man ("He actually webs me at the end of the episode!"). On *Six Million*, she also predicts her *Buck Rogers* character when she describes herself and her friends as "bird people."

"*Buck Rogers in the 25th Century* was so much fun—I played this bird woman named Koori. When they asked me to play her as a recurring character, I actually turned it down because I was doing *A Chorus Line* at the time. Because of that, they hired another girl but two days later, they called me up again and said 'You have to play her!' I reminded them I couldn't do it regularly and the producer, John Mantley, said 'That's okay—we decided to kill you!' They killed me off, but they still managed to bring me back in a later episode (The Guardians)."

On *Buck Rogers*, her death means the extinction of her species, which her mate Hawk blames on all humans in general and Buck in particular, in the second season opener, "Time Of The Hawk."

"Koori was a beautiful character to portray, very well written. Also, wonderful to look at," BarBara Luna opines. "Producer John Mantley was very involved in Koori's look—he worked closely with make-up artist Werner Keppler (who also designed Lou Ferrigno's Hulk and the aliens in *V*). Together, they designed my feathered lashes, eyebrows and cap..."

BarBara Luna, photo by Pat Jankiewicz.

She felt her costume was for the birds. "At that time, I wished they had cut holes in the rubber cap on which the feathers were glued so that I could hear better! I don't know how Thom did it, wearing that cap for 11 episodes!"

Reportedly, Buck producer John Mantley was proud that "Time of The Hawk" was a reworked *Gunsmoke* episode ("He Learned About Women," where she played a Native American maiden named Chavela) which also starred BarBara Luna, and merely switched "Indian" for "Alien."

Did the actress realize she was remaking one of her past works? "I don't think I did," she giggles. "In either role, I just couldn't escape those Mexican Indian feathers! On my *Gunsmoke*, my *Star Trek*, my *Buck Rogers* episodes—I was a captive in all of 'em, Captive Captive Captive...I just loved it!"

Working with Thom Christopher as Hawk "was very enjoyable, as we both come from a shared theatre and soap opera experience, which helps when it comes to one's work system. Generally in theatre, actors prefer to rehearse, while most film actors I've worked with like saving it for camera. They prefer spontaneity, like when I worked with Frank Sinatra, his choice was NO rehearsals."

To play an alien bird, "I tried to give her birdlike mannerisms—like when I tilted my head like a bird when I played her, and also made a bird move whenever I called for Hawk, my husband," Luna explains. "The make-up wasn't up to today's modern *Star Trek* standards—my headpiece was just a rubber bathing cap with feathers glued on it!

"As I said, they never cut out the ears, so I couldn't hear anything. The producer, John Mantley, designed Koori's feathered eyelashes and eyebrows, which moulted all over the soundstage. I think they wanted me because I only weighed 100 pounds and Thom Christopher, who played Hawk, my birdman husband, had to carry me.

"Poor Thom had to carry Koori as she's dying and he tripped! In the show, you actually see us fall down—that was real! Thom got tired, but they didn't even stop the camera, so we just kept going. It was a long shot of him carrying me across this alien world and I bit my lip, because if I laughed they would have to do that long shot again, and they would have killed me for laughing and ruining it! In television, you never stop until they yell 'cut.'"

Doing a long shot of Hawk carrying his leading lady "almost killed Thom...He was almost hyperventilating in that suit out on location in that oppressive heat! Having to carry me while wearing his heavy Hawk costume almost finished him."

"Time Of The Hawk" director Vince McEveety "was one of my all time favorite directors," she states. "Prior to *Buck Rogers*, he directed me in a film with Jimmy Stewart called *Firecreek*."(which John Mantley produced.)

Koori came back as a ghost on a later *Buck Rogers* episode. "I return and then go up in smoke...It's never fun going up in smoke," she says, of her character's conclusion. "She wasn't really a ghost though, was she? Koori was coming out of Pandora's box, so to speak...I thought she was more like a genie or something out of Hawk's imagination on that episode."

"Journey To Oasis"

Season 2, Episodes 27 & 28

Original Airdate Jan 22, 1981
Written by Robert Mitchell & Esther Mitchell
Directed by Daniel Haller

Cast
Buck Rogers...Gil Gerard
Wilma Deering...Erin Gray
Hawk...Thom Christopher
Admiral Asimov...Jay Garner
Dr. Goodfellow... Wilfrid Hyde-White
Ambassador Duvoe...Mark Lenard
Admiral Zite...Len Birman
Lt. Devlin...Paul Carr
Zykarian Jr...Donn Whyte
Odee-x...Felix Silla
Twiki...Felix Silla
Voice of Twiki...Bob Elyea
Rolla...Michael Stroka
Technician...Alex Hyde-White

To prevent a war between Earth and planet Zykaria. Their lead negotiator, Zykarian Ambassador Duvoe, is personally shuttled by Buck to the city of Oasis, on the barren planet R-4 to hopefully draw up a truce.

Buck is shocked to find Duvoe is an old flame of Wilma's. The shuttle crash lands and Zykaria threatens war if their ambassador is not returned. Trudging on to Oasis to prevent an interplanetary incident, the party evades mutants and winds up with an extremely annoying blue skinned gnome (Played by Twiki's Felix Silla!)with eye beams and other powers. He has a whiny voice and calls himself Odee X. The little creature teases and taunts Hawk, calling him "Birdman" and "overgrown chicken," before the two bond.

They are caught between a force field and winds so strong, they can rip the flesh off a man's body. Buck realizes there's even more danger when they find skulls mounted on pikes. Wilma and Duvoe rekindle their romance as Buck learns Duvoe's secret—his people can unscrew and remove their heads, which he is understandably nervous about sharing with Wilma. The ambassador thanks Buck for not telling Wilma of his unique ability.

When they are finally attacked by the man-beasts, Duvoe uses his ability to frighten them into bowing, believing he is a god. Wilma is stunned and horrified to learn his secret. When Buck successfully gets them to Oasis, she and Duvoe part as friends.

"Journey To Oasis" is a strange two-parter. With a wise gnome, a rough planet and revelations in a cave, it seems to be the show's answer to *The Empire Strikes Back*, with some of classic *Star Trek*'s 'Journey To Babel' thrown in for good measure. Ironically, that also featured guest star Mark Lenard in a major role.

Silla did double duty on the 'Journey To Oasis,' when he played both Twiki and the blue-skinned gnome, Odee-x. Unfortunately, the awful Odee-x is no Yoda, although one must give Felix Silla credit for changing his mannerisms so Odee x doesn't resemble Twiki in a different mask. It's also cute when Wilma kisses the little blue man, to thank him for his help.

The love interest between Duvoe and Wilma seems to be an extended penis metaphor, with the removable head creating a wedge between them. It's discussed metaphorically, as he worries (literally) what Wilma will think of his head! He begs Buck not to let her know. When she finally sees it and freaks out, Duvoe gets depressed. "I hope you understand it was only the shock, it wasn't a judgment," Wilma says consolingly to Duvoe.

ERIN GRAY: "I think that my line 'Not a judgment' was prevalent by the powers behind the scenes to get away with whatever we could get away with. My intention on *Buck Rogers* was no matter how unreal, silly or farfetched the situation was, be it my Starfighter or flip open phone, my intent was to treat it as real as I possibly could. It's not up to me to comment in the episode on the absurdity of it. The man I loved from my past has returned and I find he can unscrew his head and take it off his body! When I tell him it's not a judgment, it could have been a variation on other things, like race or creed, like 'I didn't know you were black,' so I tried to be who I am and play it honest and caring. A lot of my humor comes out of being genuine. The comedy means I'm the straight person for sure.

"As for the scene where I bang into the invisible wall, Gil preferred I be the one to bump into the force field and feel the invisible wall in the cave. There's something to a scene like that. I was fearless and stupid, which I think you have to be to be an actor. Sometimes you just can't over think it. You just have to leap off the cliff, you know? That fearlessness has gotten me through life. Gil had a tendency to not want to participate in those mime like scenes anyway, so who can blame him? I'm the one flailing my arms shouting, 'there's an invisible wall!'

FELIX SILLA (Twiki/Odee-x): "They asked me if I could play another character besides Twiki in this two parter, I said 'No problem' and I did it. I was Twiki and this little blue alien for double pay and double credit, so it was fun. "

PAUL CARR (Lt. Devlin) "That one was hilarious, that whole show with Mark Lenard as the alien who can unscrew his head like a light bulb—that was so damn funny!"

Buck Facts

- Mark Lenard was best known as Mr. Spock's father, Sarek, on *Star Trek*.
- Daniel Haller, director of the pilot, returns!

"The Guardians"

Season 2, Episode 29

Original Airdate Jan 29, 1981
Written by Paul Schneider & Margaret Schneider
Directed by Jack Arnold

Cast
Buck Rogers...Gil Gerard
Wilma Deering...Erin Gray
Hawk...Thom Christopher
Admiral Asimov....Jay Garner
Dr. Goodfellow... Wilfrid Hyde-White
The Guardian...Harry Townes
Buck's Mother...Rosemary De Camp
Lt. Devlin...Paul Carr
Koori...BarBara Luna
Twiki...Felix Silla
Voice of Twiki...Bob Elyea
Boy...Shawn Stevens
Helmsman...Dennis Haysbert
1st Guardian...Vic Perrin
Mailman...Howard Culver

Trapped in a freak windstorm, Buck and Hawk take shelter on
an uncharted planet. They find a dying old man who insists he
knows Buck and gives him a glowing jade box, which is supposed
to go to "The next Guardian." Once on The Searcher, the box
causes all sorts of problems for the crew whenever they touch it.

When Lt. Devlin brushes against it, he sees his lover dead—This
comes at a bad time for Devlin, who is about to get married. Buck
promises him everything will be all right for The Searcher and that
he'll "dance at your wedding."

Disturbing visions, tragic events and other nightmares continue
to befall them. Admiral Asimov sees the crew starving to death,

Buck and Hawk lead a blinded Wilma to the Guardians.

in another vision, Wilma and Lt. Devlin die. Wilma sees herself blinded—which comes to pass.

Buck has a flashback to the 20th Century, where he wakes up from a daydream in a chair to have lunch with his Mom. He tells his Mother he dreamed of being in the 25th Century, 'meeting interesting people."

His Mother frets about a recent Space Shuttle crash killing it's pilot. Buck assures her "The fuel problem that caused it had been long since corrected." He tells his Mom he's taking The Ranger III Mission because he wants to be the top of the heap at NASA.

We also see the heating system on Ranger III fail, as the shuttle ices up, freezing Buck into suspended animation. "My Mother was warning me of the sin of pride," Buck realizes.

Touching the box causes Hawk to see his dead wife Koori again. Her ghostly face appears from the box. "A moment again with you Hawk," Koori cries in happiness to the surprised Hawk, "Even a moment." She says that they are of two worlds "and we are now hurting each other."

When Devlin tries to destroy the box, Wilma punches him, unleashing a blinding flash from the box that causes the prophecy to come true—she's blinded. Asimov flushes it into Space, only to have it re-appear sitting in his command chair.

Buck, Wilma and Hawk go down to the planet to search for a cure and meet with The Guardian. It's an ancient city that Wilma feels "is still beautiful." This is amusing, as she's supposed to be blind at the time. The three befriend a lame shepherd boy. Unfortunately, the boy falls into a fissure that erupts during a sudden planet quake.

The Old Man, 'The Guardian' reappears to thank Buck for helping them find the tenth Guardian. The Shepherd boy returns, no longer lame, and cures Wilma of her blindness before he takes his place as the tenth Guardian.

An entertaining second season episode, "The Guardians" gives the cast a chance to stretch. Gil Gerard is quite good in the scenes with his Mother, as is Thom Christopher playing Hawk as a noble, proud and heartbroken alien. Dennis Haysbert shows up again as The Searcher's Helmsman, uttering the line, "My screen is starting to show some crazy readouts!"

Guest Harry Townes was an ordained Episcopal priest, which he clearly uses to give The Guardian a serene, almost angelic personality.

Episode Highlight: The welcome return of Koori (BarBara Luna) and a 20th Century flashback where we met Buck's Mom.

BarBara LUNA(Koori): "It was fun to come back, if only for a moment!"

Paul Carr, photo by Pat Jankiewicz.

DAVID JONES (FX Man): "Usually we worked on the space ships. For this episode, there was a green jade ark that glowed on the show—we built that. As a matter of fact, as soon as I finished spray painting it, they took it right over to the lot to shoot it. That's where it got Erin's print from her dress on it because it was still wet! I haven't seen it since it was first on the air."

ERIN GRAY: "My stunt double Donna Keegan did a lot of my blind Wilma scenes, on location on the rocks of the planet. We had the same jaw line, she always looked great, so I was happy with it."

PAUL CARR (Lt Devlin): "I was on The Searcher in the show's second season. What I loved about being on *Buck Rogers In The 25th Century* was Erin Gray. Erin was a sweetheart—she played Wilma Deering and it was always good to see her. She was trapped in a bad marriage at the time, but she was always fun to be around. I had fun on that show, but it was highly technical. You found your-self talking to a light stand that was standing in for a monster. I was a recurring character— I even mention I have a fiancée in one episode, but you never see her! It was just another job...A job with Erin, but still just a job!"

Buck facts

- Paul Carr (Lt Devlin) was the first Red Shirt to die on *Star Trek* under Captain Kirk's command in "Where No Man Has Gone Before."
- Buck's Mother fretting about the fuel causing a shuttle crash is prophetic. This episode was made in 1981. In 1986, The Space Shuttle Challenger exploded due to faulty O rings and fuel. Buck's Shuttle is supposed to launch in 1987.
- The first 20th Century flashback for Buck since Season One's "A Dream Of Jennifer."
- Character actress Rosemary De Camp had the perfect look to play Buck's Mom, she specialized in beloved maternal figures— she was Marlo Thomas' Mother on *That Girl*, Claude Akins' Mom on *The Misadventures Of Sheriff Lobo*, as well as Grandmother to *The Partridge Family*.
- The episode seems loosely based on Ray Bradbury's short story, "Mars Is Heaven," where an astronaut is tricked into believing he's back in his hometown.
- Guest Harry Townes played an older man who was also a Hulk in "The First," an *Incredible Hulk* two-parter the same year he did Buck.

- Buck's jokey promise to dance at Lt. Devlin's wedding was a line stolen from that year's bestselling novel, *Red Dragon* by Thomas Harris.

"The Mark Of The Saurian"

Season 2, Episode 30

Original Airdate Feb 5, 1981
Written by Francis Moss
Directed by Barry Crane

Cast
Buck Rogers...Gil Gerard
Wilma Deering...Erin Gray
Hawk...Thom Christopher
Admiral Asimov...Jay Garner
Dr. Goodfellow... Wilfrid Hyde-White
Ambassador Cabot...Linden Chiles
Dr. Moray...Vernon Weddle
Nurse Paulton...Kim Hamilton
 Lt. Devlin...Paul Carr
Twiki...Felix Silla
Voice of Twiki...Bob Elyea
Senior Officer...Stacy Keach Sr.
Major Elif...Barry Cahill
Technician...Alex Hyde-White
Wing Man...Allan Hunt
Captain...Frank Parker

Sick in bed with Cignus Fever, Buck is told by Nurse Paulton, "people who go traipsing around on unexplored planets without a respirator are asking for an infection!" Being mechanical, Twiki notes that "Buck is malfunctioning."

A sweaty, disoriented Buck sees Ambassador Cabot and his party with a strange green aura around them, sometimes seeing them with reptilian faces. Cabot is on the ship to broker peace with The Saurians, a fierce race of lizard people. The real Cabot and his team have been killed and replaced with a gang

Mark Of The Saurian *Lizard Man headshot.*

of evil Saurians who, thanks to an 'image screen,' appear as exact doubles. When Buck repeatedly tries to warn his friends and colleagues of the impending danger, no one believes him, even Hawk and Wilma find his story dubious and think he's hallucinating.

What Buck sees—but no one else does—is that they are Saurians in disguise. They are going to secretly take over The Delta Quadrant and kill anyone who gets in their way. Being from the 20th Century, Buck has a slightly different body chemistry, which allows him to see them as they truly are. The Saurian Cabot plans to assassinate Buck, while he keeps trying to prove the ambassador and his men are not human.

"How much more proof do you need to see we are who we say we are," sneers Cabot. "I'm just crazy enough to know the difference between my enemies and my friends," replies Buck.

When no one believes him, Buck cleverly thwarts the Saurians by adjusting the thermostat. The change in temperature throws the reptile men into a torpor, revealing them in their real scaly forms for all to see. The evil alien lizard men are quickly taken into custody.

"They're reptiles," Buck notes. "Therefore, they're cold-blooded. They go into hibernation once the temperature goes below Scale 3."

A cool episode, one of the very best of the second season, "Mark Of The Saurian" introduces a new alien race and puts Buck into a clever predicament. Buck's solution is smart and Gerard seems to enjoy playing the usually stoic and confident Buck Rogers dazed and disoriented. It's also fun to see Buck, too sick for a fight or space battle, outsmart his enemies simply by adjusting the thermostat.

Usually, aliens that Buck Rogers and Wilma Deering face are human, like The Draconians, or have mild differences, like Hawk's race. Having him face scaly lizard men like something out of an old Buster Crabbe Flash Gordon serial is a lot of fun.

The idea of aliens in disguise waging a secret war on humans was explored to better and bigger effect in Kenneth Johnson's allegorical sci-fi miniseries *V*, one of NBC's biggest hits of the 1980s and in John Carpenter's *They Live*, where a homeless man realizes that the rich are actually aliens.

Twiki says "Top O' The Morning" in a cloying childlike voice. You immediately miss Mel Blanc's rumbling "BeetyBeetyBeety." By stripping him of his personality, Twiki loses a lot of his charm.

Episode Highlight: Check out that circular gadget on the ailing Buck's bedside. Clearly some high tech futuristic medical device

Mark Of The Saurian *Lizard.*

to help him feel better, right? Actually it's a toy from 1980—an early electronic game called '*Computer Perfection,*' a knock off on the then-popular game, *Simon!*

Buck Facts

- We finally get to see what 25th century pajamas look like!
- Stacy Keach's father and Wilfrid Hyde-White's son, Alex, appear in this episode.
- Alex Hyde White was the first man to play Reed Richards in live action, with Roger Corman's hilariously bad *Fantastic Four.*

FRANCIS MOSS (Writer, 'Mark Of The Saurian,' in Starlog Magazine): "(The episode) was kind of Hitchcockian, where one guy, all by himself, is aware of something and nobody else is. The producers liked it a lot and they were willing to go ahead when I announced this was going to be my first TV writing assignment. It was fun and they were very cooperative. I had a good time working with them. I had ideas about how I saw it and (the producers) threw in their ideas and we put together a beginning, middle and end. The premise was simply this: Buck is sick with something and sees these people as aliens, while everyone else sees them as humans. Buck can't get anyone to believe him.

"The fever played to the fact that Buck is from five centuries earlier and he would be susceptible to viruses that people in the 25th Century wouldn't be. They've built up genetic immunities to these diseases. That gave me a hook to get into the story. Most of the other stories in that season and even the previous season dealt with Buck Rogers as a guy in the show, the hero. I can't remember any other show that capitalized on his 20th Century background.

"(*Buck Rogers'* makeup man John Stephens) complained to me every once in a while about the damn lizard men that I had come up with in the story, and what a hard time they were having in Special FX with these guys. I thought they did a great job. The look of the aliens was close enough to what I envisioned. I had a vision of real aliens and obviously, these were actors in alien masks, but what are you going to do in television? They were on a limited budget. I described the image screen effect as kind of a shimmering haze when they hit the controllers on their wrists and that's what I got."

"The Golden Man"

Season 2, Episode 31
Original Airdate Feb 19, 1981
Written by Calvin Clements &
Stephen McPherson
Directed by Vincent McEveety

Cast
Buck Rogers...Gil Gerard
Wilma Deering...Erin Gray
Hawk...Thom Christopher
Admiral Asimov...Jay Garner
Dr. Goodfellow... Wilfrid Hyde-White
Velis...David Hollander
Mr. Graf...Anthony James
Loran...Bruce M. Fischer
Relcos...Russell Wiggins
Lt. Devlin...Paul Carr
Twiki...Felix Silla
Voice of Twiki...Bob Elyea
Hag...Diana Chesney
Onlooker #1...Richard Wright
Onlooker #2...Arthur Eisner
Marcos...Roger Rose
Jailer...Michael Masters
Alphie...Bob Elyea

When The Searcher finds a life pod in an asteroid field contain-
ing a golden-skinned boy, they bring him aboard and discover that
he can alter properties of anything he touches to change it to gold.
The golden boy, Velis, is worried for his traveling companion,
Relcos, a simple-minded golden man, whose own life pod has

crashed on another asteroid, Iris 7. This is a problem, as Iris 7 is a penal colony, where all the local criminals have been exiled.

The greedy, medieval locals have discovered Relcos is there and are hunting him with pitchforks. One greedy villager is even painting himself gold to look like The Golden Man and collect any potential reward

As Buck and Velis search for him, they find Relcos has been caught and is being hauled through the streets of Iris 7 (actually, the European village street and Court of Miracles, from which villagers would chase all the monsters, werewolves and vampires in the old *Frankenstein* and *Dracula* movies from the '30s and '40s.)

Scared, Relcos turns their weapons into jade, silver and gold. Temporarily saved by Hawk, he and Relcos find themselves once again hunted. The leader of the colony, Mr. Graf, wants to use Relcos to get himself off-planet.

Naturally, Buck saves Relcos and returns him to Velis. He and Hawk are stunned to learn that Relcos is only five years old and that young Velis is his father! The golden boy is the adult, the gold man his child. "Our lifecycles are reversed," Velis explains.

With this episode, *Buck Rogers in the 25th Century* Season 2 goes full Irwin Allen. In the 1960s, there was cerebral, smart sci fi like Gene Roddenberry's *Star Trek*, which struggled for ratings in three seasons. On the other end of the spectrum was Irwin Allen's dopey but popular space shows, *Lost In Space, Land of The Giants, Voyage To The Bottom Of The Sea* and *Time Tunnel*. While *Star Trek* would have an occasional green girl, Irwin Allen's shows always had aliens in glittery gold or silver face paint, because, well, that's how aliens were supposed to look in Irwin Allen shows.

"The Golden Man" is totally in the Irwin Allen vein, right down to the silly 'shock' ending. There is still a lot to like in this episode, including the tropes of villagers chasing a 'monster' on the Universal backlot. It's also nice to see Anthony James return, although his character, Mr. Graf, is a lot less interesting than Varek in season One's superior 'Plot To Kill A City.'

ANTHONY JAMES (Mr. Graf): "I was a guy who wants to capture the golden man to use his power to turn anything into gold and silver. While the character wasn't as deep as Varek, the challenge for me was always to make each villain as different as the one I had played before. Whether it was a cowboy, gangster or alien, I tried to bring some kind of personality to it. Most of the bad guys are one-dimensional. They're bad, do bad things and say bad things. They have no other qualities to them. The challenge for me is to find out how I can bring other personality traits to the role without diminishing what the director wanted for the role, which is a bad guy. Especially in television, where everything goes so fast, they don't want anyone to be more than one dimensional.

"Heroes can have other qualities, they're smart, they're good, they try the best they can, but they have no other qualities to them. As a villain, I always tried to be unpredictable! For 'The Golden Man' episode, I was a different kind of villain that wasn't repeating any of the other villains I had done, a greedy guy. Thom Christopher, one of the regulars who played the bird man(Hawk), was a great actor and great guy—they had added him since the last time I was on the show. Having done three episodes, I found the regulars on *Buck Rogers in the 25th Century* to be really nice."

Buck Facts

- Buck mentions Mardi Gras for the first time since Season One's "A Dream Of Jennifer."
- Bob Elyea (Alphie) makes an on camera appearance as the inmate painting himself gold. Mercifully, this also marks his last time voicing Twiki.
- David Hollander (Velis, the golden boy) now does music for film, but he will always be remembered as the Young Boy With Coffee in the classic comedy *Airplane.*
- Russell Wiggins (Relcos) was a frequent guest on *Adam-12.*
- Wilma looks great this episode, with her hair pulled back.
- Roger Rose (Marcos) is an incredibly busy voiceover actor, who provided many voices for the popular game, *Batman: Arkham Asylum.*
- Co-writer Calvin Clements was the Supervising Producer of Season 2.
- Buck sneaking in to a land of criminals to save an innocent was the same plot to that year's John Carpenter movie, *Escape From New York.*

"The Crystals"

Season 2, Episode 32
Original airdate: March 5, 1981
Written by Robert Mitchell & Esther Mitchell
Directed by John Patterson

Cast
Buck Rogers...Gil Gerard
Wilma Deering...Erin Gray
Hawk...Thom Christopher
Admiral Asimov...Jay Garner
Dr. Goodfellow... Wilfrid Hyde-White
Laura...Amanda Wyss
Twiki...Felix Silla
Voice of Twiki...Mel Blanc
Chief Petty Officer Hall...Sandy-Alexander Champion
Lt. Martin...Alex Hyde-White
Kovick...James Parkes
Johnson...Gary Bolen
Petrie...Leigh C. Kim
Mummy Monster...Hubie Kearns, JR.

On the mist-shrouded planet Phibocetes, Buck, Wilma, Hawk and their landing party encounter Laura, a beautiful girl with am-nesia and a dangerous Mummy pursuing her, as they search for fuel crystals to power the ship. Wilma and Hawk return to The Searcher while Rogers stays on the planet. Buck's never been the kind of guy to leave a beautiful blonde in a toga alone to fend for herself against a Mummy. "Be aware, Buck," is Hawk's utterly use-less advice.

Laura goes into a trance before the Mummy attacks, Wilma and Hawk warn Buck that Laura has the same blood type as the Mummy. Wilma is essentially in "Lt Uhura" mode this episode,

Amanda Wyss has mummy trouble in The Crystals.

feeding Buck info from the ship whenever he needs it.

Twiki and Crichton are apparently being set up to have an antagonistic R2D2/C-3PO relationship. The problem is Crichton is an unfunny, useless one-joke prop and the show proved it didn't need this type of character when it ditched Dr. Theopolis. Dr. Goodfellow tells Twiki they need him to keep Crichton in line.

Twiki then says that "Crichton is far from an obedient son," which is strange, as Twiki being Crichton's father had never been established. From this point, everyone starts treating Twiki as if he were Crichton's father, another example of Season Two's sloppy disregard of the show's continuity.

Meanwhile, on the planet of horror, Buck realizes that the Mummy is part of Laura's race and their evolutionary process, before the mummy evolves into a generically handsome contract actor and Buck theorizes they are the Adam and Eve of this new world. Our hero never wonders why part of the aliens' birthing process is to wrap up in fleshy covering and chase people like they're in an old *Scooby Doo* cartoon.

'The Crystals' could just as easily have been called 'Buck Meets The Mummy,' but since he already met a Space Vampire in Season

One, a Space mummy is entirely appropriate. Buck would do a Space werewolf episode next, where he transforms into a hairy man beast— except he's changed into a satyr, not a wolf.

The Mummy on display here is very much an old school *Lost In Space* growling and lurching man-in-a-suit monster. This is appropriate, as this episode was written by people who wrote many of Irwin Allen's *Land Of The Giants* TV series. A space mummy is typical of the cockamamie plots that Irwin Allen shows specialized in.

Using a mummy may have been inspired by

Twiki and Crichton make an unlikely father and son.

The Awakening, a painfully dull Charlton Heston/Susannah York "Our daughter is being taken over by a Mummy" melodrama that flopped six months before this episode aired.

Episode Highlight: MEL BLANC RETURNS AS TWIKI! This marks the first 'Beety! Beety! Beety!" this season. The character lost its acerbic charm without him.

Buck Facts

- Amanda Wyss went on to co-star with Johnny Depp as one of the terrified teens in the original *A Nightmare On Elm Street*— She's also the very first person ever killed onscreen by Freddy Krueger!
- Director John Patterson went on to do 13 episodes of *The Sopranos*.
- Wilma reveals that she took nursing courses.

BUCK BABE: AMANDA WYSS "Laura"

"Doing *Buck Rogers in the 25th Century* was a lot of fun—in the episode, Gil Gerard and I are being chased around a futuristic set on the Universal Studios backlot by a mummy. It was one of my very first gigs, so I found it all very exciting and new...I really liked that little dress I wear in it! Gil was nice and I had a lot of fun doing it."

"The Satyr"

Season 2, Episode 33

Original Airdate March 12, 1981
Written By Paul Schneider & Margaret Schneider
Directed by Victor French

Cast
Buck Rogers...Gil Gerard
Wilma Deering...Erin Gray
Hawk...Thom Christopher
Admiral Asimov...Jay Garner
Dr. Goodfellow... Wilfrid Hyde-White
Cyra Samos ...Anne E. Curry ...
Major Jason Samos/Pangor...Dave Cass
Twiki...Felix Silla
Voice of Twiki...Mel Blanc
Delph...Bobby P. Lane
Midshipman...Dennis Freeman

On the planet Arcadus, Buck and Twiki befriend a little boy, Delph, and his terrified mother, Cyra. Buck finds they are actually facing a greater danger. The woman and child are being raided daily by a brutal creature named Pangor, a Satyr, half-man/half-goat, who rides what appears to be a hellish mechanical steed. Buck cannot convince Cyra and Delph to leave the planet and when the whip wielding Satyr attacks Buck's ship, he realizes he has to fight the creature. After a short but brutal skirmish, The Satyr seemingly drowns, but not before it's bitten Buck.

This upsets Cyra, who reveals that the creature was actually her husband, Major Jason Samos with the other men who arrived to colonize Arcadus, but they were transformed into these monsters by a virus. That's why they wouldn't leave with Buck.

Buck goes full Satyr.

Worse, two other Satyrs move in, hoping to take over the seemingly dead Pangor's turf...and his woman. Poor Buck also realizes the bite has infected him with the virus, as he sprouts horns, curly hair and a beard, as he transforms into a Satyr. To his horror, he realizes that he's becoming more angry and inhuman towards Cyra and Delph. As with Wilma in 'Space Vampire,' 'The Satyr' gives Buck a chance to transform and show a dark side.

One of the justifiably remembered episodes of the much maligned second season, "The Satyr" is disturbing and full of interesting imagery. There's no shortage of kink in this episode as it's clear Pangor is interested in more than food from Cyra. After saving the boy from a savage Z Wolf, Buck Rogers receives a request from Delph regarding the Satyr: "Please make him go 'way and leave my Mother alone."

The kink factor increases when we learn the Satyr is actually the boy's Dad transformed. Mom, Cyra, is bruised by her nightly attention from the satyrs, When Buck begins changing into one himself, he informs the other Satyrs, "The woman is mine—and so is the wine!"

The show is a cut above the usual damsel-in-distress episodes of the second season, and feels like a third season episode of classic *Star Trek*, with Gil Gerard standing in for William Shatner's Captain Kirk. This is no accident, as Paul Schneider was a writer for the original *Trek*.

Makeup and wardrobe departments rise to the occasion with both the Satyr design and the demonic/metallic headpieces on their horses.. Dave Cass makes a scary, disturbing Satyr. The opening teaser is also disturbing—a lustful satyr grabs Delph, a young boy, who is then thrown bodily out of his hovel so that the half-goat/half-man can be alone with the boy's striking young Mom...Until they make it clear he's only looking for wine and food (wink!) Anne E. Curry plays the pretty Mom.

Dave Cass is an actor and stuntman, which explains why the fight between Buck and Pangor is so good.

BUCK FACTS

- Erin Gray is back in her spandex cat suit!
- The Satyr continues this season's obsession with Greek myths and legends, including Pandora's Box (The Guardians'), The Underworld and aliens with Greek names("The Golden Man").
- Director Victor French is the actor from *Little House On The Prairie*, where he worked with Gil Gerard.
- Paul Schneider wrote two great episodes of classic *Star Trek*— "Balance Of Terror" and "The Squire Of Gothos," which *Buck* rips off this season with "The Hand Of Goral."
- Composer Bruce Broughton won a Primetime Emmy in Outstanding Achievement in Music Composition for a Series (Dramatic Underscore) for "The Satyr."
- Episode highlights: Wilma calls Twiki "Sweetie" and it's great to have Mel Blanc back.

25th Century Guest: Dave Cass: The Satyr

As an astronaut who lands on the planet Arcadus and transforms into Pangor, a violent satyr, who attacks his own wife and son, actor/director/stuntman Dave Cass is the best remembered villain from the second season of *Buck Rogers in the 25th Century*.

Cass had also stunted as Bigfoot on *The Six Million Dollar Man* and as The Hulk in the lab explosion in the pilot for *The Incredible Hulk*("on the original *Hulk*, I doubled Lou Ferrigno, jumping down into a lab that was on fire...That was enough green makeup for me!")

Satyr Dave Cass with electro whip.

His half-man/half-goat, and the metallic horse he rode, are the best remembered elements of all of *Buck Rogers'* Season Two.

"I got my *Buck* role when John Mantley was producing the show and Vic French was directing. I knew both of them from my *Gunsmoke* days, where they both knew me as an actor/stuntman, so they called me to do the part, as Guest Star. Playing Pangor, I actually did my own stunts, including my fight with Gil (Gerard), the horse stuff, all of it; because I was much younger then!"

Cass says "I could never forget doing *Buck Rogers in the 25th Century*—that show sent me to the Emergency Room in Westlake Village one night, when the horse I was on tripped and fell over backwards when I reared him! That gave me a concussion, but the concussion did not stop the show."

"Universal actually sent a limo to my home every morning to take me to and from the studio. They even had a nurse to watch over me," he recalls. "Wars and Movies do not stop for the wounded."

"The exteriors of the planet, where the house was, was actually in Hidden Valley, near Westlake Village. The big fight with Buck Rogers and I was shot on the Universal backlot and the interior of the house was shot on a soundstage at the studio. I cannot re-member if I had any contact with the robot (Twiki)."

The Satyr on his hellish horse.

Wearing so much latex, horns, wig and prosthetics as The Satyr was not a problem. "Makeup bother me? Are you kidding," he says defiantly, "I was in showbiz, *of course* it bothered me (wearing it) when not in front of the camera! When in front of the camera, my mind was on other things - After doubling Bigfoot on *The Six Million Dollar Man*, being a Bear Man in *The Island of Doctor Moreau*, a Swamp Monster on *Logan's Run* TV series and a few other heavy makeup jobs, you would think one would get used to it, but that did not happen. The green paint when I was The Hulk made me a little crazy."

"The hardest part of the gig was wearing the makeup and outfit, but my favorite part was taking the makeup off and, of course, playing this fun part in a Sci Fi TV series. I found Gil a very pleasant fellow to work with and be around, because he took the job very seriously."

On the show, he torments his family after he becomes a a satyr. "Both my wife and son on that show were great. The boy (Bobby P. Lane) and I had a great time playing monster when we weren't shooting. Of course there wasn't much playing when we shot the interiors at the studio, because that's when I was walking around with a concussion.

"Anne Curry played my wife Cyra. We had a great time working together on *Buck*. Around 1989, I was stunt coordinator on (the western TV movie) *Desperado* with Alex McArthur, when Anne did a part on that show—it was grand seeing her again."

"Shgoratchx!"

Season 2, Episode 34

Original Airdate March 19, 1981
Written By William Keys
Directed by Vincent McEveety

Cast
Buck Rogers...Gil Gerard
Wilma Deering...Erin Gray
Hawk...Thom Christopher
Admiral Asimov....Jay Garner
Dr. Goodfellow... Wilfrid Hyde-White
General Xenos...Tommy Madden
 Twiki...Felix Silla
Voice of Twiki...Mel Blanc
Ensign Moore...Alex Hyde-White
General Zoman....John Edward Allen
 Private Zedht...Tony Cox
General Yoomak...Billy Curtis
General Sothoz...Harry Monty
General Towtuk...Spencer Russell
General Kuzan ... Charles Secor

   Searching through a derelict freighter after it drifts dangerously
through space lanes, Buck and Hawk find it contains deadly solar
bombs and seven dwarves with telekinetic powers. To their credit,
the first thing they try to do is strip Wilma with their amazing powers, showing they have the network's best interests at heart—as
well as those of teenage boy viewers.. They plan to detonate the
bombs before they can explode (they're old and unstable), while
poor Wilma has to deal with the alien dwarves who mischievously
give her a hard time. The alien little people keep saying the same
things in unison in an attempt to be cute, in an otherwise forget-
table episode."Shgoratchx!" is as inane as its title.

Buck and Wilma have to deal with a ship full of little telekinetic aliens in Shgoratch.

ERIN GRAY: "Oh, Shgoratchx!— I actually liked that episode, I had a nice part in that one, even when the little guys use their powers to strip me! I liked the short skirt I wore in that."

BUCK FACTS

- Vincent McEveety's brother directs a later *Buck* episode.
- Guest John Edward Allen appeared in *Blade Runner* as one of Sebastian's toys.
- Alex Hyde-White (Ensign Moore) returns.
- Billy Curtis was title character in the sci fi horror classic from Howard Hawks, *The Thing* (1951), when it was shrunk by electricity.
- The episode has a "Who's Who" of Hollywood little people.
- One wonders why Felix Silla wasn't one of the seven little dwarves on the spaceship, but he was also a stunt double for kids on other shows, so he may have been too busy!
- In the episode, Buck is told that Twiki and Crichton are programmed by Isaac Asimov's Three Laws Of Robotics, which Twiki broke in the first season when he was blowing up enemy craft piloted by living beings and making jokes about it.

"The Hand Of The Goral"

Season 2, Episode 35

Original Airdate March 26, 1981
Written By Francis Moss
Directed by David G. Phinney

Cast
Buck Rogers...Gil Gerard
Wilma Deering...Erin Gray
Hawk...Thom Christopher
Admiral Asimov...Jay Garner
Dr. Goodfellow... Wilfrid Hyde-White
Hand of Goral...John Fujioka
Cowan...William Bryant
Reardon...Peter Kastner
Twiki...Felix Silla
Voice of Twiki...Mel Blanc
Lt. Parsons...Dennis Haysbert
Yeoman James... Michael Horsley

The Searcher journeys to Deeth, a supposed "Planet of Death," where Buck, Wilma and Hawk meet Rickard, a mysterious survivor of a crashed ship. Buck and Hawk find their friends behaving quite differently than they usually do.

Wilma takes Buck on The Searcher, Twiki is a rebel, Goodfellow is evil, Admiral Asimov a bully, even Crichton the robot is subservient to humans. The ruins of the ship disappears before Buck and Hawk's eyes. They deduce that this Searcher, is a fake, packed with duplicates who behave abnormally from the people they are posing as. To save their friends, they must deal with a mystical old man who calls himself "The Hand of the Goral." Before they can rejoin their friends, they have one final test to go through or The Searcher will be destroyed.

There are some similarities to "The Guardians," where Buck and Hawk encounter another godlike alien posing as an old man, but "The Hand Of The Goral" is an interesting episode, very reminiscent of classic *Star Trek*'s "The Squire Of Gothos" and "Mirror Mirror."

BUCK FACTS

- Dennis Haysbert returns as Lt. Parsons!
- Buck Guest Michael Horsley also appeared on *The Six Million Dollar Man* with a pre-Ardala Pamela Hensley ("Sharks," Part 2).
- Guest Actor John Fujioka played everything from losing Japanese Generals in WW II movies like Pearl Harbor to samurai and ninjas.

"Testimony Of A Traitor"

Season 2, Episode 36
Original Airdate April 9, 1981
Written By Stephen McPherson
Directed by Bernard McEveety

Cast
Buck Rogers...Gil Gerard
Wilma Deering...Erin Gray
Hawk...Thom Christopher
Admiral Asimov...Jay Garner
Dr. Goodfellow... Wilfrid Hyde-White
Commissioner Bergstrom...Ramon Bieri
Lt. General Preston Myers... William Sylvester
Gen. Armheim...David Hooks
US President...Walter Brooke
Air Force General...John Milford
Twiki...Felix Silla
Voice of Twiki...Mel Blanc
Major Peterson...John O'Connell
Crawford...Thomas Bellin
Brigadier General Biles ...Buck Young
Air Force Sergeant...Carl Reindel

The Searcher returns to Earth for the only time this season for a grim task: Turn Buck over to the authorities. Buck is being put on trial for allegedly helping the group that started the nuclear war that destroyed Earth (and created Anarchia, the place that can never be mentioned on the series!)

Basically, an inexpensive bottle show, where Buck's memories are probed. While it's nice to see Buck and Wilma share a meaningful kiss, we the audience already know Buck isn't a traitor, so this becomes a routine 'Who Framed Buck' episode. The question of whether or not Buck is a traitor was solved in the pilot, when Dr. Theopolis' fellow computers put him on trial and Wilma realized he wasn't a pirate.

That the second to last episode of the series is a lazy, generic recycling of clips and plots, using the same mind probe gimmick employed in the first season bottle show "A Blast For Buck" is a sad statement on this season.

BUCK FACTS

- Hawk uses the Talons on his ship for the first time since he accidentally killed his wife Koori with them in "Time Of The Hawk."
- Third episode written by Buck's Executive Story Consultant McPherson.
- David Hooks appeared in Kenneth Johnson's landmark sci-fi miniseries, "V."
- Ramon Bieri frequently played Native American Chiefs on Universal TV shows like The Incredible Hulk and Kolchak: The Night Stalker.
- Director Bernard McEveety had done a virtual "Who's who" of TV genre shows, including *Planet Of The Apes, Misfits Of Science, Knight Rider, Hulk, Voyagers, The A Team, Blue Thunder, Airwolf, Outlaws* and many more.
- Guest Actor John O'Connell guested on *The Incredible Hulk* and *Wonder Woman.*

"The Dorian Secret"

Season 2, Episode 37 of 37

Original Airdate April 16, 1981
Written By Stephen McPherson
Directed by Jack Arnold

Cast
Buck Rogers...Gil Gerard
Wilma Deering...Erin Gray
Hawk...Thom Christopher
Admiral Asimov...Jay Garner
Dr. Goodfellow... Wilfrid Hyde-White
Joham...Keith Atkinson ...
Darel...Lachelle Chamberlain
Demeter...William Kirby Cullen
Koldar... Walker Edmiston
Asteria Eleefa...Devon Ericson
Ensign...Dennis Haysbert
Cleis...Michele Marsh
Saurus...Denny Miller

When Buck and Hawk help refugees board The Searcher, Buck accidentally starts an interplanetary incident when he lets a woman named Asteria Eleefa aboard. Asteria is a member of mutants known as Dorians, who have to wear masks to hide their ugliness.

Dorian leader Koldar demands Eleefa be turned over to him for the crime of murder, Buck refuses, because that's what heroes do. It also doesn't hurt that she's actually a beautiful woman, so Koldar decides to heat up The Searcher—literally. Buck easily saves the girl of the week with little zeal.

Buck Rogers in the 25th Century limps to a close with this utterly dull episode. Generic aliens in a generic conflict, before Buck saves the day when he comes up with a generic solution, in one of the series' most stultifying episodes. The Searcher was sent to dry-dock, in the face of the second season's precipitous ratings drop. As former Story Editor Alan Brennert predicted, *Buck Rogers in the 25th Century* was now headed for "The Sargasso Of Lost Space Shows."

BUCK FACTS

- Jack Arnold, the Steven Spielberg of the 1950s, directed *The Creature From The Black Lagoon, The Incredible Shrinking Man* and *It Came from Outer Space.*
- Guest Actress Devon Ericson later co-starred in '80s Cult classic *Night of the Comet* with Buck villainess Mary Woronov.
- Dennis Haysbert makes his final appearance on the show.
- Denny Miller made the rounds on all the late '70s/early '80s superhero shows, including *The Incredible Hulk* and *Wonder Woman.*
- A character named 'Demeter' may be a Dracula reference, a nod to the freighter in the "Space Vampire" episode or, more than likely, just a grasp at re-using a futuristic sounding name.

The Future

Since the end of his TV series in the early '80s, *Buck Rogers* has lain dormant. There were no new movies or shows based on the character, although interest has built up in the last five years.

There was an internet series memorable for having Samantha Hissong, Erin Gray's daughter, play a Wilma Deering-type character. "It was fun to follow in Mom's footsteps," Hissong jokes.

Comic book artist/writer Howard Chaykin did a *Buck Rogers* miniseries and in 2014, Leisure Concepts and Licensing Works released a life size Twiki figure (Felix Silla not included). Buck, Wilma and Twiki tee shirts are sold in the back pages of genre mags like *Famous Monsters Of Filmland*.

In 2008, OddLot Entertainment announced they were in talks with Nu Image/Millienium Films to have comics impresario Frank Miller (*300*, *Sin City*) write and direct a new version of *Buck Rogers*, after he adapted Will Eisner's *The Spirit* into a film for them. The Hollywood Reporter noted that Miller's take was expected to be "darker" and touch on "Miller's signature visual elements and themes, such as corruption and redemption."

Slash Film expressed surprise that OddLot would "put their trust in Miller at this point ... as early buzz has begun to leak and the consensus is that Miller's directorial debut *The Spirit* is beyond disastrous." They noted, "It seems like it would be smarter to do this deal after *The Spirit*'s box office debut."

Sure enough, when his terrible, incoherent all star version of *The Spirit* opened to terrible reviews (It made over 50 "Worst Of The Year" lists) and worse box office, all talk of him doing *Buck* was scrapped.

In 2015, *Transformers* producer Don Murphy received massive applause in a crowded convention hall when he announced plans to do a big screen version of *Buck Rogers* through his Angry Films banner at The San Diego Comic Con.

His script for the film is by RoboCop creator Ed Neumeier and Flint Dille, grandson of original *Buck Rogers* publisher John Flint

Dille. When Murphy was unable to come to an agreement with The Dille Family Trust to license *Buck* for a feature film, he realized the source novel, *Armageddon 2419 A.D.*, by Philip Nowlan, which introduced Buck as 'Anthony Rogers' and Wilma Deering, had been in the public domain since the 1950s when no one bothered to renew the copyright. Since Murphy wants to base the film on that, he seeks to have *Buck Rogers* declared public domain so he can make the film. That legal battle was not resolved as this book went to press.

Of course, history has shown that the heroic Buck Rogers is always able to jump into immediate action after a long sleep.

NOTES AND SOURCES

"Buck Rogers Begins"
"Buck Rogers In The 25th Century " pilot script by Glen Larson and
    Leslie Stevens, 1978
"The Right Stuff" by Tom Wolfe

"An Interview with Glen Larson, writer/producer" by James Delson,
    Fantastic Films #9, July 1979
"An Interview with Gil Gerard" by James Delson, Fantastic Films #9,
    July 1979

In-person interview with Glen Larson
In-person interview with C.Z. Wick
In-person interview with Ralph McQuarrie
In-person interview with William Stout
In-person interview with Paul Peters
In-person interview with Peter Anderson
In-person interview with Erin Gray

"Awakening"
"Buck Rogers In The 25th Century " pilot script by Glen Larson and
    Leslie Stevens, feb 2, '78
"An Interview with Glen Larson, writer/producer" by James Delson,
    Fantastic Films #9, July 1979
In-person interview with Glen Larson
Interview with Alen Brennert
Interview with Anne Collins Ludwick
In-person Interview with Mike Lantieri
In-person interview with Erin Gray
"Dressed To Thrill"
In-person interview with Jean-Pierre Dorléac
In-person interview with Larson
Cinefantastique's 25th Anniversary "Buck Rogers" screening Egyptian
    Theater, 2005

"Composer Stu Phillips"
Interview with Stu Phillips

"Art Director"
In-person interview withLarson
In-person interview withv Daniel Haller

In-person interview with-Paul Peters
In-person interview with Dorléac

"Two Tigermen"
In-person interview with Dorléac
"Anarchia"
Interview with Alen Brennert
In-person interview with Gil Gerard

"Buck Memories"
In-person interview with Erin Gray
In-person interview withLarson
In-person interview with Samantha Hissong

"Weekly Series"
Bruce Lansbury quotes from "Buck Rogers In The 25th Century" by
   David Houston, Starlog #28

"Gil Gerard: Buck Rogers Lives!"
In-person interview with Gil Gerard

"Erin Gray: 25th Century Fox"
In-person interview with Erin Gray

"Tim O'Connor: Dr. Huer"
In-person interview with Tim O'Connor.

"Felix Silla: Talking With Twiki"
In-person interview with Felix Silla

"Story Editors Anne Collins & Alan Brennert"
-Interviews with Anne Collins Ludwick and Alan Brennert

"Planet Of The Slave Girls"
In-person interview with-Paul Peters
In pertson interview with Gil Gerard
In-person interview with Erin Gray
Interview with Alan Brennert
BUSTER CRABBE: HIS LAST INTERVIEW By Jeff Rovin, from BEST
   OF STARLOG 1980
In-person interview with Mike Caffey

SEASON ONE

In-person interview with Pamela Susan Shoop

Interview with Anthony James

"Architects of Imperfect Futures", David Bennett Carren interview, STARLOG Platinuim, by Lee Goldberg

"Confessions Of A Story Editor" by Alan Brennert, STARLOG Magazine 1980

Interview with Katherine Ann Wiberg

In-person Interview with Mary Woronov

In-person interview with Dennis "Danger" Madalone

In-person interview with Eric Server

In-person interview with Samantha Hissong

In-person interview with Michael Ansara

In-person interview with Kimberly Beck

In-person interview with Grace Gaynor

In-person interview with Anne Lockhart

In-person interview with Nicholas Hormann

Interview with Jeannie Fitzsimmons

"Scribe Of The Serpent God"(Interview with David Wise), by Bill Florence , STARLOG Platinuim Magazine #1, "

Interview with Dee Walllace Stone

In-person interview with – Morgan Brittany

In-person interview with Anne Lockhart

Interview with Allan Cole

Interview with Guy Magar

Kiss Me Quick Before I Shoot" by Guy Magar, Sea Scipt Company, 2011

Interview with Judy Landers-Niedenfuer

"The 25th Century That Almost Wasn't: An interview with Gil Gerard" by Karen E. Wilson, Starlog Magazine #40, 1980

Interview with Judith Chapman

"Rogers Over & Out", parts one and two, by Bill Florence, Starlog Magazine issues #231 & 232, October, November 1996.

In-person interview with Donald Petrie

In-person interview with Sid Haig

In-person interview with Julie Newmar

SEASON TWO

In-person interview with David Jones

"Architects of Imperfect Futures", David Bennett Carren interview,

STARLOG Platinuim, by Lee Goldberg
In-person interview with BarBara Luna
In-person interview with Sid Haig
Interview with Silla.
Interview with Alex Hyde White.
Starlog interview with Francis Moss.
In-person interview with Amanda Wyss

"Rogers Over & Out", parts one and two, by Bill Florence, Starlog
    Magazine issues #231 & 232, October, November 1996.

"Scribe Of The Serpent God", by Bill Florence , STARLOG Platinuim
    Magazine #1, "

The Future
Samantha Hissong interview
"Frank Miller to Direct Buck Rogers"
By Peter Sciretta/Slash Film, December 18th, 2008
"New Buck Rogers Movie Happening If A Court Decides The Name is
    In Public Domain" GEEK. Com, by Ryan Whitwam, October 27, 2015

ACKNOWLEDGEMENTS

A book like this depends on the cooperation, stories and help of the people who made that show. Luckily, the cast and crew of *Buck Rogers In The 25th Century* are some of the nicest people you could ever hope to meet.

Truly appreciated the gregarious Gil Gerard, enchanting Erin Gray, and fun Felix Silla for participating in this book. Erin writing the foreword was an awesome honor and thrill. Erin is sweet, and I appreciated her participation, as well as that of her daughter, Samantha Hissong. Felix, who scared the shit out of me as a child when I saw him playing the lead Goblin in *Don't Be Afraid Of The Dark*, has been a friend since I met him on a commercial audition. He and his wife Sue are delightful. He answered all my questions and more.

Tim O'Connor was funny, kind and sweet, even when discussing unpleasant things, such as his unjust dismissal from the series, which led to the weak second season. Great stories came from Michael Caffey, Thom Christopher, Daniel Haller and Paul Peters, who were all nice and more importantly, highly quotable.

Thanks to Amanda Wyss, Anthony James and the great Sid Haig, who told me to call him "Uncle Sid, because everyone else does!"

BarBara Luna, who I adore, was an amazing help on this book, She knows (and is loved by) everybody. If there was anybody who couldn't be found or didn't have time to do an interview about the show, the beautiful BarBara not only found 'em, but told them to talk. You just can't say no to BarBara Luna.

Anne Collins Ludwick was simply incredible. She endured my many, many questions, answered them all with aplomb and then wrote me a long treatise on her not always pleasant experiences writing for *Buck*, which she generously allowed me to quote here. She also helped me cajole Alan Brennert into taking part in the book.

Julie Newmar was a treat. Interviewing this enthralling actress, I made the mistake of telling her that I thought her campy War Witch on *Buck* was one of her best roles. Horrified, the Tony winning performer spent the rest of the interview mentioning all her other work. In between answering my questions, she would throw in a line like "A lot of people think Stanley Donen's *Seven Brides For Seven Broithers* is pretty good, dear—you should take a look at that." Thanks for everything, Julie Newmar, you rock. Your invitation to meditate in your secret garden is something I will always treasure.

Damsels in distress Kimberly Beck, Grace Gaynor, Mary Woronov, Judy Landers-Niedenfur were helpful. Morgan Brittany. Morgan, despite her soap opera siren career is actually a huge sci fi fan, truly proud to have been in *The Birds, The Twilight Zone, Death Car On The Freeway* and *Buck*. Her ability to remember her Buck Rogers character's name and quote her lines even today was simply stunning.

Judith Chapman was also impressive, recalling anecdotes from her one crazy episode, as did Katherine Ann Wiberg. That Dave Cass could tell so many neat facts from "The Satyr" despite having a concussion from when he made it (His demonic horse on the show had thrown him) only adds to my admiration of him.

In putting this book together, Buck know it all Steve Jankiewicz had all sorts of advice and the lovely Lisa Jankiewicz was also a big help, even if she kept urging me to do "a book on the original *Battlestar Galactica!*" (No!) AL "The Pal" Callaci suggested the title "25th Century Fox" for my piece on Erin, which I thought was inspired. Neil D'Monte spent our weekly Starbucks bull sessions patiently listening to me rattling off Buck facts, while he was merely designing things for the year's highest grossing film *Jurassic World*.

When I needed a shot of *Buck Rogers* toys, I made a Hail Mary pass and called Gina Sheridan, who has an impossibly huge toy collection. She photographed them and offered some insights on certain episodes. To make her even cooler, she worked as a Popcorn Girl at Michigan's greatest movie house, The Showcase Cinema Sterling Heights.

Gina, Darren Roberts, Allision Sweeney and Staci "Pippi" Hammon acted as my Computer Council . Each of them giving copious thoughts and suggestions in covering the series. The fact that Darren and I were at a party, music blasting, lights flashing, drinking wine when he leaned in to yell in my ear "DON'T FORGET— BUCK MENTIONS JAWS IN A DREAM OF JENNIFER!" Duly noted, Darren—and thanks!

As always, thank you to publisher Ben Ohmart and special grateful acknowledgement and appreciation to tireless Robbie Adkins, an amazing designer. She came up with the jaw dropping cover and layouts. Robbie had never seen an episode of the show and wouldn't be able to identify Twiki in a police lineup, which makes her skills here all the more impressive. By the time we finished, she could identify Ardala from her wardrobe in any episode, Dr. Theopolis from Dr. Apol or Mr. DeBronin. Danke, Robbie!

Calling the hokey judo moves Buck uses in the show "Buck Fu" was something I got from the very funny website Topless Robot.

Thank you, Hilari Scarl for finding me Katherine Ann Wiberg, Joe Williamson for finding me my satyr, Dave Cass, Dawn Mead for getting a difficult to obtain photo at the very last minute.

Special kudos to the usual suspects Don Jankiewicz (The Thomas Crown of Meijer Thrifty Acres), Conan & Ajax Jankiewicz, Matty Almanzar, Troy & Allie Nelson, Tara Mairead Meisner.

INDEX

ABOUT THE AUTHOR

PATRICK JANKIEWICZ is the result of a Detroit, Michigan breeding experiment between an Aerospace Engineer and a Registered Nurse. He is a writer, journalist, actor. This is his third book. He's written for Marvel Comics, Titan Publishing, *Fangoria Magazine* and *Nuke The Fridge*.

As an actor, he's been in the films *Chastity Bites, American High School, The Eric Andree Show* and multiple episodes of *Tim & Erics Awesome Show*, Great Job! Jankiewicz also starred in commercials for Coca-Cola, Liberty-Mutual, Dippin' Dots, Burger King, Hardee's/Carl's Jr (His spots

Photo copyright Albert L. Ortega

as a singing waiter introduced the world to The Six Dollar Burger), Turner Classic Movies (Which he did with a three legged pitbull named "Rocket") and this year's popular GEICO spot, "Prisoner", as the cheerful giant prisoner.

He feels being frozen for 504 years to wake in a world where you get a talking robot sidekick and womens' business attire is spandex is a fair trade. New Detroit has to be better than the one he grew up in.

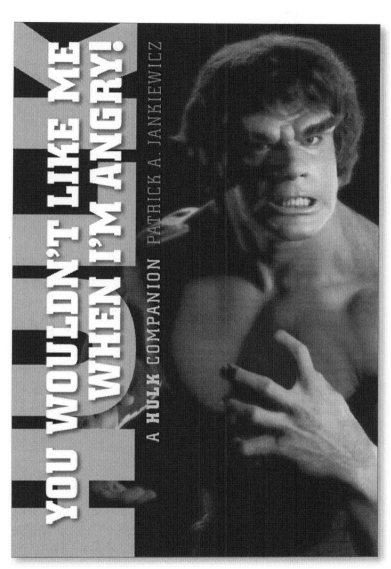

Also from bearmanormedia.com

18127531R00185

Printed in Poland
by Amazon Fulfillment
Poland Sp. z o.o., Wrocław